Supercharge Your Slack Productivity

Discover hacks and tips for managing and automating your workflow with Slack and Slack bots

Moshe Markovich

BIRMINGHAM—MUMBAI

Supercharge Your Slack Productivity

Group Product Manager: Ashwin Nair

Publishing Product Manager: Ashitosh Gupta

Senior Editor: Sofi Rogers

Content Development Editor: Rakhi Patel

Technical Editor: Saurabh Kadave

Copy Editor: Safis Editing

Project Coordinator: Kinjal Bari

Proofreader: Safis Editing

Indexer: Tejal Soni

Production Designer: Joshua Misquitta

First published: March 2021

Production reference: 2200721

Published by Packt Publishing Ltd.

Livery Place

35 Livery Street

Birmingham

B3 2PB, UK.

ISBN 978-1-80056-962-1

www.packt.com

I dedicate this book to the kindest people I know; my mother, father, and all five of my siblings. They continuously accept and support me unconditionally throughout my journey in life. They also taught me life skills, like to always wear a winter jacket, macaroni and cheese is the easiest and most filling meal, and it doesn't matter what you're going through, just keep going and it'll all work out in the end.

– Moshe Markovich

Contributors

About the author

Moshe Markovich is a marketing and Slack consultant who has worked with governments, venture capitalists, and dozens of corporations and brands, including Johnson & Johnson, Google, Keybank, and Comedy Central. He runs a company called Online Geniuses, which has grown to become the largest real-time marketing community in the world with over 25,000 vetted members.

I want to thank my family and friends who came along for the journey.

About the reviewer

Vikrant Singh is an experienced collaboration solution architect with a demonstrated history of working in the entertainment industry. He has architected, designed, and developed customization on major collaboration platforms, such as Slack, MS Teams, Yammer, SharePoint, and G Suite. He is also sufficiently skilled with the Google and Microsoft Cloud platforms to fulfill industry needs at the enterprise level.

Table of Contents

3
Slack Features, Tips, and Tricks

4

Onboarding Your Team to Slack

5

Using Slack Externally with Live Chats, Guests, and Partners

Section 2: How to Use Third-Party Applications and Bots

6

Your Workspace Slackbot

7

Integrating Your Favorite Tools

8
Automate Your Workflow with Zapier

9
Slack API, Webhooks, Block Kit, and Sandboxes

Section 3: How to Build Your Own Bots

10
Building Your Own Bot

11
Buying, Building, and Outsourcing Your Bot

12

Distributing Your App in the Slack App Directory

Other Books You May Enjoy

Index

Preface

Slack is an online communication tool that allows workplace teams to collaborate efficiently, effectively, and securely. Through Slack, your team opens the doors to endless opportunities to engage and create in a unified place. In this book, we'll walk you through the basic elements that comprise the app's workspace as well as added features both internally and externally that work to individualize your team's experience based on the needs and requirements for your company's success.

Who this book is for

The beauty of Slack is that it can be used by anyone. Beginners and master developers alike are encouraged to participate in the Slack experience, using it as either a basic communication channel or an advanced workspace for coding and creating bots and applications.

As a developer, you can use Slack to create tools such as bots to handle and maintain routine and time-consuming tasks. The only background required of a Slacker is the motivation of someone searching for a unified place to build and create with others.

What this book covers

Chapter 1, Getting Started with Slack, explains what Slack is and how to know whether it is the right fit for you and your company. We go through the pros and cons of Slack and whether it's useful for people deciding to use Slack internally.

Chapter 2, Setting Up Your Slack Workplace, covers setting up the logistics of your Slack workspace, as well as understanding the three tiers of Slack's hierarchy.

Chapter 3, Slack Features, Tips, and Tricks, covers the best Slack tips and tricks for your business team. This chapter covers tons of Slack features that are normally unknown to the bulk of its users.

Chapter 4, Onboarding Your Team to Slack, helps you understand how to provide the most helpful and welcoming experience for new hires and already existing team members.

Chapter 5, Using Slack Externally with Live Chats, Guests, and Partners, covers branching beyond your direct team to bring agencies, consultants, freelancers, and external partners into your workspace.

Chapter 6, Your Workspace Slackbot, takes a deeper dive into the ways that bots can impact your workspace and help things run more efficiently by understanding Slack's in-app bot: Slackbot.

Chapter 7, Integrating Your Favorite Tools, shows you how to implement helpful additional tools to help manage time, increase productivity, and engage users once your team is up and running.

Chapter 8, Automate Your Workflow with Zapier, walks you through how to get the most out of Zapier, one of the most popular and useful integrations for Slack.

Chapter 9, Slack API, Webhooks, Block Kit, and Sandbox, covers learning how to integrate complex services with the Slack API to go beyond the integrations provided through the app.

Chapter 10, Building Your Own Bot, covers understanding which platform is best to build your bot on using existing code, pushing the bot live, and testing it.

Chapter 11, Buying, Building, and Outsourcing Your Bot, and Outsource, teaches you how to recognize when it's best to buy, build, or outsource your own bot.

Chapter 12, Distributing Your App in the Slack App Directory, covers placing your bot on the market for others to utilize in their own workspace through the Slack App Directory.

To get the most out of this book

In this book, we'll walk through scenarios on how to set up a Slack workplace, build a Slack bot, and integrate your favorite tools. You'll learn how Slack can create a more collaborative, efficient, and coordinated work environment from anywhere. You'll then progress to more advanced features, including creating a Slack bot to assist with the completion of tasks such as automatic message responses or accessing personal reminders and tasks.

Slack users can enter a workspace with very little or extremely detailed knowledge of the app, bot creation, or code. This book will focus on specific tools meant to guide you through a general understanding that could then be expanded upon later. The following features and requirements will 100% be utilized throughout the book.

Tools utilized throughout this book	OS requirements
Zapier	Windows or macOS for desktop
ebhooks, Block Kit, a sandbox	iOS or Android for mobile
API, scopes, basic code	

Setup features will be explained in detail in Chapter 2, Setting Up Your Slack Workplace. Additional tools can be utilized depending on the user and their unique workspace.

If you are using the digital version of this book, we advise you to type the code yourself or access the code via the GitHub repository (link available in the next section). Doing so will help you avoid any potential errors related to the copying and pasting of code.

By the end of this book, you will be able to set up a Slack account, know how to share files and communicate with your team, be able to build bots, and be knowledgeable about the platform and how it can help you progress in your industry.

Conventions used

There are a number of text conventions used throughout this book.

`Code in text`: Indicates code words in text, database table names, folder names, filenames, file extensions, pathnames, dummy URLs, user input, and Twitter handles. Here is an example: `admin.conversations.invite`: Invite a user to a public or private channel.

A block of code is set as follows:

```
{
"type": "button",
"text": {
"type": "plain_text",
"text": "Click Me"
},
"value": "click_me_123",
"action_id": "button"
}
```

Bold: Indicates a new term, an important word, or words that you see onscreen. For example, words in menus or dialog boxes appear in the text like this. Here is an example: "From your email invitation, select the **Finish Setup** link."

> **Tips or important notes**
> Appear like this.

Get in touch

Feedback from our readers is always welcome.

General feedback: If you have questions about any aspect of this book, mention the book title in the subject of your message and email us at customercare@packtpub.com.

Errata: Although we have taken every care to ensure the accuracy of our content, mistakes do happen. If you have found a mistake in this book, we would be grateful if you would report this to us. Please visit www.packtpub.com/support/errata, selecting your book, clicking on the Errata Submission Form link, and entering the details.

Piracy: If you come across any illegal copies of our works in any form on the Internet, we would be grateful if you would provide us with the location address or website name. Please contact us at copyright@packt.com with a link to the material.

If you are interested in becoming an author: If there is a topic that you have expertise in and you are interested in either writing or contributing to a book, please visit authors.packtpub.com.

Reviews

Please leave a review. Once you have read and used this book, why not leave a review on the site that you purchased it from? Potential readers can then see and use your unbiased opinion to make purchase decisions, we at Packt can understand what you think about our products, and our authors can see your feedback on their book. Thank you!

For more information about Packt, please visit packt.com.

Section 1: Slack Overview

Slack is an extremely useful tool for any member, at any level, in any area of any industry. The communication platform allows users to interact, communicate, and share information, skills, and files all in one unified place. This section focuses on the basics of the application, as well as developing a general understanding of what Slack is and how it can be beneficial to you and your team.

We will first look at how to approach the app itself by getting started with your Slack workspace. We'll break down the basic terms and features to familiarize you with the application. Then we'll set up an account and profile and invite members of your team as well as external members, such as guests, clients, and partners, to join. Let's get started!

In this section, we will cover the following chapters:

- *Chapter 1, Getting Started with Slack*
- *Chapter 2, Setting Up Your Slack Workplace*
- *Chapter 3, Slack Features, Tips, and Tricks*
- *Chapter 4, Onboarding Your Team to Slack*
- *Chapter 5, Using Slack Externally with Live Chats, Guests, and Partners*

1
Getting Started with Slack

Does a coordinated team, moving in unison, sound like something you need? In order to build this type of team structure, you need a supportive communication and collaboration tool where your team can streamline conversations and push development forward. Slack is the platform that allows for that type of top-notch conversation, and this book will show you the ins and outs of bringing that to life.

This book is organized in a way that allows you to first master the basics before diving into technology that you didn't even know was accessible to you. Each chapter is meant to push you to a higher level of understanding of Slack technology so that you can build a Slack workspace that is unique to you.

Chapter 1, *Getting Started with Slack*, will get you familiar with the platform and its functionality. After you have built a deep understanding and familiarity with Slack, you will be ready to build your Slack workspace and create the type of real-time communication that your team requires. So, let's dive right in and start your journey.

This chapter will cover the following main topics:

- What is Slack?
- Slack versus other tools

- Slack versus email
- The pros and cons of Slack
- Slack versus Microsoft Teams

What is Slack?

That is the ultimate question, isn't it? What is Slack and how does it pertain to you? Slack is a business communication platform that allows you and your company to communicate through easily accessible channels and threads to create a simple and efficient working environment.

Communication is an integral factor in any working community. Moreover, in a time where face-to-face communication is not always possible, Slack is a quick and easy way to connect all members of your organization through one simple tool.

Why communication spells success

Whether you are a founder with a small team, a leader with several hundred employees, or a freelancer with dozens of clients, the chances are you that are searching for a better way to keep everybody connected.

You've sat through various TED Talks, MasterClasses, and keynote speeches about leadership that all share the same message: communication is the key to success. There is an excellent reason why this message appears repeatedly. So, let's start this book by stating that communication is the foundation to your success.

Living in the 21st century means that you are continually bombarded with digital communications. Your phone lights up with every notification from a friend, team member, or brand trying to get in front of you. You've been annoyed by receiving the short "OK" messages that seemed pointless to receive. In team communications, that annoyance can quickly permeate a negative culture and breed disassociation across the team. This is the exact opposite of what you want and what this book will teach you.

A simple restructuring of the preceding statement is needed to ensure that digital communications carry importance and value connectivity; that is, *intentional connections are the foundation to your success.*

Do you want to be the next Steve Jobs and take over a market? How about taking over your street block with a booming small business? You need to nail intentional and consistent communication in order to do all of these things. It's good that you have powerful technology at your fingertips to make this process seamless – after you learn the basics, of course.

The digital communication tool you need

Slack has become a standard tool that is mentioned in every entrepreneurial ecosystem you are likely to come across. It has even taken on cultural significance as the brand name is used as a verb (for example, "Let me slack you when I'm done" or "I'll slack that link over to you"). A tool taking on this kind of importance deserves its own book to explain why and how a platform can be so powerful at keeping people connected.

Voila! The book is resting in your hands now.

Having found this book means that you've heard of Slack. You know it's defined as an online communication tool that allows workplace teams to collaborate with each other. You might even have a Slack profile for a workplace somewhere. But there is so much more to Slack than a high-level glance will show. *Slack is the tool that will help you to build the next Facebook, Nike, or Apple.*

You can build your company's very culture by utilizing Slack and creating a bustling ecosystem that is unique to the needs and desires of your company. Through customization, team members can feel the mission and values of their company come to life. Through the integration of tools, a team has the information they need at their fingertips. Through the creation of bots, an organization becomes more coordinated than ever.

There is power in having a comprehensive digital workspace that keeps remote and in-office personnel connected. Slack is that comprehensive tool, and, when done right, your team will be one that prioritizes communication for the broader success of your company's vision.

Understanding the platform

Slack is a channel-based messaging platform that connects teams and systems so that they operate more efficiently and effectively. This digital communication tool helps build a company's ecosystem by streamlining communications and processes across the organization to drive the business forward.

Simply put, Slack is the digital communication tool that keeps companies growing and scaling successfully. Take it from the following major brands who utilize Slack to keep their team connected:

- Airbnb
- Lyft
- Pinterest

- Amazon
- BuzzFeed
- Salesforce

Have you ever wanted to implement a piece of software into your team's processes to keep everything together? For instance, a storing ground for files, past messages, notifications, and more? Slack is the organized portal that gives you answers with the click of a search button.

Slack is not just useful for the major brands we mentioned earlier (and thousands of others not listed here). Many early-stage start-ups use Slack as the primary communication hub for their thriving ventures, and solo contractors apply its functionality to stay in touch with clients around the world. Slack is a tool that allows you to grow with it, no matter what stage of development you are at.

With a reported 12 million-plus daily active users and over 119 thousand paid customer accounts, Slack has quickly become a leader in its market. Competitor platforms such as Google Workspace, Miro, and Blizz (explained in more detail in an upcoming section) offer attractive functions to teams seeking more on-demand communications, yet Slack has paved the way and has captured a lot of market potential with its user-friendly interface, capability for integration with other tools, and overall simplicity.

Simplicity and familiarity are two qualities that Slack has leaned into for its design. Living in the social media generation means that you want quick access and easy-to-read communications. Think about some of your favorite posts on Twitter. Avid users love the platform for the following reasons:

- They can keep up to date with the latest news and developments.
- They can contribute to conversations in a way that doesn't take up too much time.
- They can create content that isn't time-consuming or overwhelming.
- They can search and share rapidly with a click of a button or by typing in a search word.

These reasons, and more, are not exclusive to Twitter but also Slack and its millions of users. A team can communicate and collaborate in a way that feels very social and quick to manage. Rather than getting into an hour-long meeting to discuss updates on a project, Slack creates a space for that conversation to happen quickly and efficiently – with some of the messages that are shared being no longer than a tweet.

The social aspect of Slack is an outstanding quality, and many teams are attracted to the platform because of this. Building a strongly united team and culture shouldn't take more time out of a busy founder or manager's schedule. Slack's easy-to-use technology creates a connected team through up-to-date and engaging communication; it is as though a social network vibe comes to life for your company.

The founding story

With such a socially driven communication platform, it is no wonder that the founding story of Slack has roots in the **Massively Multiplayer Online Role-Playing Game (MMORPG)** market. Slack founder Stewart Butterfield began Slack as an internal chat tool for his gaming company, Tiny Speck. Indeed, one of the fastest-growing **Software as a Service (SaaS)** start-ups in the world didn't even start with the mission to help companies "be less busy" (Slack's tagline).

Stewart and his team aimed to revolutionize the MMORPG market with a new, nonviolent game, unlike *World of Warcraft* and other popular outlets. Their team was spread across four cities and two countries, and they found that the online chat tool at the time, **Internet Relay Chat (IRC)**, wasn't functioning smoothly or offering the type of communication they needed.

As a result, Tiny Speck built an internal chat tool and added functionality on an as-needed basis to improve their communications. It was that ad hoc approach that produced the now majorly attractive search feature within Slack, which transformed how teams connect.

After Tiny Speck's game failed due to insufficient traction and gameplay, Stewart pivoted his team to focus more on the internal tool they had already built, beginning to see how other groups might need this type of communicative functionality at their fingertips. Slack was built through dozens of feedback loops, trial and error analyses with big and small companies, and a founding team who spent an enormous amount of time using the product to identify every angle of functionality.

The early development of Slack allowed the team to discover unique factors that would give them a competitive edge, such as the following:

- A centralized hub of communication that not only brought team members together but also documents, files, past messages, and more

- A transparent and lasting record of all correspondence, so no more thoughts were lost in intra-office phone calls or meetings

From the need for more reliable internal team communications to a company now valued at $17 billion, Slack has taken the market by storm and has shown companies large and small what it means to be less busy.

The anatomy of a Slack workspace

Around 65 Fortune 100 companies and countless others utilize Slack daily, but what exactly is it that these companies use on the platform to keep their team connected? Let's dive into the full anatomy of Slack and its workspace settings. Feel free to bookmark this section as a Slack dictionary for future use when creating your own workspace.

Workspaces

A workspace is the communication hub for your team on Slack and is made up of channels where your team members can connect and work together. Team members will need to create a Slack account once they are invited to join the workspace:

Figure 1.1 – A Slack workspace

Workspaces are often named after the company, for example, the Google Workspace or the Amazon Workspace.

Channels

A channel is a single place where a team can share messages, links, tools, and more that are organized around a common theme. That theme is decided by a Slack manager who can create a channel for a particular team, product, or another concept:

Figure 1.2 – Slack channels

Channels can be one of the following:

- **Public** and open to all team members in the Slack workspace

- **Private** and open to only the team members who are invited to that channel

- **Shared** and open to an invited external organization to connect with the internal team

Topics and descriptions

A channel topic delineates what members are working on or discussing in a particular channel. A channel description shares information regarding the intended use of the channel:

Figure 1.3 – A portfolio example

Topics and descriptions are a great way to create guidance and structure for chatting intra-channel, although companies can also make a *random* channel with loose guidance to host more watercooler-type conversations.

Here are some examples of channel topics:

- Announcements
- Suggestion box
- Random
- IT Help

Direct messages

Direct messages are how team members can host private, one-off conversations that don't need to be on a channel:

Figure 1.4 – Direct message channels

Slack is known for the transparency it provides across a team, keeping everyone in the know and updated. However, some conversations don't require more than a few individuals to take part.

Direct messages can occur between two people or up to eight people at a time.

Calls

Slack calls are how team members can connect via voice or video call directly through Slack. Screen sharing is also available during a call depending on what platform you are using (note that iOS and Android are not able to screen share at this time).

Slack calls mean that your team members can keep their phones for personal use, and they do not have to make calls or send texts to other team members.

Threads

Threads are a messaging functionality and are used to organize discussions attached to an original message in channels and direct messages:

david ✅ 12:10 PM
Hello @here, I'm the founder of Online Geniuses - the largest SEO and Digital Marketing community based on Slack. Feel free to ping/direct message me with any comments or questions you may have!

Figure 1.5 – Slack threads

Thread replies don't clutter your workspace and keep everything organized below the initial outreach. Team members can view the entire conversation by clicking on **View Thread**.

Reactions

Reactions are a quick way for a team member to respond to a message, using the full emoji keyboard:

Figure 1.6 – Reactions in Slack

Reactions are another feature that makes Slack feel like a social network platform with natural, instant, and fun engagement methods.

Team members can see who has left emoji reactions to their messages, leave them for others, and remove them from posts.

Mentions

Mentions are a way to notify team members that a message or conversation requires their engagement. Team members can tag someone using the @ sign and typing in their name, which will then notify the individual that they have been mentioned in a message.

> **Important note**
> If there are multiple team members with the same name on your Slack workspace, you will need to select the appropriate individual you want to mention. If you mention someone in a private channel that they are not invited to, this individual will not be notified of the mention.

Notifications

Notifications are Slack's functionality to inform a team member when and where they are needed by others instantly. When creating a profile and deciding on your preferences, you can choose whether to receive notifications by desktop, email, or mobile device. Slack notifications can be customized by channel so that team members can stay up to date in a manner that works best for them.

Search

Searching through your team's workspace gives you quick and direct access to past messages, files, channels, and people:

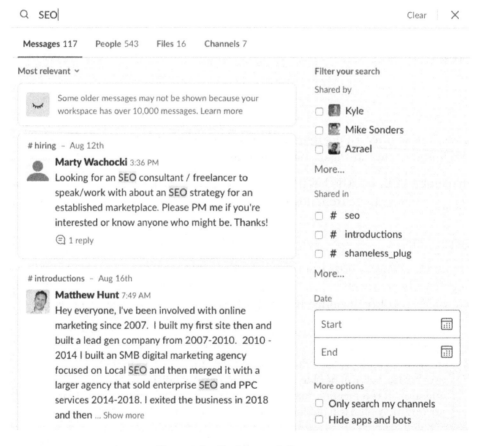

Figure 1.7 – Slack's search feature

The search feature is one of Slack's most attractive elements for teams because it allows for every interaction in Slack to be archived and then recovered when it is needed. The main navigation bar at the top of the workspace is your direct portal for searching.

You can also search using filters to narrow down precisely what you are looking for in your search.

Apps

Apps allow you to bring tools into your daily communications with teams and, by doing so, streamline your processes even further. Connecting apps to your Slack workspace brings all of the necessary information to one place, leads to quicker and sounder decisions, allows projects to progress more efficiently, and adds fun for the team.

File sharing

File sharing allows you to browse, share, and download files in your Slack workspace to keep all of your relevant documents in one place:

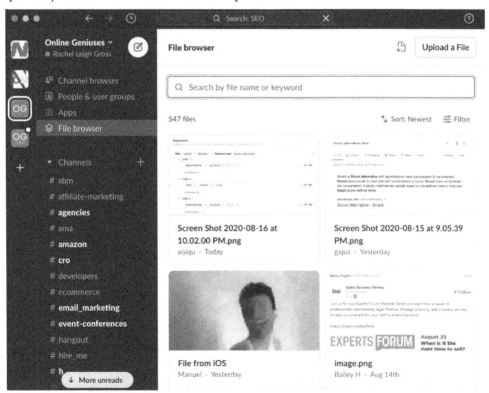

Figure 1.8 – File sharing in Slack

Utilizing the **File browser** option, you can search through files that you have shared or find those that other members of your team have added. Uploading is also simple, and you can do it by simply attaching a file to a channel or direct message text.

Main menu

The main menu is where a team member can go to personalize the Slack workspace for their needs and best processes. A team member can access their profile to add a profile picture, phone number, and other details. Some of these preferences include setting up notifications, picking a Slack theme, customizing the sidebar, and searching for advanced settings.

Sidebar

The sidebar gives team members direct access to all channels and direct messages they are a part of in the workspace:

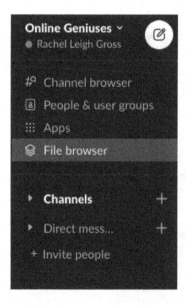

Figure 1.9 – The Slack sidebar

The sidebar organizes all recent conversations, mentions, files, and more, making it easy to build upon conversations and move projects forward. The sidebar also gives access to the main menu where team members can adjust their settings and preferences.

Statuses

A Slack status is a simple way to share your availability and accessibility with other team members:

Figure 1.10 – Slack statuses

A status includes an emoji and short text description that appears when an individual hovers over your workspace status. Popular methods of utilizing Slack statuses include the following:

- **In a meeting**
- **Online and available**
- **Busy and will respond soon**
- **Away from laptop**

This overview of various Slack features and functionalities will help you to create a workspace that best fits your team's needs. Now that you understand the basics of Slack, let's figure out whether Slack is the best tool for your team.

Slack versus other tools

Slack has become the standout in team communication tools over the past few years. Its functionality and adaptability for small and large teams attract many to its path. However, there are a number of competitors within the market that you need to be aware of:

- **Microsoft Teams**: Teams is the communication and collaboration hub that syncs well with Office 365 processes. Continue to the end of the chapter to find out more about this platform in detail.

- **Workplace by Facebook**: Workplace creates a social-like network for team members to collaborate with each other. This is a recent development by Facebook and could experience more bugs.

- **Chatter by Salesforce**: Chatter connects employees to files, data, and other team members in a manner that focuses on collaboration. This is an expensive platform and not ideal for an emerging start-up.

- **monday.com**: Monday is a project management tool that allows teams to work dynamically through the planning and execution of projects. Monday has more power within project management than daily, one-off communications.

- **Google Hangouts**: Hangouts offers a secure instant messaging platform and direct connection to Google Drive that makes sharing simple. Hangouts offers much less functionality than Slack, and it carries a more text message-like feeling than might be deemed workplace-appropriate.

While these platforms all have something different to offer, Slack is praised for its simplicity and range of capabilities that allows users of all backgrounds to instantly apply the tool to fit their company's needs. Slack permits its users to communicate safely in addition to its many other features that collaborate in a singular space.

Slack versus email

Email remains one of the most prominent communication tools among companies, both for internal and external conversations. For instance, how many times just this week did you find yourself saying, "Email that document over to me for review," or "I need to email our accountant these details"? One too many times is most likely the answer.

Billions of people spend hours every single day on their email. It is one of the most popular communication forms. However, it is also one of the most draining and time-consuming. Think about what your team has emailed you recently; this might include the following:

- An update on the current project development for your latest product

- Last week's data analytics in CSV pulled from your social media accounts

- A proposal document for an upcoming sales call

- A request for 15 minutes on your calendar to discuss a team member's progress

These items have merit and are essential for your company's growth, yet they should not need to suck up the time they take to write, send, and respond to another email among hundreds received each day.

So, what if there was a platform that could decrease your presence (and hours) on email and increase your time spent on meaningful company growth and project development? There is, and it just so happens to be the topic of this book.

Slack has given teams another option besides inundating team members' inboxes with more emails during the day. For all of the examples we have listed previously, and countless others, a channel or direct message with the appropriate individuals mentioned would create the communication needed to move a task forward.

An email takes away the real-time notifications and updates that your team needs to move swiftly. Every email is measured with the same significance because it goes to the same inbox. A Slack message is given the proper importance (whether that is high or low on the totem pole of company urgency) by delivering it in the right channel, to the right person, and at the exact moment that it is needed.

Email still has an essential place in your day-to-day communication, and Slack does not erase that need completely nor replace all of your email connectivity. The majority of companies who use Slack still have an email in place for their team. Google and Salesforce team members all have email addresses just as they all have Slack profiles, and smaller companies function similarly. However, Slack can, and should, decrease the number of emails you receive and send internally because you have a better and smarter method for communicating with your team.

If email and Slack are a marriage of communication channels, how should each platform be used most effectively? Let's get into these nitty-gritty details together.

Perfect examples of when to use Slack

The following is a list of examples of when you can use Slack:

- **The "Reply all" message**:

  If you send an email where "Reply all" is a response that a team member can make, you will get more engagement and less annoyance if sending through Slack. For instance, there could be a team brainstorm where every individual member needs to get involved, there might be an update that you need people to confirm the receipt of, or there might be a company-wide update that needs to be shared across the team.

  Before Slack, sending an email with dozens of people CC'd in was a go-to move, but this also led to pointless replies crowding coworkers' inboxes. Slack is a simple way to share information or updates across a team and declutter an already full inbox.

- **Quick answers or immediate responses**:

  Have you ever sent an email and crossed your fingers, hoping for an immediate response or urgent approval? Slack eliminates that fear and, instead, functions as the perfect space for direct communications to occur. No longer do you need to wait and let a partner sale slip through your fingers or share an urgent request for time off because of a sudden illness. Slack alerts the appropriate person to your concern, and your need is answered efficiently in real time.

- **Off-topic conversations**:

  An essential part of building your company's culture is team communications, business topics, and more personal watercooler conversations. The beauty of building strong relationships with other team members happens in random conversations, photo shares, last-minute happy hours, and more personal chitchats.

  Rather than sending a formal email to communicate these items, Slack is the perfect place to host the random and off-topic chats that lead to a thriving company culture that focuses on positive relationship building. Create a channel in your workspace, titled **random**, and watch as your team fills the feed with memories of their first day at the office, photos from last year's New Year's party, and rapid-fire questions to get to know one another better.

Perfect examples of when to use email

The following is a list of examples of when you can use email:

- **Long messages**:

  You have received or written a multitude of long emails that took you an hour or more to put together. They come with bulleted sub-sections, headers, tagged team members, and call to actions to move a project forward. Slack is perfect for real-time conversations and quick connectivity; however, these longer messages are a great example of how to continue using emails.

  Email communication is not great for quick responses, but it is a place for full project reports and other necessities that need to be conveyed to all the right team members. Information stays the front of the mind in an email message when an intense priority must be given to the topic at hand.

  So, what could be a perfect union of Slack and email in this instance? Well, you could send your detailed email to critical stakeholders and follow up with a Slack message to get everyone to confirm the receipt and timeline of response to the call to action.

- **Initiation over email**

  It is only a matter of time until a team member reaches out over email with a particular request or need for communication. If they are to initiate this interaction over email, you can do them a service by continuing the conversation over email rather than trying to shift it to Slack.

  There could be a reason they have decided on an email instead of a Slack message, or maybe this individual prefers the sense of privacy that an email carries with it. Whatever the reason, shifting a conversation initiated over email will result in a loss of important communication in the transition and make it hard to continue in Slack.

- **External stakeholders are needed**

  External organizations, partners, and other contributors are far more likely to communicate with your team over email. Whether or not they appear in a shared channel on your Slack workspace, respecting their decision to contribute over email creates a culture of respect and understanding. The organization may not prioritize Slack as your team does, or its IT department may frown upon Slack messaging as they can't track it as easily. Meeting your external stakeholders in an email is a great example of how best to utilize this communication portal.

  However, you can set these Slack versus email standards with your partners to fit your relationship best and make all parties feel valued.

The pros and cons of utilizing Slack

Fully understanding Slack's pros and cons will allow you to make an easier decision over the best way to communicate your intended message. Slack has been built to make working both easier and smoother for your whole team; however, there are some elements that you might want to consider when looking into the platform.

The pros of Slack

Here is a list of some of the pros of using Slack:

- **User interface (UI)**: Slack is continuously raved about for its user-friendly design. The onboarding process is simple for getting all of your team members onto the platform on their first day with the company. Additionally, the clear directions given on the platform for sending messages, finding documents, and searching for them make it simple for daily use. Other pros, along with those already mentioned, include the following:

    a. A beautiful **user experience (UX)** and UI

    b. Clear channel and message designations

    c. Intuitive for first-time users

- **Quick connections**: Group and individual messaging functions are as simple as writing a message and clicking on **Send**. There is no longer a need to triple-check recipients who are BCC'd in, nor question the best method for quickly pinging a large group. One of Slack's most significant pros is its quick and efficient messaging to maintain communication across your company. Other advantages in this category include the following:

    a. Notifications for new messages

    b. Easy-to-create group messaging

    c. In-platform calls

    d. Ability to add external parties to a channel

    e. Transparency across the team

- **Search**: Slack's ability to save and archive all threads of conversation that occur on the platform is game-changing for many companies. Slack eliminates the fear of losing any information shared with another team member or accidentally throwing away a meeting communication with an important to-do list. Housing these items, and many more, on Slack means that everything is stored for you to find at a moment's notice. Other pros, along with those already mentioned, include the following:

    a. A detailed history of communications

    b. Time and date details per message

    c. Stored files shared on the platform

    d. A filtering system when searching for a specific item

- **Integration**: A final significant and attractive part of Slack is its ability to integrate with other tools, apps, and bots to streamline your work even more. This is an important topic for later in this book where we teach you how to build bots for Slack integration. Here are the pros of Slack's integration function:

     a. Dozens of Slack apps are available to integrate.

     b. You have the ability to develop your own tool.

     c. Multiple data points can be accessed from one platform.

Let's move on to the cons of Slack next.

The cons of Slack

Slack is an incredibly powerful platform to bring into your team's toolbox. However, there are a few elements where Slack falls short of in its development. They include the following:

Overwhelming: Many individuals are drawn to Slack for ease of communication and a social-like feel, yet this can easily be a con for many people. The line between work life and home life can start to blur when a message ping comes through, and you are compelled to respond. Other disadvantages in this space include the following:

- It is easy to respond during out-of-office hours when it feels like a "chat" rather than work.
- Notifications can become overwhelming.
- Messages can become unorganized quickly.
- Context switching occurs easily.

Disorganization: Communications move so quickly on Slack that individuals can sometimes feel lost by the rapid pace. The platform also loses out on a number of customization features that could make the disorganization and faster pace easier to handle. Cons in this area include the following:

- Fast-paced communications can be hard to keep track of.
- There is no automated messaging (without the need for a bot or an app).
- There is limited customization.
- Screen sharing is not accessible via iOS or Android
- The Free plan has a minimal number of features.

Though, like any platform, there are aspects of Slack that do not quite meet every team member's satisfaction, Slack has overwhelmingly proved to be a positive tool in the workplace. In comparison to its competitors, Slack provides a scale, from beginner start-ups to big-name corporations, that allows for a wide range of growth that other applications simply can't compete with.

Slack versus Microsoft Teams

Slack has become the top contender among work communication platforms, and many other brands have paled in comparison to this $17 billion company. One tool that continues to be a strong competitor in the battle against Slack is Teams from Microsoft.

Microsoft Teams is a communication and collaboration platform that connects people, content, and tools to streamline a company's processes. This tool is very similar to Slack and has many of the same appealing features, yet there are distinctive reasons for choosing Slack over Microsoft Teams.

Teams that already have an Office 365 subscription may find that Microsoft Teams functions best for their needs. Teams integrates with Microsoft's full suite of products to make sharing projects and other details quick and easy. Teams can easily be customized to meet a company's needs, including APIs, bots, and third-party services. This platform scales with your company and can be utilized across many industries.

However, Microsoft Teams has some steep limitations that make Slack a worthy contender in this discussion. Teams does not allow external parties to be welcomed onto a company's team portal. This would get expensive if you frequently work with external organizations, and that is a significant win for Slack as external stakeholders can be welcomed onto a shared channel. Teams also has limited access to different functions, including a lack of notifications, a set number of channels, and storage that fills quickly with shared files.

Teams is perfect for those with Office 365 subscriptions; however, many small businesses, early-stage start-ups, and solo entrepreneurs may not find it accessible. These individuals and many others rely heavily on Google Drive to create content, track projects, and more. Slack offers full integration with your Google Workspace that makes sharing files simple.

The following reasons would make your company a fit for Microsoft Teams:

- It utilizes Office 365.
- It is a large enterprise.
- It has an IT team that can do a complex Teams setup.

Overall, Microsoft Teams was created with large enterprises in mind, whereas Slack caters to those across different levels of development. Your local start-up can find success on Slack just as 65 Fortune 100 companies do. That transformative functionality is what makes Slack a leader in this space.

Summary

This chapter has laid the groundwork of your Slack knowledge to begin preparing you for what's ahead. In this chapter, we began with an overview of Slack and discussed several of its important features that aid companies in streamlining their communications and collaborations. We discussed other contenders for team communications and how Slack features match or perform better than those platforms. Then, we discussed the pros and cons of Slack to identify whether it would be the best fit for your company's needs. Lastly, we discussed Slack versus email and Microsoft Teams for internal communication methods to show you how Slack can add to your team's overall structure.

You now understand what Slack is, whether or not it is the best platform fit for what you need, and what situations call for communication via email or Slack depending on the context.

In the next chapter, we will look at how to set up your Slack workspace and walk you through a step-by-step description to set you up for success. We will explain, in depth, what a workspace is, how to download Slack applications, how to set up a profile, and how to join existing workspaces. Then, we will make sure you fully understand the roles and permissions that are allowed within Slack and how to migrate your existing workspaces to your organization. Finally, we will dive into the power of Slack for remote teams and how this platform is a great way to build a thriving remote culture.

You can return to this chapter as often as you need for the Slack dictionary mentioned here. Now, move on to the next chapter to continue your Slack journey.

2
Setting Up Your Slack Workspace

Becoming a highly efficient and effective team begins with top-notch communication and collaboration. As we have already discussed, Slack is the right tool that can bring this type of coordination to life and ensure that you reach all of your business goals, build a thriving culture, and prepare your team for ultimate success.

In the previous chapter, we provided you with information that enabled you to become familiar with the Slack platform and begin to gain an understanding of its functionality. You have mastered the basic knowledge of this tool and are now ready to dive into the next phase of your technological journey.

In this chapter, we will cover the following topics:

- Understanding what a workspace is
- Creating a Slack workspace
- Downloading Slack applications
- Inviting and tracking team members

- How to join a Slack workspace as a new member or guest

- Different roles, levels of permissions, and access in Slack

- Migrating existing workspaces to your organization

- Best practices of how to set up your workplace for a remote team

Reading this chapter will bring you in-depth knowledge of setting up a Slack workplace so that you can utilize this tool within your business. A workplace is just the beginning of the type of real-time communications that will level your company up for success.

What is a workspace?

Simply put, a Slack workspace is your digital office, and it ensures that your team is set in a place where its members can thrive together.

From its original conception to what it has evolved into today, Slack is a popular and high-quality team connectivity platform. The channel-based messenger powerfully connects your team members, files, apps, and more for instant and real-time communication and collaboration. The technology on the platform makes it not only comfortable but effortless, enabling you to keep your team connected, no matter the time or location barriers that may be present for remote or divided teams.

Slack's many features for collaboration

Slack was developed with a team's operations and processes in mind. Real-time updates can lead to much faster business growth, sales results, and culture. If you aim to be the next Mark Zuckerberg or category-defining business, then Slack is the tool for you.

Slack's dozens of features ensure that sharing, creating, and ideating with team members is almost instantaneous. Some of these features are listed here:

- Customizable **channels** to create the perfect place for every conversation

- Detailed **topics and descriptions** to guide your team members on the use of each channel

- **Direct messages** to host private conversations between yourself and up to eight others

- **Threads** that keep one topic of communication organized and trackable

- Social-like **reactions** to ensure team members feel supported and heard in their messages

- Robust **search** capabilities for direct access to messages, files, channels, and people
- **App** integrations to streamline your current workflows into your communication channels
- Individualized **statuses** so team members can quickly share availability

A Slack workspace as a digital office

Slack's many features are organized into a workspace. A workspace is the central communication hub for your team on Slack. This is where your team members can collaborate and discuss once they have created a Slack account and have been invited onto a particular workspace.

Customized channels make up your Slack workspace and create various lines of communication. Channels can cover topics such as watercooler talk, social media, announcements, general, and more.

All of your channels build the workspace into the hub you aim to develop for top team efficiency. Slacks workspaces can have an unlimited number of channels, and this type of customizability has been created with the user in mind.

Dozens of Fortune 100 companies utilize Slack workspaces as their leading communication portal for team members. These organizations may need to have dozens of channels to support their communication workflows. On the other hand, early-stage start-ups and small businesses who find themselves on Slack may use a much smaller number of channels. Whatever fits your company's process is accessible to you on the platform.

Workspaces and Slack plans

Slack offers several different plans depending upon the workspace capabilities you are seeking. All Slack plans present you with unlimited channels, but a free or paid for plan might be a better option based on your other necessities.

The Free, Standard, and Plus plans are the different options you have available, and each comes with a different number of features and level of flexibility. A plan is attached to a single workspace for you to customize to your needs.

Free

The Free plan for a Slack workspace is an excellent option for teams trying out Slack for the first time and making sure it's the proper collaboration tool for your business. With a Free plan, you have access to the following:

- Message history with your 10,000 most recent messages
- Searchable messages
- 10 app integrations
- 5 GB of file storage per workspace
- General channel posting permissions
- One-to-one calls
- Essential support from Slack's team

Those on a Free plan have access to these features for an unlimited amount of time.

Standard

The Standard plan is the next step up in terms of efficiency and effectiveness for your team. This fits well for small- and medium-sized businesses with its additional features. With a Standard plan, your workspace will have the following:

- All elements of the Free plan
- Unlimited message history
- Unlimited app integrations
- 10 GB of file storage per member (a significant distinction from the Free plan)
- Customizable sidebar sections
- Share channels externally
- Single-channel and multi-channel guest invites with external collaborators
- Up to 15 participants on calls
- Screen sharing
- Detailed analytics to understand your company's workflows
- Priority support

As detailed in all of these features, the Standard plan offers a more robust level of individualization for your company. Building a thriving hub for sharing messages, files, and updates becomes more streamlined with the Standard features. The Standard plan is around $7 a month per active user on an annual contract.

Plus

The Plus plan is Slack's top tier workspace option for larger businesses or those with more administrative needs. With a bigger team comes more requirements to stay on track with real-time collaborations, and the Plus plan allows for that organization to occur. The Plus workspace includes the following:

- All elements of the Standard plan
- 20 GB of file storage per member
- Compliancy settings and options
- An active directory
- Ability to set posting permissions on any channel
- Full message activity history
- 24/7 support and a 4-hour first response time

The Plus plan is around $13 a month per active user on an annual contract.

No matter what plan works best for your team and team size, you will find that any Slack workspace provides the organization and structure you are looking for in a communication tool.

No matter what stage your business is at, Slack is a platform that grows with you.

Many smaller-sized businesses start with the Free plan to explore Slack's capabilities before moving to a Standard or Plus plan as they grow. With each additional member, both your company and messaging platform continue to expand. Slack is designed to never be outgrown.

Downloading Slack applications

As a 21st century application, Slack acknowledges that each person's workspace no longer looks the same. For many, it's based on preference; however, in certain situations, it's based on availability and resources. Not every member of your team can be expected to operate on the same systems. Slack has a solution for this.

Different options for use

Team members can join a Slack team only after being invited and accepting the invitation to join the individual workspace. This process keeps logins separate for individuals on multiple workspaces – another streamlined feature that keeps your team organized for success.

Slack has built its platform for several different applications so that individuals can decide how they best work in the workspace. Slack applications include desktop and browser clients and mobile apps, and every update in one platform automatically updates across the others. This allows your team to stay updated on the move with just a glance at a computer screen or cell phone notification:

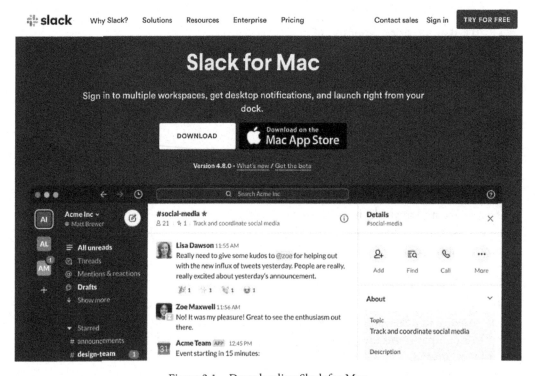

Figure 2.1 – Downloading Slack for Mac

Let's explore each download option for different applications.

Desktop

Slack's desktop application makes it seamless to connect with team members on both Windows and Mac computers. Downloading Slack to your desktop allows you to customize the notifications you receive and how you receive them.

Integrating Slack directly onto your work computer provides instant access to team members and files. This creates the real-time updates Slack has built for a team's operations. Answers to your questions, brainstorms for your products, and celebrations for your wins are a click away with the desktop application:

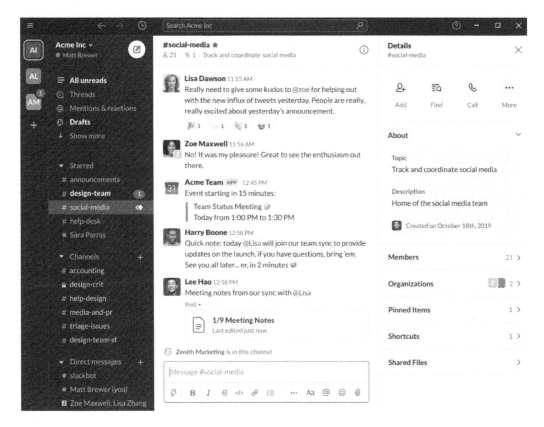

Figure 2.2 – Slack on a desktop

The iOS app

The iOS Slack application brings ease of use and social-like updates to your workspace. With the iOS application, Slack notifications can be delivered directly to your phone so that you do not miss out on any essential conversations or exciting news.

Some individuals may find that the iOS application blurs the line between the personal and professional world. However, using the iOS screen time technology, you can easily create boundaries and turn off notifications quickly during non-working hours:

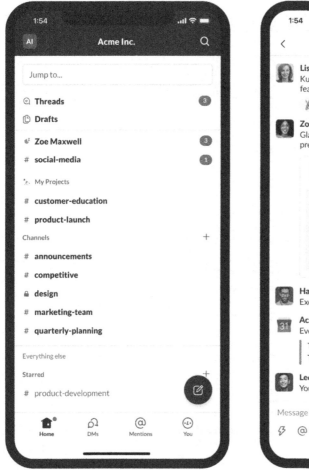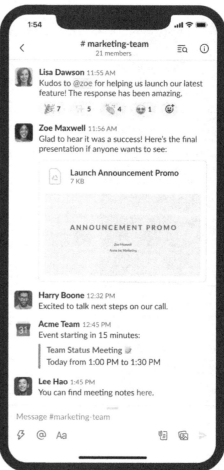

Figure 2.3 – Slack on iOS

The Android app

The Android Slack application is very similar to the iOS application, but it makes it accessible for those without iOS technology (think about all Android devices versus iPhones). The Android platform offers all of the Slack capabilities that you would find on the desktop version right on your Android device. Real-time notifications, reactions, and conversations exist right through your phone:

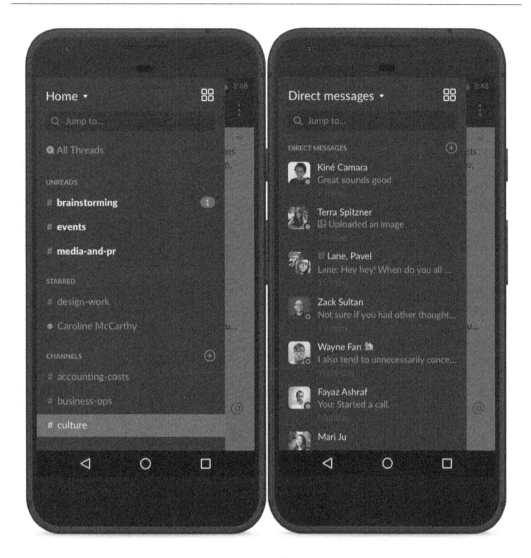

Figure 2.4 – The Slack Android app

Now, let's take a look at how we can download the application option of our choice.

Downloading your application choice

Beginning your journey toward the complete synchronization of your team is simple with the Slack download process. Remember that Slack is not just for businesses with full teams already integrated into workflows and cultures. Slack is an excellent destination for a solo entrepreneur or early-stage company with one or two team members who wish to stay organized and on track. The platform is also perfect for a freelance contractor who works with various external individuals or organizations.

The high-quality connectivity and collaboration you receive on Slack suitable are for many different types of entrepreneurs. Your platform choices and workspace growth can be customized to fit those needs.

In creating a Slack workspace for your team, a solo entrepreneurial venture, or contractor relationships, you first need to download the platform or platforms that you aim to work from.

Slack's website is incredibly useful for getting direct access to what you need. Not only has Slack created a tool that is easy to use, but its website emphasizes user ease and support across every page.

Desktop downloads

There are two options that you can use to download the Slack desktop applications for Mac systems (macOS) and Windows systems, depending on your computer. Having both of these system options available means that every individual on your team can easily find and download the platform that works best for them. You can download Slack in one of two ways:

- Download it directly from the Slack website at `slack.com/downloads`.
- Download it from the Windows Store or App Store by simply searching for `Slack`.

After finding the application through either option in the preceding list, you can click on **Download** or **Install** to get the process started. It will only take a few minutes for the download to complete, and then you can launch Slack on your desktop with a double-click of the newly installed file.

Mac users that download from Slack directly will need to drag and drop the Slack icon into the **Applications** folder in the window that appears before being launched. A Mac computer will automatically guide the user through this process.

You are now one step closer to having an organized team that will beat any of your business goals!

iOS and Android downloads

Downloading Slack for iOS and Android products is simple. The individual will search for **Slack** in either the Google Play Store (for Android users) or App Store (for iOS users), click on **Download**, and launch Slack on their devices with a tap of the icon. Slack will automatically begin running once this process is complete, and you are now able to keep track of your company on the go.

As highlighted previously, a few simple motions are all it takes to download Slack across different platforms and begin your workspace mastery. Once you've downloaded the actual application to your respective device, it's time to log in to your workspace.

Logging in to Slack

There are a number of different ways in which to actually access your workspace. If you're joining an existing workspace, there are instances where you can utilize a company link to easily find your organization's workspace on Slack. You can also choose to sign in with your email or Google account information. Let's take a look at some of the different ways you can log into Slack for the first time.

Signing in with your email account

As simple as it sounds, you can use your email address to sign up with Slack as you would for any online service. Once you open the Slack app, choose the **Sign in with Email** option and enter your email address. You should immediately receive a confirmation code in your inbox from Slack. Enter the code and your workspace will open automatically.

If you're a member of multiple workspaces, Slack will provide the option to **Launch** whichever workspace you'd like to open.

Signing in with Google

Similar to signing in with your email address, signing in with Google allows you to automatically choose your Google account to proceed with Slack. Open the app, choose the **Continue with Google** option, and select the Google account you'd like to use. Your workspace should open immediately.

If you're a member of multiple workspaces, Slack will provide the option to **Launch** whichever workspace you'd like to open.

Signing in with multiple workspaces

Once you've signed into one Slack account, you can access multiple workspaces you belong to. From your desktop version of Slack, select the workspace name in the top left-hand corner of your workspace. Choose **Sign in to another workspace** and sign in to your other workspace accounts with their login information.

After you've signed in, click on the **plus** icon on the left side of the app below the icons of your other workspaces. Follow the regular steps to sign into the workspace, and you'll have access to all of your workspaces through the sidebar of your desktop Slack application.

Now that you've officially logged into your workspace, it's time to begin the more personalized aspects of your Slack experience. So, what's next? Let's create a workspace and your profile.

Setting up your profile

You are now entering the next phase of your Slack learning: setting up the full workspace where your team will collide in a roar of conversation, teamwork, and excitement. Just like downloading Slack applications, creating a workspace is a simple process and can be done via the Slack website.

What is a workspace primary owner?

As the creator of the workspace, you become the workspace primary owner, and this holds a lot of management power when it comes to your workspace. Primary owners act as the administrative authority in a Slack workspace and have final decision-making capabilities. This individual also becomes the Slack customer, and your identity is intertwined with the Slack account.

> **Tip**
> As is likely within any company, leadership can change over time. To avoid messy handovers that could happen with the passing of leadership, make a service account for the owner, or share the account information with other members of your team. This is so that if the person chooses to leave the organization, for whatever reason, the workspace primary owner account still stays within the company.

With the highest level of authority, a workspace primary owner should represent a senior-level manager at the company or an IT administrator who can best understand Slack's technical role for your business. Transferring primary ownership is an option, and it is especially useful if and when the primary owner leaves the company. However, the individual who holds this title should align with the company's best practices to ensure your Slack remains a strong haven for team collaboration, efficiency, and culture.

Here are some top things to keep in mind:

- Ensure all Slack members use their work email addresses to create their profiles.
- Add billing information and contacts to maintain on-time payments.
- Promote team members to admin roles to aid in day-to-day work.
- Maintain your company's culture through clear channel rules.

The workspace primary owner holds power over a business's Slack workspace – this comes with great responsibility and can be great fun when done well.

While this kind of accountability can become overwhelming, there are several key tips to creating a proper and creative workspace for everyone involved. Let's start with the basics.

Creating a Slack workspace

Upon identifying the workspace primary owner (probably the individual holding this book right now), it is time to create your workspace with ease through Slack's website.

Head to `slack.com/create` to find the workspace creation funnel. Then, perform these steps:

Enter your email address and the confirmation code that will be sent to you. Remember to use the business email address that you want associated with the Slack account!

Name your workspace. This should reflect the workspace's purpose; more often than not, it is named after the company name.

Create a new channel for your workspace. You will have the chance to create channels on-demand after setting the workspace up, so don't fret if you haven't thought of all the channels you need at this point.

Add your team members' emails if you are ready. If not, you can invite them on an ongoing basis after creating the workspace.

Click to see your channel in Slack and visit your newly created workspace.

Finishing signing up by clicking on the button at the top of the screen and entering your name and password.

Finally, review your workspace name and URL before clicking on **Save**.

Completing these seven steps brings your workspace to life instantly. While there are numerous fun, personalized steps in which to create your individualized workspace, do remember to set up the proper security measures as well. For instance, make sure you utilize **Single-Sign-On (SSO)** for your members, which we'll discuss in more detail in *Chapter 9, Slack API, Webhooks, Block Kit, and Sandbox*.

If you're an Enterprise Grid-level company, you might also want to claim your domain if the organization currently operates under multiple web domains. This will make your workspaces easier to find, prevent access to those with unsanctioned workspaces outside of your company, and allow team members with specific domains in their email addresses easier access to join. To claim or remove a domain, follow these steps:

1. Select the **Contact Us** button in the top right-hand corner of your Enterprise Grid Slack page.

2. Click on **Write a message**.

3. In the **How we can help?** field, describe for the Slack Help team which domains you'd like to claim for your organization, or if you'd like to remove any existing ones. For example, if Google wanted to create a Slack and designate the name "Google" for just their company workspaces.

    This feature is exclusively available on the Enterprise Grid plan option.

As the workspace primary owner, you can dive further into your workspace's setup and organization at this point. You can configure the full workspace's permissions and settings, such as enabling multifactor authentication for guests, adding an icon and custom emojis, creating "Do Not Disturb" hours, and managing the channels you want your company to use.

Channels were explained further in *Chapter 1, Getting Started with Slack*, so please refer to that chapter to build out your workspace. Channels are the main thoroughfares of conversation, so creating guidelines for names, exact topics, and descriptions, and setting up default channels so that they appear for newly invited members will direct the flow of connectivity you want across your organization.

Now you can move onto setting up your profile to ensure it's customized with your preferences.

Creating your profile

Creating a Slack profile begins with the workspace primary owner, but all individuals invited to the workspace need to follow this process. Slack is your team's digital office, so team members should show up as themselves on the platform.

With Slack's individualized features, making a profile that reflects your professional image occurs in the first few steps of getting onto the platform:

Figure 2.5 – An example of a Slack profile picture

After joining (or creating) the workspace, you can find the profile edit options by navigating to the dashboard and selecting **View Profile** and **Edit Profile**. A couple of details that you can customize include the following:

- Add a profile picture, so you are quickly identified in the channels.
- Add a full name that is associated with your Slack account.
- Add a display name that appears in Slack channels (often, a display name is shortened from the full name).
- Add a job title so that team members can identify your role.
- Add a phone number so that you can be reached in case of emergencies.
- Change your time zone as needed to reflect your current location.

Here is an example of a Slack profile:

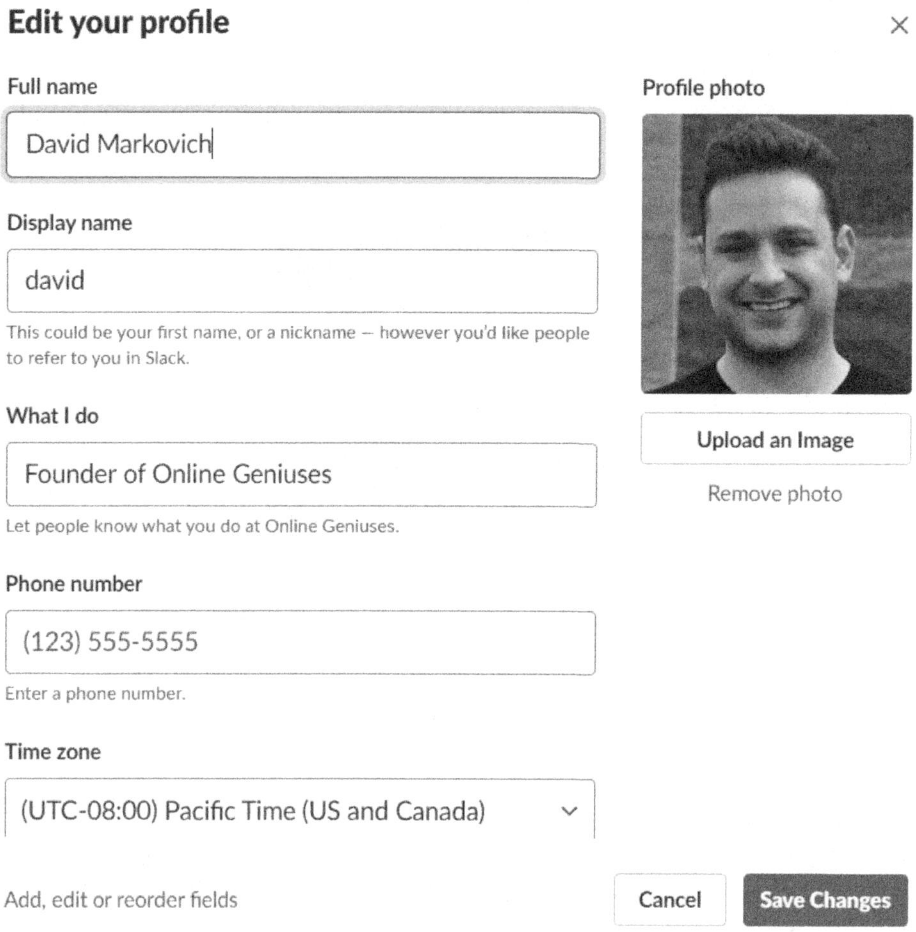

Edit your profile   ✕

Full name

```
David Markovich
```

Profile photo

Display name

```
david
```

This could be your first name, or a nickname — however you'd like people to refer to you in Slack.

Upload an Image

Remove photo

What I do

```
Founder of Online Geniuses
```

Let people know what you do at Online Geniuses.

Phone number

```
(123) 555-5555
```

Enter a phone number.

Time zone

```
(UTC-08:00) Pacific Time (US and Canada)        ⌄
```

Add, edit or reorder fields   Cancel   **Save Changes**

Figure 2.6 – Slack profile features include your name, preferred name, job title, phone number, and time zone

Your profile will quickly set you apart from your team members on Slack, and this is crucial for streamlining conversations among team members who need to be involved. Update your profile every few weeks to reflect changes such as your job title, phone number, or maybe even a new office nickname that you've been bestowed.

Growing your workspace

You now have a brand new workspace to call your own and are on your way to total team alignment and growth. Your profile is set for success so that your team members can identify you among all Slack members. Now is the time to begin inviting your team members to the Slack workspace and boosting your Slack presence even more by joining other workspaces that will aid in your work.

Inviting and tracking team members

Getting your workspace primed for success means that you are ready to invite your team to the platform and have them interacting daily. Workspace primary owners and admins can always invite team members, but the default setup for a workspace gives everyone permission to invite members. Owners and admins can restrict that feature and take responsibility for inviting members themselves.

Other workspace members can request that individuals be invited to the Slack workspace, which sends a notification directly to the owners and admins for their approval.

There are three easy options that you can use to invite your team members:

- **Sending an email invitation** provides steps to accept the invite and get your team member set up on the account.

- **Allowing for email signup** means that individuals with an approved domain in their email address can create accounts and join automatically.

- **Sharing an invite link** with an expiration date that can be sent out in whatever manner best fits your process.

Sending an email invitation as the primary owner occurs right through your desktop app:

1. Click on the workspace name you want to invite members to.

2. Click on **Invite People to [Workspace]**. If you want to share an invite link, you will see this pop up as an option here.

3. Check whether the invitee is a multi-channel guest or a single-channel guest.

4. Enter the email addresses and add the invitee(s). You can add several email addresses at once by selecting the **Add many at once** option.

5. Choose the channel(s) the invitees will be added to.

6. Set a time the invitees will have access to the channel(s).

7. Send the invites.

The multi-channel and single-channel guests are great choices to welcome someone outside of your internal team into your workspace. An example of a multi-channel guest would be an intern who only needs access to a few channels for a specific length of time. An example of a single-channel guest would be a marketing contractor who just needs access to a marketing channel you have created for the length of their contract. Make sure that you correctly identify who these individuals are before sending the invites.

You can track and manage pending invitations as the workspace owner by viewing past invites through the invitation process. You can revoke an invitation or disable email notifications that a team member might receive before accepting or resending an invitation that may have expired or become lost.

Keeping track of where your team is in the onboarding process keeps you on the ball.

Team member notifications

A member who has been invited but has yet to accept can still be mentioned or sent direct messages through the workspace. They will receive email notifications upon each active message being sent. Upon accepting the invite and setting up their profile, they can view all notifications on the app and start the conversation from where they left off.

Team members can customize how they receive notifications once they are in the workspace. Many individuals unsubscribe from email notifications but utilize the desktop or app notifications to keep in the know. Unsubscribing from email notifications is simply done by hitting "**Unsubscribe**" in an email notification you have received.

It's the job of the workspace owner to invite new members, but it is each individual member's responsibility to add themselves to their respective workspaces and threads. As a new member or guest, there are certain basic steps you need to perform before you begin your Slack experience.

Joining a Slack workspace as a new member or guest

As we discussed earlier, joining a Slack workspace from an invitation is a simple process. Team members will click Accept on the invite, set up their profiles, and be ready for full Slack integration. Then, they can be added to channels, be mentioned in messages, and sent direct messages right through the Slack applications they download.

You can also follow this straightforward process for other workspaces you are joining as a new member! Maybe you work for another company that uses Slack for communication, or perhaps there is an open Slack group you want to participate in to build your professional skills. Following the steps from an emailed invite, direct email signup, or shared invite link looks the same every time.

Joining a workspace as a guest includes different permissions and access options. Single-channel guests enter a workspace from an invitation and only have access to one specific channel. Multi-channel guests enter a workspace from an invitation and can access one or more specified channels.

Guests can follow the same setup procedure as a Slack member:

1. They can join a workspace through an invitation.

2. They can set up a profile.

3. They can adjust notifications.

4. They can download Slack applications.

A critical distinction for joining a workspace as a guest is becoming familiar with the company's Slack workspace habits and rules. Guests are welcomed with a specific purpose, but they might not be familiar with the company's culture. Reviewing any company Slack guides, looking at Slack interactions on the workspace, and reaching out to the workspace owner are significant steps that either you (as a guest to another workspace) or a guest of yours can take to familiarize themselves with the new territory.

Company guidelines are crucial for any guest or outside member coming into a Slack workspace, but they are just as relevant – if not more important – for direct team members. Each member, from the workspace owner to the average employee, plays a specific role and has their own list of instructions to follow in order to keep the complete unit afloat.

Understanding roles and permissions

Slack workspaces welcome members with different roles, levels of permission, and access to features. These help you to create a secure workspace that places people in the best roles for them to succeed. Let's dive into the five role types and the permissions associated with each.

Owner

Slack owners have the highest level of permission on workspaces. Owners can join any public channel, send messages in any channel, upload files, and delete their messages. Additionally, owners have full access to the channel management, notifications, workspace management and settings, administration, and app integration.

Not all owners are workspace primary owners who have top-level access to permissions. Owners cannot delete a workspace, demote an owner, or transfer primary ownership as these are specific permissions of the primary owner.

Admin

Slack admins have the second-highest level of permissions in the workspace. Admins have the same access as owners do, apart from setting up channel retention and having fewer workspace, administration, and app integration settings.

Members

Slack members have access to Slack in all communication and collaboration permissions, including joining public channels, sending messages, uploading files, and deleting their messages. Members can also create public channels, private channels, and utilize notification strategies. Workspace management, settings, and administration permissions are generally not available for members.

Multi-channel and single-channel guests

Multi and single-channel guests can join the channels they are invited to, send messages, upload files, and delete messages if that feature is made accessible to them. These individuals do not have many other permissions as Slack acts merely as a portal for messages with these role types.

As you build out your optimal workspace, keep in mind the various roles and permissions associated with each level. This will streamline the onboarding process and enable everyone to get the tools and capabilities they need. Reference back to this section often while you build your workspace online.

Roles within a Slack space maintain their own hierarchy, but many companies join the communication tool with a set organization of members and prior history. Although starting fresh can have its own benefits, importing existing data allows for a seamless transition from one workspace to another.

Migrating existing workspaces to your organization

At this point in the chapter, you should now have a deep understanding of how to set up a Slack workspace and invite members with different permissions attached to their accounts. However, what if you have already built a workspace and now need to migrate that information over to your new (and improved) workspace? Slack's search feature means that your messages never get lost and your old workspaces shouldn't either.

Slack's import and export tools make this merge possible, allowing you to move members, messages, and channel data from one workspace to the next. Slack also offers two export options for you to choose from:

- A Standard export for those on the Free, Standard, or Plus plan
- A Corporate export for those on the Plus plan who apply for the option

A Standard export will move public channels (such as messages and members), links to files, and member profile information. A Corporate export will move public and private channels (such as messages and members), direct messages, links to files, and member profile information. The Corporate option allows for a much more robust transition of information.

To export your data from one workspace to the other, follow these steps:

1. Export the data into a file (transitioning from a smaller to a larger workspace will make this process much simpler).
2. Sign in to the workspace you are importing the data to.
3. Upload the export file in the **Settings & Administration** panel under workspace settings.
4. Choose the members to import either through batch action or manual selection (you must decide how members with matching email addresses are imported along with those without a matching email address in the new workspace).
5. Choose the channels to import (private and shared channels cannot be merged into existing channels on the new workspace due to privacy reasons).
6. Review all of your import choices and run.

Once you have successfully moved your existing information into your Slack workspace, the rest is up to you. All of the communication possibilities Slack has to offer is now in the hands of you and your unique team to utilize in any way you see fit.

While Slack can address the needs of any type of team, the tool was created for those incapable of an in-person workspace to be their one-stop-shop for all materials and communication. As many companies have turned to remote work to expand their options, Slack has become that resource.

Slack for remote teams

Slack was built with digital teams in mind, specifically, *for remote teams and by remote teams*. The founding team built the platform out of the need to connect remote team members from different countries and cities on a real-time basis.

Slack is meant to immediately create a digital office experience with up-to-date communication and collaboration that is accessible with a click of a button. As you set up your workspace, keep in mind that Slack is here to support your remote and in-person teams.

Here are some ideas for you to keep in mind as you build a workspace for your remote team:

- Set "Do Not Disturb" hours.

- Encourage team members to utilize Slack statuses and "Away" notifications.

- Ensure time zones are accounted for in team members' profiles.

- Create a specific channel for out-of-hours communication to retain a personal/ professional divide.

It can be hard for team members to distinguish between working hours and non-working hours when there is no set office space or commute time to remind them of the difference. It's important to encourage a separation to prevent an overworked environment and to stimulate those working in different locations/time periods to be able to work and share when the time is appropriate for them.

Summary

This chapter has set you up for success with a deep understanding of Slack workspaces and how they will change your team's connectivity from the outset. In this chapter, we discussed how you can create a workspace that is optimized for your team and workflow. You have learned how to invite members and join other workspaces yourself to continue your education. We discussed different roles and permissions that guide the user experience of an individual with a particular role. We also walked you through how to transfer old workspaces to new ones to keep up with your company's growth.

You know how to build a workspace and get your team onboarded to Slack, which is the next level of your learning.

In the next chapter, we will dive further into the differences between paid and free Slack workspaces and how to utilize direct messages versus group chats, tagged mentions, and public announcements to the fullest. We will hone in on how to use Slack effectively without sacrificing your focus, and we will learn more functionalities, shortcuts, and demands to make your work even more efficient.

3
Slack Features, Tips, and Tricks

Slack has replaced many other team connectivity platforms – and for the better. No longer is there a need for winding email chains, chat rooms connected to personal cell phones, or even the daily standup meeting (in office or via video). Slack has become the overwhelming chosen platform for all of your team's connecting and collaborating purposes.

Chapter 1, Getting Started with Slack, got you familiar with Slack as a whole, while *Chapter 2, Setting Up Your Workspace,* shared detailed information on how to set up a Slack workspace that best fits your team's needs. You now understand what a workspace is, how to create and invite team members with different permission levels, and how to join other workspaces for your own personal and professional development. This is just the beginning of what you need to learn about Slack, and this chapter will dive into further customization. While doing so, you will learn about the best Slack tips and tricks for your business team. There are tons of Slack features that are normally unknown to the bulk of its users.

In this chapter, we will cover these crucial topics:

- Learning the difference between paid and free Slack accounts
- Learning how to use private messages versus group chats

- Knowing the power of @ mentions and channel announcements

- Using public versus private channels

- Tricks to increasing your productivity

- How to use Slack effectively without sacrificing focus

- Notification tricks

This chapter will make your newly created Slack workspace into a customized hub of intentional connection and collaboration across your team. We recommend that you come back to this chapter often and bookmark the Slack shortcuts that will make your team a dream.

A simple versus powerful Slack application

Slack has become the most used connectivity platform for companies, ranging from Fortune 100 to early-stage startups, because of its ease of use and brand familiarity. Slack functions smoothly for your team to enjoy and utilize by providing the following:

- Real-time messaging and integration with other important platforms

- Channel-specific conversations to aid in organization

- Private messages and invite-only channels to keep conversations with the right team members

Slack, in its simplest form, is a fantastic portal for communication where team members can dive into real-time talks that ease development and project growth. But Slack is a much more powerful tool when you understand the many features it holds. Although you now understand how to create a custom workspace for your team, do you know how to do any of the following?

- Star messages for easy access.

- Notify all your team members who are online and active by using @.

- Delete unnecessary channels from your Slack search engine.

- Change the default download location.

- Create reminders for that all-important weekly team meeting.

If your answer to this question is a resounding "no", then don't worry – this chapter is here to help by providing all of the insider knowledge you'll ever need to make Slack an even more customized, effective platform for your team's needs and desires.

The importance of intentional communication

As the leading collaboration platform built for entrepreneurs by entrepreneurs, it is no wonder that your business's needs for up-to-date connection will be met on your customized Slack workspace. Slack brings communication to the forefront, yet it is effective and intentional communication that will truly level up your company's development and team synchronicity.

Real-time chat and updates can become overwhelming, unnecessary, and, worst of all, annoying when done so with repetition. Think back to a time when you looked at your cell phone's lock screen, saw 20+ notifications, and quickly went to your settings tab to turn off everything but the essential pings. You likely felt overwhelmed by the amount of updates your apps were telling you that you needed. In a world of minute-by-minute connectivity, true importance can be lost and priorities can be muddled.

That is why this chapter becomes so important since by using Slack's features, tips, and tricks, you can create a culture of intentional and efficient conversation.

Earlier in this book, Slack was compared to Twitter because of its amazing likeness to that particular social media stream. Short messages are combined with threaded conversations and reactions to create an ongoing stream of conversation. What are your Twitter notifications set to? You are most likely not sent a notification when every user sends a Tweet into the Twitter-sphere.

It is much more likely that you receive notifications about what's important, keep tabs on your own content and conversations, and disregard the unnecessary information that can become annoying.

Slack is that real-time platform that plays host to a multitude of crucial conversations, unessential yet fun watercooler chats, and companywide updates that affect every team member. The sheer amount of connectivity that occurs on Slack can be overwhelming if you don't create a Slack culture that encourages, empowers, and enforces intentional collaboration.

Slack is a business tool that should be customized and edited to fit your business goals, company culture, and, on a more personal basis, individual preferences.

Now, let's dive into how all of these points can come to life, starting with paid versus free accounts.

Paid versus free Slack features

Slack is a tool meant for both large corporations and solo entrepreneurs who are seeking a hub for conversation, file sharing, and integrations. Well-known Fortune 500 companies such as Google and Pinterest use Slack's features just as small companies and freelance contractors do, and Slack caters to its widespread audience by creating different account tiers to suit a company and its budget.

Slack has built four different accounts that all vary in terms of their prices and accessible functionality:

1. **Free**: Perfect for Slack beginnings or early-stage startups

2. **Standard**: Perfect for small- and medium-sized businesses

3. **Plus**: Great for larger businesses and those with more in-depth administrative needs

4. **Enterprise**: Meant for very large businesses and regulated industries

Depending on the size of your company and your current needs for a tool such as Slack, you have a choice to make between a free and paid platform that best fits your budget.

The free option

Slack's free option presents a number of different features that make building your workspace easy and efficient. The free plan also presents a great starter option if you are new to Slack and hoping to test out the highest-level features that are available. Slack's free features include the following:

*   Access to 10k most recent messages, giving you the option to test out Slack's search engine and see the power of a storage hub for collaboration.

*   10 integrations, which gives you access to your team's most loved and used platforms, such as Google Drive, Dropbox, and Google Calendar.

*   Private voice and video calls between teammates, which is a quick way to talk more in-depth with someone at the click of a button.

*   File sharing, so that all your important documents can be accessed from one main location.

*   Unlimited private and public channels so that you can organize your team's conversations.

*   Notifications that can be personalized for each individual and the way they work best.

Slack's free plan is a strong option for starting your technological journey and allows your team the space to grow further until you are ready for the next step: a paid Slack account.

The paid options

Slack offers a myriad of paid account options that best fit the level of customization and administration your company needs for its success. These accounts range anywhere from $7 - $12.50 a month per active user, and they offer specials when you're paying for an annual subscription. Standard and Plus accounts include features such as the following:

- All benefits from the previous plan.

- Full, saved history of messages and interactions.

- Smart search features that make your archived history easy to access and can locate specific information.

- Google authentication for your team so that you can utilize a Google sign-in to gain access to their Slacks.

- Unlimited integrations to bring one of your tools into one main storehouse.

- Group video and voice calls with up to 15 members so that conversations can quickly go from text to talk.

- Outside collaboration through shared channels with external guests.

- Identity management, to ensure your team is secure in their logins and activity. This includes features such as **Just In Time** (**JIT**) provisioning, which allows new users logging in for the first time to trigger a flow of information needed to create the account from the identify provider to Slack.

- Corporate exports for all messages, links, files, and conversations.

- 24/7 support with a 4-hour response time so that you always receive the answers you need in a timely manner.

The Enterprise account is yet another paid Slack account that is offered and is particularly useful for major corporations and those in regulated industries. This plan offers all the benefits of the previous account options, plus enterprise-grade security and compliance, large-scale collaboration for up to 500,000 users, deep administrative power, and tailored support with designated customer support agents.

Standard and Plus are the best options for small- to large-sized businesses and offer a strong plethora of features to keep your team updated. Enterprise is the stronger option for massive corporations since it provides special tools and various customizable options.

Effective communication in Slack

Slack can and should be one of the most powerful tools your team uses on a daily basis. Whether you're utilizing a free or paid workspace, Slack's features allow your team to stay updated and connected at a moment's notice.

Making this instant communication effective is key to having a powerful and synchronized company. The previous chapters started to highlight key features for effectiveness, including social-like reactions, statuses, file sharing, and archived messages. Some of Slack's most powerful tricks focus on how you and your team are interacting with each other on an individual or group level. This section will provide you with detailed information on using private versus group chat features, mentions, and public announcements.

Stylistic choices for adding urgency or excitement

Your Slack workspace is meant to share teamwide updates, important information, and urgent requests quickly to illicit the immediate responses needed. Have you ever tried to share an important text message and wished there was a way that your urgency could be understood at a quick glance?

You can utilize the power of **bold** and *italic* text to share that sense of importance or grandeur by selecting (highlighting) the text you want to format and selecting the proper icon:

 david ☑ 1:25 AM
Attention! Online Geniuses has some *major* job openings coming to our **Job Board** this month. Check some of them out here ‼️

> 🆗 **Online Geniuses**
> **Director of Acquisition and Growth Marketing Job at Animoto in New York, New York**
> Apply for ANIMOTO Director of Acquisition and Growth Marketing Job in New York, New York

Figure 3.1 – Bold and italic text can be used in separate messages or in the same one for further emphasis

Slack not only gives you the power of bold and italic information, but also a host of other stylistic text formats so that you can share your messages in a way that they carry the emotion or information clearly. Let's take a look at text formatting in Slack.

Strikethrough

Strikethrough is great for sharing real-time edits of messages or other text, as well as providing emphasis (or de-emphasis) on something stated. Highlight the text you want to format and choose the strikethrough icon:

@channel the Marketing meeting will be at ~~2pm~~ 1pm EST today ! Don't forget to accept your invitation if you're planning on joining.

Figure 3.2 – Strikethrough messages to amend your edits in real time and avoid confusion

Code blocks or inline code

Inline code is a useful method for sharing a block of text in a compact and organized manner. This makes it easy to share a paragraph of text or several lines of code for your latest app development. Select the text and click the code icon to transform it into a code block:

We will be having a guest from `Online Geniuses` available for a Q&A today at 3pm.

```
For reference: Online Geniuses is the largest SEO and Digital Marketing community based on
Slack.
```

Figure 3.3 – Code blocks/inline code help emphasize specific messages in their own area

Blockquotes

Blockquotes are a simple way of providing major emphasis on an update or shared message. Blockquotes are often used in articles when sharing a significant quote, and your Slack messages should be treated with the same gravitas. Select the text you want to appear in this manner and choose the blockquote icon:

Quick Update:

> **I will be away from Slack this coming week as I transfer my office to LA.**

Things to know while I'm gone:

> If you need to reach me in my absence, please first reach out to me via direct message before proceeding to my personal email.

Thank you for your understanding!

Figure 3.4 – Blockquotes are an easy way to break up your text into an easy-to-read format

Hyperlinks

Hyperlinks play a major role in a company's day-to-day conversation, and Slack has made it possible to hyperlink a Slack message to a website you want to flag for others. Select the text, click the link icon, and paste the website link you want to share:

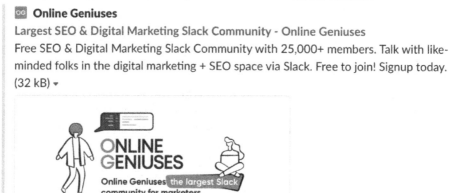

Figure 3.5 – Hyperlinking allows for a clean way to share links with your team

Traditionally, a message you hyperlink will appear as in the preceding figure with an image of the website/document/PDF you're choosing to link to. If you don't wish to have an image preview like the preceding one, simply hover over the link preview once it's displayed in your message box and click the "x" that appears on the left side of the link. This will remove the image from your message once it's sent, leaving only the text and the hyperlinked word or phrase.

All these stylistic choices offer an easy way to provide the urgency you need behind a message while also offering a way for your team to personalize their words. Maybe some of your team is extra enthusiastic and bold text emphasizes that. Whatever the case, Slack's text styles are only a click away to make conversation engaging.

Listicles for any occasion

Everyone loves a great to-do list, especially those Type A individuals on your team who thrive on having organizational habits. Seeing and making a clear list of items brings about deep satisfaction and clear communication when you need something done.

Slack has built a handy feature into its stylistic options for creating two types of lists: ordered lists and bulleted lists.

Ordered lists

An ordered list shares information in a numerical order that can be helpful to emphasize priority, sequences, or options. Select the ordered list icon from Slack's text toolbar. The number 1 will immediately appear in the textbox, and you can begin creating. Each time you need a new ordered line to appear, you will need to use *Shift + Enter*.

Bulleted lists

A bulleted list is a great communication tool for when you need to share several items, such as to-dos, that don't need a numerical order. Need to share a list of team members who will be involved in a meeting? How about a shopping list for your next office party? Creating a bulleted list in Slack can be done to get your message across with organization and ease. Select the bullet list icon, and it will immediately appear in the textbox. Write your first item and continue adding to your list using *Shift + Enter*:

Today's agenda includes:
1. Team leaders check in with me to update your weekly progress.
2. Marketing meeting at 1pm EST.
3. Q&A with Online Geniuses co-founder at 3pm EST.
- Don't forget to accept your invitation to virtual Happy Hour Friday night!! 🍻

Figure 3.6 – Create lists with bullets/sequential numbers to simplify your message

Any list you need to share, whether that's with an individual, a group, or even yourself, can be done efficiently in Slack. This, combined with other stylistic text features, makes effective communication a breeze.

The power of @

Whether you are a small team of five or a major corporation of 5,000, the power to notify just a single individual, channel, or group of team members is a necessity for effective and clear communication. Slack has built the capability to create these individualized alerts and notifications with a simple press of one key: @.

Notifications can create on a host of alerts based on who you direct the message to, including the following:

- A full channel
- All member of your team active and online
- Everyone in your workspace
- A single individual

Depending on your needs and the person(s) you hope to alert, you will want to be selective of the message you type up and send. Utilizing @ and a keyword or name will create the type of real-time alerts you'll need to create important results.

@[name]

Let's set the scene: you have a dedicated Slack channel for a brand redesign your company is undergoing with 12 people invited to it. One individual from your team is in charge of the color palette, and you want an update on color progress. Rather than sending a message to the whole channel and hoping the proper individual views and responds, you can write a message in the channel and direct it to the specific person.

Using @[name] sends a desktop or mobile notification to the person and gets the message across clearly. No longer do team members need to dig through message chains and channels to find items that are specific to them. If the messenger directs the notice to a specific person, that person is guaranteed to see and respond, pushing conversations forward swiftly.

@channel

Using the same situation we used previously, let's imagine you need to alert the full brand redesign team about a crucial update. You don't need to ping each individual separately or send a channel message and hope everyone sees it. Instead, you can write your message using @channel to send a notification to every person in that specific channel so that everyone gets a real-time ping.

Slack has built a genius feature into their @channel notification system. When sending an @channel message, Slack will alert you to the various time zones that are currently present in the channel. This gives you immediate comfort that your message will be seen by all but that it may take longer for individuals who are in different time zones to respond:

Figure 3.7 – The @channel function notifies everyone in that channel

@here

The @here notification alert is a great system for keeping the personal and professional divide on such a real-time communication platform. Earlier, we discussed how Slack can become overwhelming as it carries with it an "always on" connotation. However, Slack continues to build intelligent features that ease those concerns. This type of notification is an example of such.

Working with a team means working with potentially different schedules, time zones, and out of office notices. Simply put, not every team member will be online at the same time as everyone else. Using the @here notification gives you the ability to alert those who are online and working while maintaining the privacy of those who are offline. Only team members who are online and active will be sent a desktop or mobile notification.

This is a two-fold win: you get the attention of those working for your needs and your team gets to retain their personal and professional time:

@here Reminder to come join our virtual Happy Hour going on right now !!

Figure 3.8 – @here notifies all active members that you've sent a message

@everyone

The @everyone alert is a great tool at your disposal when you need the attention of everyone on your team in a company-wide channel. This will trigger a desktop or mobile notification being created for every team member and will get them involved in the conversation or make them aware of an update.

Your own @ activity

One major reason that Slack notifications aid in creating clear and effective communication is the organization it creates for everyone. Your workspace may be dozens of channels and hundreds of team members large (or the opposite). If there is no easy way to access your messages, you would be lost digging through all these channels and message threads to remind yourself of what you need to get to the most:

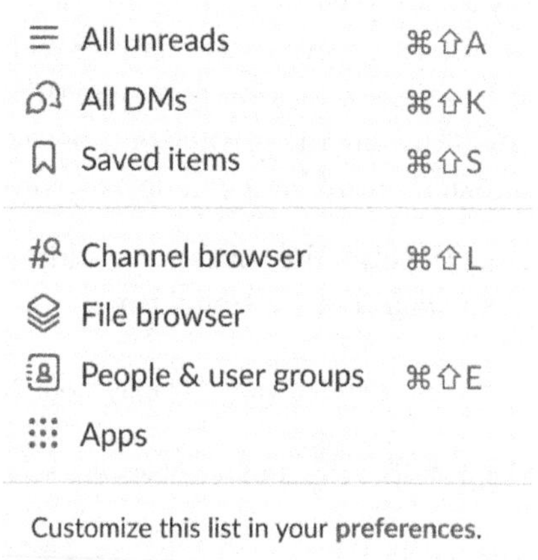

☰	All unreads	⌘⇧A
🗩	All DMs	⌘⇧K
🔖	Saved items	⌘⇧S
#ᵠ	Channel browser	⌘⇧L
⬙	File browser	
🗟	People & user groups	⌘⇧E
⋮⋮⋮	Apps	

Customize this list in your **preferences**.

Figure 3.9 – You can also access unreads by pressing Ctrl, the up arrow, and "A"

Slack makes it simple for you to keep track of any notifications that you have been sent using the **All unreads channel**, which is specifically built for you. Unread messages you have been notified of will appear in this space until you take action on them, whether that action is reading, reacting, or responding. Think of this as your own personal to-do list that keeps you on track and aware.

Sharing your screen through Slack

Not only has Slack built a call and video call technology into its communication portal, but also offers a screen share option that makes presenting ideas to your team easy. Sharing your screen is helpful for a myriad of reasons:

- When you are experiencing an unidentified tech issue and need someone to troubleshoot.
- When you've had a creative brainstorm and need to share it.
- When you've received a completed project and need your team involved in a feedback cycle.

Sharing your screen and the information on it is a necessary part of collaboration. Whatever the reason, Slack has you covered in a few steps:

1. From your desktop, start a Slack call with a team member.

2. Once you're on the call, click the **Share screen** option at the bottom toolbar.

3. Choose which screen you want to share.

You and other team members involved in the screen share are, by default, able to draw on your screen. Whiteboarding has never been so easy with this tool. If you prefer that team members don't have access to this drawing functionality, you can turn it off by deselecting the group drawing icon.

It is important to note that screen sharing is only available on the desktop version as the call technology on mobile does not include this feature.

Using reactions for polls

Slack reactions play many roles within your Slack workspace. They can function as a response to a message – a notice that it has been read by your team. Reactions have a social-like interactivity that brings entertainment to your communications. They also function as a method of polling your team with each emoji representing a vote someone can take.

Want to know whether your team prefers tagline A, B, or C? Whether they want to work remotely on day 1, 2, or 3? Creating options and encouraging team participation is yet another Slack feature that is right at your fingertips:

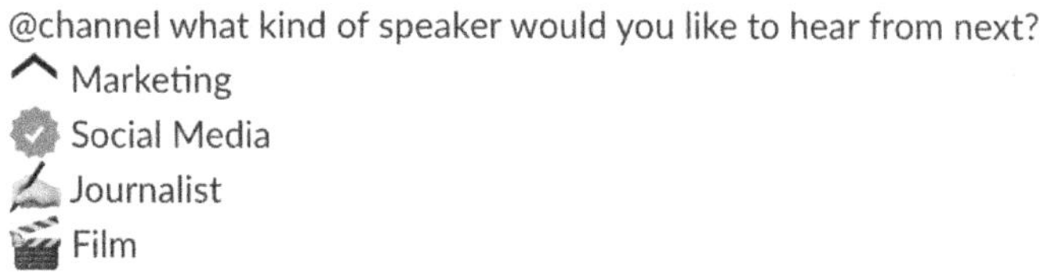

@channel what kind of speaker would you like to hear from next?
∧ Marketing
Social Media
Journalist
Film

Figure 3.10 – Using emojis to have team members easily respond with their poll choice

To make a Slack poll using reactions, follow these steps:

1. Go to the particular channel you want to host the poll in.

2. Write up the question you want answered in the poll.

3. Press *Shift + Enter* to create a new line.

4. Select an emoji and type in what that emoji corresponds next to it.

5. Continue with that process until all of your options are present.

6. Push **Send** and encourage votes with a @channel notification!

Next, we will see how to reference a past Slack message.

Referencing a past Slack message

Slack will become your daily hub for conversation among your team, and that means an endless stream of messages, reactions, and updates. Sometimes, you may need to continue a conversation that started on Slack or bring a message back to the forefront. Referencing a past message by including that direct text eases the conversation and allows for quick action to be taken, as opposed to a *he said/she said* dynamic. Let's take a look at how to implement this:

1. Hover over the past message you want to discuss and click the share icon.

2. Select which channel you want this to be shared to and write an optional note, which is encouraged to build conversation.

3. Click **Share** to send the message.

Public messages can be shared on any public or private channel. However, private channel messages can only be referenced within the private space.

Communication is the foundation on which Slack was created. Now that you've mastered a variety of ways to communicate with your team, the next logical step is to learn about where these conversations will take place.

Types of channels

All the different Slack features listed in this channel come to life in your Slack workspace, as discussed in *Chapter 2, Setting Up Your Slack Workspace*. To ensure your team is primed for effective collaboration on Slack, you will want to utilize Slack channels to create a flow of conversation, teams, and projects right through your workspace.

A channel is a place for your team to share messages, files, and tools around a particular topic, as stated in the channel's topic and description. Some common channels you can utilize on Slack would be `#general` (for companywide updates and messages), `#random` (for water-cooler conversation), and `#support` (for tech troubleshooting).

There are many different channel types, and each has a particular purpose when it comes to making your Slack conversations efficient and purposeful.

Public versus private Slack channels

Slack understands that certain collaborations need to happen with either a full team or select members present, and public versus private channels are how those necessary points of communication occur.

A public channel can be accessed by every member of your Slack team and is open for anyone to join once they get invited into the workspace. All messages and files shared in a public Slack channel can be accessed and searched for by anyone. Furthermore, any member of your team (except guests) can create a public channel.

A private channel is only accessible to the team members you or the channel creator specifically invite and join. Often, private channels are used for conversations that not all team members need or should have access to. Private channels are also a great avenue for gathering particular team members who are working on a singular project together. Messages and files shared in a private channel can be accessed and searched for by anyone in the channel. Any member of your team (including some guests) can create private channels.

> **Important note**
> Once a channel becomes private, it cannot be converted back to public use.

To create either a public or private channel, follow these steps:

1. Click the workspace name and select **Create a channel** from the dropdown. You can also select the + icon next to the **Channels** menu in the sidebar.

2. Enter a channel name that is correlated to the channel's use. This must be in lowercase, without periods or spaces.

3. Enter a channel description to set the rules and guidelines for using the channel.

4. Toggle to make the channel private if this is supposed to be a private channel (this may already be toggled, depending on the Slack member's permissions).

5. Click **Create** and then invite team members by typing in their names and selecting them from the dropdown.

6. Invite more team members once the channel has been created by clicking the **Invite** button at the top of the channel.

Next, let's see what external Slack channels are.

External Slack channels

For conversations that need to occur with someone outside of your company or organization, Slack has built shared channels into its workspace options. Shared channels allow for external and internal individuals to collaborate, allowing for progress and updates to be made in real time.

Shared channels have the option to be either public or private, so you can rest easy knowing only the right people have access to them. Creating a shared channel follows the same process as creating a private or public channel. The only difference is that a shared channel cannot be officially shared with both parties until both organizations accept the invite. Let's take a look at the different types of Slack channels and how to join them.

Joining Slack channels

Slack channels will create a major focus and organization for your team's communications, yet the right people need to be in the right channels for that to come to life. Joining a Slack channel depends on the type of channel you are trying to join:

- **Public Channels**: Browse channels to join by selecting the + icon next to **Channels** in the left sidebar menu. Browse through or type in a specific name and click **join**.

- **Private Channels**: Members must be invited to private channels to join them. The creator of the channel should be alerted if someone needs to be added.

- **Shared Channels**: These channels can be public or private, and how you join them depends on which type of channel it is.

Next, we will see how to prioritize your Slack channels.

Slack channel prioritization

Your Slack workspace may quickly flood with different Slack channels, all of which have an important need for your team's connectivity. However, they may not be all conducive to your work or that of a team member's. Rather than becoming overwhelmed by the sheer number of channels and lost in a sea of notifications, give yourself quick access to the most important channels by starring them.

Any team member has the ability to star Slack channels. This creates another field of organization in the sidebar menu and features these starred channels and their notifications at the very top of the menu. By utilizing this feature, team members can keep track of messages and files that are the most crucial to their work and get involved without the need to dredge through other channels.

Slack channels are another part of Slack's functionality that is meant to change the way you converse and collaborate with your team. There are dozens of other tricks that are meant to increase your productivity past organized channels and communication. By knowing this, you are on your way to becoming a Slack pro.

Slack features that increase productivity

Slack was built for teams by a team who felt the need for increased productivity and connection themselves. With such a close connection to this need, the development that has gone into building one of the most powerful collaboration tools for teams across the world is immense. This development has led to dozens of features being built into the platform that you may not even be aware of.

Let's prime you with the knowledge you'll need to continue your Slack pro journey.

File features

One of Slack's most popular features is its file-sharing capabilities, which allows a team to stay within one platform for all their collaboration needs. Sharing files is as easy as clicking the **Upload** option on a new message or message reply. Suddenly, your communication tool becomes a storehouse for all the documents that your team needs for efficiency.

Slackbot can store any files shared in your workspace into your personal Slackbot thread so that you have quick access to any file that you have shared. Furthermore, anyone can view all the files across all channels by utilizing the File browser tool:

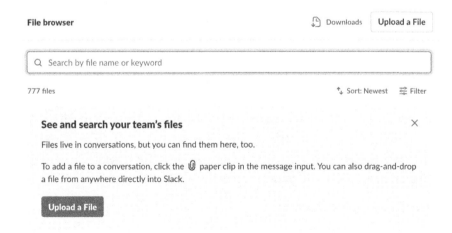

Figure 3.11 – File browser can be found by clicking on "More" from your Slack sidebar

Oftentimes, you will need to download a file that has been shared with you via Slack. You can customize the download location your files appear in to ensure Slack works in tandem with your personalized processes. From your profile, click **Preferences** and change the download location to one that fits your needs best.

Message features

Slack runs on messages, and all of its features are meant to make messaging a quick and easy process. However, there are several messaging tricks that many don't realize are available to them on the platform. This includes the following:

- Streamlining chats using message threads to organize and contain conversation
- Editing and deleting messages that you send (so your typos are never seen)
- Starring important messages that keep them accessible within the **Starred Items** section located in the main sidebar
- Pinning messages to a channel or direct message so that they can be found within the channel information section
- Locating your unread messages through the **All unreads** feature on the main sidebar so that you can see what you missed and what needs your attention urgently
- Clicking the **Mark as Read** option when you go to a channel whose messages don't need your attention
- Customizing the **Mark as Read** option in your preferences so that you can do the following:

    a. Start where you left off.

    b. Start at the newest message and mark the rest as read.

    c. Start at the newest message and mark the rest as unread until you get to them.

- Marking a message as unread that needs your attention at a later time by clicking the **More Actions** icon next to a message and selecting **Unread**
- Talking in third person to create a message that alerts your team to what you are doing by typing /me [message]
- Sharing color swatches on a message using color hex codes, which is perfect for deciding on new colors with your company rebrand

Let's look at some search features next.

Search features

Slack's search feature is one of the most powerful tools that a collaboration hub has, and it is the reason many teams find themselves drawn to Slack from the start. Having an archived history of conversations, files, and tools and finding those items with a search can ease any conversation your team has.

Slack has a comprehensive search tool located at the top of the platform on both desktop and mobile options. You can utilize the advanced search by using modifiers and stringing them together to hone in on the specifics you are seeking. Some of these modifiers are as follows:

- Specific individual: `from:@display name`
- Specific channel: `in:channel name` or `in:@display name`
- **Direct messages (DMs)** sent to you: `to:@your display name`
- Date or time frame: `before:date`, `after:date`, `on:date`, and `during:month` or `year`
- Emoji reaction: `has::emoji-code:`
- Others: `has:pin`, `is:saved`, and `has:link`

You can also use these modifiers and type them into a textbox of a specific channel to search directly within that space. This eases the need to type modifiers into the main search tool but directs your focus to the channel you need.

Channel features

As we mentioned previously, all of your messages are organized into particular channels. Slack channels themselves come with several different tricks that further aid in creating that intentional conversation.

Slack's Quick Switcher allows you to hop from one channel or DM to the next by pressing *Ctrl + K* or *Command + K* and typing in the place you want to be sent to. This is especially useful when you have dozens of channels and DMs that need your attention.

Having dozens of channels may mean that some are unnecessary and irrelevant to your team's successful collaboration. Workplace owners and admins can delete or archive any channel they find unnecessary. Deleting a channel will not delete the files that have been shared as those will live on in the File browser.

Personal Slack features

Within the DMs of Slack, you will find one attached to your own account. Using your private Slack space to store files, links, to-dos, and more is essential to keeping yourself on track. This acts as your own personal message and collaboration playground you can use for your own needs.

You can also set up a forwarding email address that will send DMs to your Slack when a new email comes through. These types of real-time updates encourage the constant growth and progress of your company's projects.

While your private channel can serve as a crucial tool when it comes to reminders, agendas, calendars, and more, it's important to remove yourself from your work when appropriate. Your presence on Slack should reflect your work hours, so, like for any communication application, we must now focus on the importance of managing your account properly.

Learning how to maintain a published Slack app

Using Slack effectively means creating a space that doesn't sacrifice your focus in the face of real-time connection. Being "on" all of the time should lead to more progress, focus, and growth as opposed to distraction, overwhelm, and annoyance. Slack's permissions, reminders, mute features, and other capabilities bring focus and intention to the forefront.

Muting notifications

Sometimes, the best thing for our productivity is canceling out other distractions and losing yourself to a flow state of work. Muting notifications on Slack is a simple way to create that space from constant updates and build a more focused work culture. You can mute a channel or DM by opening the channel, clicking the **More** icon, and selecting the **Mute** option. You can do this for all channels or DMs you don't want to receive pings from.

Do Not Disturb (DND) is another useful trick for muting notifications and building focus on your work. DND pauses all notifications and @mentions when turned on, and you will receive notifications when you turn DND off. This feature also creates a special icon next to your status so that team members know that you are in focused work mode.

Cleaning up Slack channels

Even with a clear topic and description, Slack channels can become a bit overwhelming with various team members and conversations occurring at once. This can eat away at your focus and pull you away from the important conversations and collaborations that are occurring. Some easy ways to clean up Slack channels and build focus are as follows:

- Hide all image inline previews so that your feed isn't overwhelmed with files, GIFs, and graphics by using the `/collapse` and `/expand` slash commands to reset this.

- Hide all channels and keep only starred and unread messages in your sidebar by selecting your channel's **Preferences** under your profile.

- Remove team members from a channel using the `/kick` slash command (the ability to remove someone from a channel must be set by the Workspace Owner).

Let's look at how to use reminders in the next section.

Using reminders

Everyone needs a gentle nudge once in a while so that they keep account of their work, events, or other items. Slack understands that reminders are a quintessential part of team communication and has built a reminder function directly into the platform.

The `/remind` slash command can be used to gently nudge several different people on your Slack workspace:

- `/remind` yourself

- `/remind` a particular channel

- `/remind` a single person

You can also set reminders to recur by including phrases such as `every day` or `every Friday`. Not only will you and your team receive the reminders at the time they need them, but you will never forget to remind them weekly as Slack will have your back.

Integrating your company's Google Suite can also level up your reminder features with your workspace. Connecting Slack to your Google Calendar can allow for reminders to ping particular channels based on calendar events. Your team won't forget to show up at your weekly standup or monthly retreat! Connecting a Google Sheet account means pings can be sent when a document is updated, acting as a reminder that a document may need someone's attention.

Admin and account maintenance

Finally, creating an effective Slack workspace without distractions may need an administrative hand. The workspace owner and other admins will want the proper team members and external guests in your Slack workspace at all times. Members who don't need access may only create distractions and frustration. Owners and admins can track logins across their team to identify if unauthorized access is being granted.

Furthermore, all team members have the ability to sign out from everywhere in the case of logging into a public computer. Someone may have access to your account accidentally if this were to occur, so logging out of all accounts is a safety measure to help keep a workspace private.

Through muting, cleaning up channels, using reminders, integrating a Google Suite, and tracking logins, your Slack can be made a place of true focus toward company development.

Most useful Slack shortcuts and customization

Most of Slack's features and tricks can occur with minimal effort since Slack has built a full range of keyboard shortcuts and commands into its functionality. Mark this chapter for future reference as a full directory of shortcuts that you can use.

The following is a list of **keyboard shortcuts** you can use:

- Browse direct messages: *Command + Shift + K*
- Browse channels: *Command + Shift + L*
- Compose new message: *Command + N*
- Open threads: *Command + Shift + T*
- Open preferences: *Command + ,*
- Channel info pane: *Command + Shift + I*
- Mentions and reactions: *Command + Shift + M*
- Saved items: *Command + Shift + S*
- Set status: *Command + Shift + Y*
- Search current channel: *Command + F*
- Full screen view: *^ + Command + F*
- Collapse left sidebar: *Command + Shift + D*
- Open all unreads: *Command + Shift + A*

- Mark messages as unread: *Option + [Click message]*
- Mark messages as read: *Shift + Escape*
- Set message as oldest unread message: *Option + [Click message]*
- Move between messages: Up or down arrow
- Edit a message: *E*
- Add reaction: *R*
- Pin or unpin: *P*
- Share a message: *S*
- Save a message or remove from saved: *A*
- Delete your message: *Delete*
- Create a reminder on a message: *M*
- Select text to the beginning of the current line: *Shift + up arrow*
- Select text to the end of the current line: *Shift + down arrow*
- Create a new line in a message: *Shift + Enter*
- Bold selected text: *Command + B*
- Italicize selected text: *Command + I*
- Strikethrough selected text: *Command + Shift + X*
- Quote selected text: *Command + Shift + 9*
- Turn selected text into numbered list: *Command + Shift + 7*
- Turn selected text into bulleted list: *Command + Shift + 8*
- Undo message formatting: *Command + Z*
- Upload file: *Command + U*
- View all downloaded files: *Command + Shift + J*

The following is a list of **slash commands** you can use:

- Search for Slack apps: `/apps`
- Archive: `/archive`
- Change away status: `/away`
- Collapse inline images: `/collapse`

- Expand inline images: `/expand`

- Start or end DND: `/dnd`

- Send feedback to Slack: `/feedback`

- Invite a member to a channel: `/invite`

- Become a member of a channel: `/join`

- Leave a channel: `/leave`

- Share a third-person status: `/me`

- Send a message: `/msg [channel]`

- Send a direct message: `/dm @someone`

- Mute a channel: `/mute`

- Open a channel: `/open`

- Create a reminder: `/remind`

- Rename a channel: `/rename [new name]`

- Open the keyboard shortcuts menu: `/shortcuts`

- Set or clear status: `/status`

- Set a channel topic: `/topic [text]`

In the next section, we will see how to customize your workspace.

Customizing your workspace

Slack commands and shortcuts are one way to make your team's connections effective and efficient. Customizing your workspace adds an additional flair and sense of company culture that aids in intentional conversation. Several customization tricks you can perform are as follows:

- Add custom emojis by clicking **Add Emoji** in the emoji menu and uploading an image.

- Integrate Giphy by finding it in the Slack App Directory and adding it to Slack.

- Edit your sidebar with custom sections by hovering over channels and selecting the three dots icon to create new sections or edit a sidebar.

- Customize Slackbot responses any time a specific word or phrase is posted in Slack.

All of these shortcuts, commands, and customization tricks will allow you to build a Slack workspace that thrives in your company's culture and encourages quick actions.

Notification tricks

Notifications in Slack are a powerful thing. They can encourage immediate actions and responses from your team members, but they can also distract or overwhelm and thus obstruct positive collaboration. Slack has created some helpful tools when it comes to their notification systems that continue to bolster a space of focused connection.

Default Do Not Disturb hours

As we explained previously, DND is a resourceful tool for any team member who wishes to create a work/life divide. This also creates clear boundaries for team members that maintain one another's privacy.

Workspace owners and admins can create default DND hours that are specific to a workspace. Slack notifications will not be sent to either desktop or mobile platforms during this time. Individual team members can set their own DND schedules that work best in their workflows. However, setting a default encourages all team members to break from their work and focus on other things.

Keyword notifications

Team members can customize how they receive notifications by selecting the **Preferences** menu from their profile. Notifications can be sent to emails and appear as desktop and mobile pings, and you can even select different notification types, depending on the content.

However, one of Slack's lesser-known features is keyword notifications. Individuals can receive notifications when particular words or phrases are used in channels that they are members of. Whenever someone uses a keyword, you will receive a notification and see the word highlighted in yellow. You can select words and phrases to be notified of by going to the notification settings in **Preferences**.

Summary

This chapter has prepared you to take over your Slack workspace by providing you with knowledge of the many features, tips, and tricks that are available to you with a click (or two) of a button. In this chapter, we shared the differences between paid and free Slack accounts, as well as private and public group chats. You now deeply understand the power of @ mentions and announcements so that you can get direct attention from team members who are needed. You also learned about a host of Slack shortcuts, commands, and tricks you can use to increase productivity, focus, and decrease distractions. Finally, we shared some notification tricks that can put you in conversations when this is needed.

The next chapter will teach you how to get your whole team onboarding in Slack. This will include setting up a 2FA, building a team knowledge base and Slack etiquette guidelines, customizing Slack so that it suits your team and improves company culture, and understanding Slack stats and analytics so that you can continue building a collaboration tool that changes the game for your company.

4

Onboarding Your Team to Slack

Building a collaborative environment among your team begins with the tools and processes you choose to utilize. Slack was created to be a hub of communication that urges your company forward toward goals and growth. Slack is the tool, and now it is time to focus on ensuring your team is in the right mindset to use Slack and its features to the best of their abilities.

Chapter 3, *Slack Features, Tips, and Tricks*, provided you with the clear knowledge you need to ensure that Slack messages are effective, non-distracting, and focused on bringing your team together for top-tier collaboration. You have mastered paid and free Slack accounts, public and private channels, keyboard shortcuts and slash commands, and notification and productivity tricks. With this knowledge, you are ready to continue your Slack journey and learn how to provide the most helpful and welcoming experience for new hires and already existing team members.

In this chapter, we will cover the following crucial topics:

- Setting up a security measure to protect your Slack channel's privacy
- Customizing workspace design, creating custom emojis, organizing channels by teams, and projects

- Best practices on how to not annoy and distract your teammates and creating a Slack knowledge base for your team with pinned messages in channels

- Customizing Slack based on your department (customer support, developers, human resources, sales, project management, marketing, and project management)

- Setting the tone of communication in Slack with emoji reactions, GIFs, public shoutouts, weekly check-ins, and other best practices

- Learning about team activity, storage space usage, and what messages and files have been sent to what channel

This chapter will help you guide your team members through all of Slack's features in a way that best fits your team, culture, and individual preferences.

Setting up 2FA

Two-Factor Authentication, or **2FA**, adds a deeper layer of security to your Slack channel. The work that's completed in your workspace is unique and individual to you and your company, and it deserves privacy and security measures to make sure it remains a safe space to work in.

Both members and guests alike can turn on this safety feature on Free, Standard, Plus, and Enterprise Grid plans to prevent passwords from being stolen and allowing public access computers to log into an account.

You can avoid any general member having access to your workspace by creating your company's own Slack "instance," also known as your workspace link, as a private way of signing into the account. For example, if your company's name was Online Geniuses, your Slack "instance" would be `https://onlinegeniuses.slack.com/`. While this does direct intended members to your exact workspace login, 2FA adds another security level to ensure your organization's workspace remains private to you and your team, and therefore is highly encouraged. A simple authentication process, 2FA exists to protect your Slack channel. Let's take a look at how 2FA works.

How 2FA works

If your password is compromised or stolen, it's important to know that you know you are the only person who can sign into your account. To use 2FA, members and guests need access to a mobile phone so that they can sign into Slack. Then, the following steps will occur:

- Workspace owners and admins will set up a code to be sent out. They can also provide a workspace link that allows the user to easily be directed to the workspace and log in.

- A code will be sent to your mobile device so that you can sign in. You can choose to send your verification code by text message or from an authentication application that will generate a code for you.

- You'll enter this verification code and password each time you sign in. This does not apply to every time you use the app, should you remain logged into your workspace.

How you chose to receive your code is a personal preference. SMS text message is the more common route because of its conveniency of sending a message directly to your phone. Using an authentication application is a safer way to make sure that only you have access to the verification code through a secured app. If you do not have access to a mobile device, whether your phone is dead, lost, stolen, and so on, Slack can also provide you with a one-time code so that you're not permanently locked out of your workspace.

Signing up with an authentication app

Before you can set up 2FA on Slack, you will need to download and install an authentication app. Options vary based on the type of phone you have, but Slack can be used with most **Time-Based, One-Time Password** (**TOTP**) applications or through varying **single sign-on** (**SSO**) providers such as Google or OKTA for enterprise-grade companies. Follow these steps to sign up with an authentication app:

1. Download and install an authentication app. Some of the app options available for phone are as follows:

   a) Duo Mobile (iPhone, Android, and Windows Phone)

   b) Google Authenticator (iPhone and Android)

2. Turn on 2FA in Slack.

3. Sign into the appropriate workspace and visit your **Account** page at `my.slack.com/account/settings`.

4. Head to **Two-Factor Authentication** and click **Expand for Set Up**.

5. Enter your password and click **Use an app** to create an authentication code.

6. Add a new account.

7. Scan the QR code using your phone's camera or enter the code manually.

8. On the configuration page, enter the six-digit verification code generated by the app.

9. Last but not least, verify the code.

When you sign into Slack, just enter the code the authentication app has generated for you, along with your password.

Signing up with an SMS message

Another way to sign up is through SMS. Follow these steps to sign up through SMS:

1. Sign into the appropriate workspace and visit your **Account** page at my.slack. com/account/settings.

2. Head to **Two-Factor Authentication** and click **Expand for Set Up**.

3. Enter your password and click **SMS Text Message** to receive an authentication code via text message.

4. Select your country from the menu.

5. Enter your phone number. A six-digit verification code will be sent to your phone.

6. Enter this code on the 2FA page on Slack.

7. Last but not least, verify the code.

Every time you sign into your workspace, you'll be sent a single-use code via text message to use. If you're a member of multiple Slack workspaces, you will have to set up 2FA for each account separately. Or, for a shortcut, copy and paste https://your-url. slack.com/account/settings (making sure to add your individual workspace's domain) to enable 2FA on all your accounts.

If you ever get locked out of your account, workspace owners have the power to restore your access and can view which members have 2FA set up. The workspace owner simply has to manually disable 2FA on a person's account to allow them access again.

If you're the workspace owner or admin, follow these instructions:

1. On your desktop version of Slack, click on your workspace name in the top left-hand corner.

2. From the menu, select **Settings & administration | Manage members**.

3. Look for the **three-dot** icon to the right of the member you'd like to manage and click it.

4. Lastly, select **Disable two-factor authentication**.

Now that you've securely set up your account, it's time to take your skills into the actual workspace. The previous three chapters have prepped you on getting started, setting up your profile, and learning about the features that are available. Now, it's time to understand Slack manners while interacting with your team members and guests in a digital environment.

Slack etiquette and team knowledge

Slack can become a notification-heavy place. Members are constantly communicating with one another in channels, threads, and direct messages, where notifications can stack up over time – even when you only remove yourself from the workspace for a quick lunch break.

Since nobody wants unread messages to pile up, it's important to message others the way you'd like to be messaged when using Slack. This is what we consider proper "Slack etiquette," something that helps us avoid easily distracting and annoying our teammates throughout the workday and even in off hours.

For your benefit as well as your teammates, we will go through some tips on how to properly maintain productive and healthy communication via Slack.

Minimal messages are key

When it comes to communicating in a workspace, nobody wants to deal with overcomplicated, wordy messages. The best way to get your point across is to be quick and to the point with what you're trying to say, so that your team members can understand the announcement or task at hand.

That's why it is of the utmost importance that when you're using Slack, you make your best effort not to overwhelm the channel with unnecessary messages. Slack even allows you to edit or remove your message from the chat when you realize that you made a mistake, sent the message too soon, or simply solved the problem you were seeking clarification on.

Utilizing the proper channel

While it's important to minimalize your messages altogether, it's equally as important to make sure the messages you do send are directed to the right channel. Channels are an integral part of your Slack workspace and they divide your team into specific categories.

Channels can vary from general to a niche, such as social media where conversations can be held about that topic. This channel specifies social media:

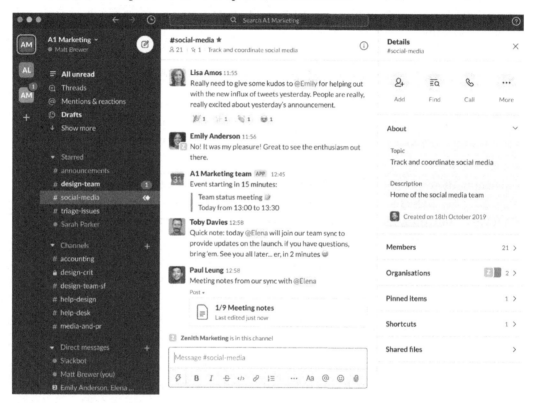

Figure 4.1 – Channel descriptions can be found in the channel's details

Each channel has its own description about the topic and its members. Direct questions about that topic to the proper channel to avoid excessive messaging in improper chats.

For important announcements that every member should see, use shortcuts such as @ here, @everyone, or @channel to notify all active members. For important messages that need to be referenced periodically, pin them to a channel so that it can be easily accessed by members whenever they need it.

While channels are the most basic division of content, threads offer an even simpler breakdown of conversation, thus keeping consistent messages in one place.

Threads, threads, threads

Threads are essentially group messaging for Slack. Although you can create direct messages with multiple people, threads are the conversations within a conversation.

You can create a thread by replying to a message that's already been sent in the general channel. Replying then opens a separate sidebar with only messages in that thread, while still giving you a view of the general channel. The following message is asking members to participate in a conversation that they can then respond to directly through its thread:

david ✅ 12:59 PM

Happy Friday **@everyone**! I hope you have had a fantastic week. Share what you accomplished this week for a chance to be featured in our newsletter 🙌

💯 4   😃⁺

👤 **2 replies** Last reply 3 days ago

Figure 4.2 – Threads take place in the replies of a message and open in a separate sidebar

Keeping ongoing chats and replies in a thread ensures that an entire conversation can be found in one place. For conveniency and organizational purposes, threads are the way to go.

When it comes to one-on-one messaging, direct messages are the next route you would take to communicate with individual team members.

Direct messaging for individual conversations

Direct messaging is the easiest form of Slack communication. Just like your basic email/text message format, direct messaging allows you to communicate with another team member in a private setting when you wish to ask individual questions or make comments. Direct messages result in a notification popping up on your mobile and laptop devices.

You can even address multiple members in a group messaging format via direct message to keep clutter away from the more general channels. Cluttered is the complete opposite of what you Slack workspace should be. That's why it's crucial to be conscious of the style and wording of the things you send.

Keeping conversations brief and succinct

I cannot stress this enough – keep your messages short and to the point. But while short messages are key, the style you write these messages in has a greater effect on how they are eventually perceived.

Keep in mind the following key factors when structuring your messages:

- Short messages in a row are unnecessary. This is what we call a "Slack bomb" – when your thoughts turn into a string of messages. Avoid these at all costs.

- Write longer messages that can be scanned quickly by using bullet points, spacing, dashes, and paragraph formatting.

- Contact unresponsive team members through direct messaging or other formats – not by sending multiple messages.

- Use mentions mindfully. Direct mentions toward the people that your message directly pertains to, but not excessively. If they are in the same channel or thread, chances are they will see your message without a mention notification.

While some of these tips may seem like common sense, it's critical that you remember them when it's time to take part in your workspace's dialogue.

An emoji is worth 1,000 words

Emoji reactions can send a message without you having to use any words at all. Emojis reduce the disarray of acknowledgement messages and reminders by instead substituting emoticons, such as a thumbs up or exclamation.

> **Tip**
> To see who responded to a message via emoji, simply hover over the emoji. You can also choose to use the same emoji someone else has used by simply clicking on the existing response to signify you mean the same.

Not every message expects a verbal response and not every message deserves one. Emojis are a simple solution to excessive responses and can also be a fun way to express yourself. There are hundreds of different emojis to choose from. Read the room and those you are interacting with to determine the kind of range you have to use emojis in a playful but professional manner.

Make sure not to overdo it. Never treat your Slack channel like a social media feed. Always keep your emojis tasteful and classy.

Respecting the Do Not Disturb sign

It's natural for a devoted team member, such as yourself, to become lost in the work that you do – no matter the hour of the day. And while it's okay every now and then to work into your off hours, it's important to respect your colleagues' time away from work.

The easiest way to achieve this is by announcing arrival and departure times. Members of your team should send a message in the channel when they are signing on for the day and when they are signing off so that other members know what their active hours are. These serve as your Slack statuses. You can turn your Do Not Disturb on and off or set a specific time for notifications to turn on, such as 8:00 A.M. for the workday:

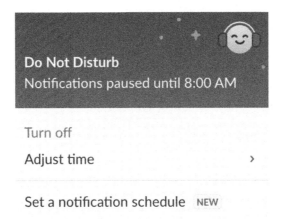

Figure 4.3 – Do Not Disturb can be found under your profile icon in the top-right corner

To reduce messages in off hours, simply turn on **Do Not Disturb** to remove any possible notifications – even from people who have directly messaged to you. You can set yourself as "away" or pause your notifications entirely for intervals such as 30 minutes, 1 hour, 2 hours, tomorrow, or customize it to fit your schedule.

Now that you've learned to appreciate proper Slack etiquette, it's time to customize your personal workspace.

Customizing Slack to suit your team

Each workspace is unique to your company/organization's motives and composition. While it's important to keep etiquette in mind, it's critical that you develop your own workspace culture.

Whether it's by color coding or alphabetical organization, each Slack workspace should be individually designed to create the most optimal working environment for its members through its aesthetic, emojis, and functionality.

Aesthetic

Slack maintains a specific formatting across all its platforms that can become confusing to members with multiple Slack workspaces. This is why Slack offers varying themes and coloring so that you can customize your unique workspace design.

This is where your creative side comes into play. You can match company colors or style with your own Slack workspace by either picking an existing theme or creating one of your own. The following screenshot shows the default color and theme of Slack:

Color for each wkspace

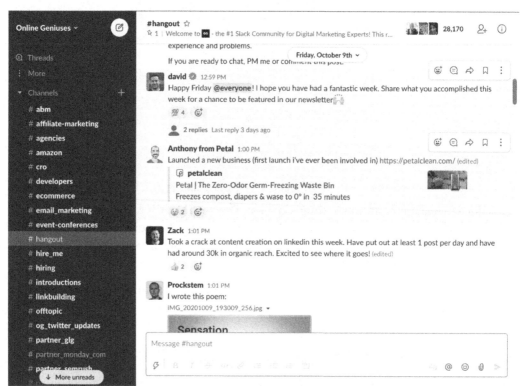

Figure 4.4 – Typical Slack formatting and coloring

Once you've selected a new theme, it will appear on all of your platforms, from mobile to desktop, whenever you open the application.

To choose a new workspace theme, follow these steps:

1. From a desktop, click your profile icon in the upper right-hand corner.

2. Select **Preferences**.

3. Select **Themes**.

4. After that, select **Colors** to then select a theme. From there, you can proceed to customize your theme.

5. From your desktop, again, click on your profile icon.

6. Select **Preferences**.

7. Select **Themes**.

8. Click on **Colors** and select **Create a custom theme**.

9. Enter any six-digit HTML color value or a pre-formatted color on offer.

Once you've finished customizing your theme, you can share it with other members. Some examples of customized themes can be seen in the following screenshot:

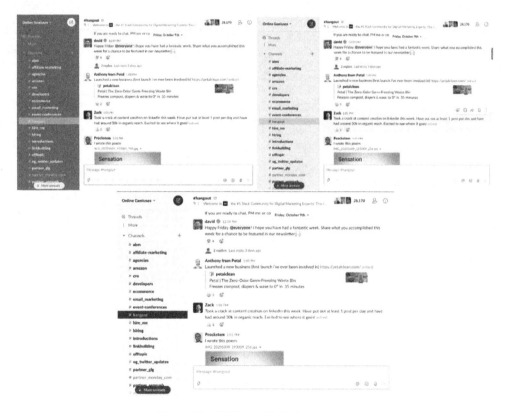

Figure 4.5 – Different Slack theme options

Your theme is only visible to you unless you choose to share it with others. To share your theme, copy the values in the **Copy and paste these values to share your custom theme with others** section and paste them into any channel or direct message. Members can click the **Switch sidebar theme** button via their desktop to start using the theme in Slack.

Slack also offers a "dark mode" preference to make working in Slack easier on your eyes with a darker contrast theme. In the following screenshot, you can see what Slack's dark mode looks like:

Figure 4.6 – Slack dark mode

You can adjust your dark mode preference by following the same steps we just followed while customizing. You can also do this by turning off the **Sync with OS** setting, which adjusts your light and dark themes as your computer does, and then selecting the dark **Slackbot**. You can switch back and forth between the light and dark settings, as shown in the following screenshot:

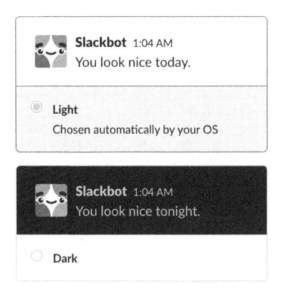

Figure 4.7 – The dark mode Slackbot is featured below the regular Slackbot mode

In addition to the aesthetically pleasing theme of a workspace, you can also individualize custom emojis for the team members that represent you and your company.

Creating your own emojis

Emojis serve fun and functional purposes that you can add to your overall workspace design. As we mentioned previously, emojis can act as a message without you having to use any words at all. For example, you can notify others that you're looking into something with the eyes emoji or signify that you're present with a wave emoji. You can see the already available emoticons in the following screenshot:

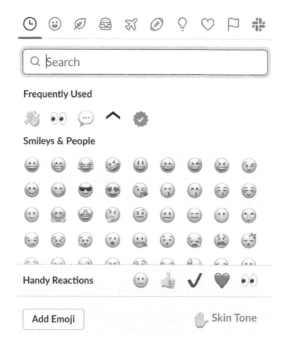

Figure 4.8 – Emoji options available in Slack

But what if the emotion/action you're trying to portray doesn't currently exist in your emoji selection? This is where you have the creativity to individualize emojis for you and your team.

You can only add custom emojis via the desktop version of Slack through images in JPG, GIF, or PNG formatting. Slack then resizes the image to the proper emoji size. You'll get the best-looking emoji with small, square images that fit this formatting. Follow these steps to add a custom emoji:

1. On your desktop, click the smiley face icon in response to a message in the message field to open the emoji menu (see *Figure 4.8*).

2. Click the **Add Emoji** button in the bottom-left corner.

3. Select **Upload Image** and pick the file you wish to upload.

4. Enter a name for your emoji and then save it.

The name you give your emoji will be the way other team members can look for it in the menu. Once you've completed these steps, you will have successfully uploaded your own emoji, fit for your company's workspace! In addition to custom emojis, you can also add a variety of emoji packs by following the same steps mentioned previously, but instead clicking the **Emoji packs** tab at the top of the page and choosing from the available packs.

Aesthetic is an important aspect of developing a creative and stimulating workspace, but, of course, it isn't everything. Now that you've created a color scheme, personalized emojis, and selected a level of brightness suited for you, it's time to create a functioning workspace that's appropriate for you and your team.

Functionality

A team doesn't work unless its workspace does. And, while it may seem like a tedious aspect of the platform, the way you choose to organize your workspace can play a critical role in overall productivity.

Slack is automatically organized by channels followed by direct messages, but the arrangement of those channels in your sidebar can be moved and adjusted to your liking, as well as the members that are included in each channel.

Departmentalizing Slack

Chances are your company/organization is broken down by departments or sections based on the various teams that work together to push out the unified product. Some people may overlap into multiple teams, whereas others may only focus on one. It's important that your Slack channels reflect each of these sections and are organized by need.

Customize Slack based on your departments (customer support, developers, human resources, sales, project management, marketing, and project management, and so on). Each section gets its own channel. If you are the workspace owner, you have the power to invite your team members into each channel as an active member or with a read-only view, so that they can view information but can't necessarily communicate.

It's vital that each department gets their own individual channel to work in so that the general channels don't get overwhelmed with information that doesn't always pertain to every member. On theme with keeping messages to a minimum and brief, channels help eliminate any clutter and keep the right information with the right people in the right places.

Organizing channels

The actual succession of channels in your Slack sidebar is equally as valuable as including each team member in the proper section. Organize your channels and sidebars in a way that makes for efficiency.

Create a general channel for all the members of the company to participate in at the top of your channel thread and then proceed down by department in whatever way makes sense for you; whether it's by team size, relevancy, importance, and so on. This will allow for a smooth flow throughout the workday for members that need to travel from channel to channel.

Once you've organized the technical and aesthetic aspects of your workspace, it's time to move toward creating your company culture. Mechanical details only go so far as cultivating a dynamic environment for you and your team. Every company has its own story, and that story should be visible – as well as felt – in your Slack workspace.

Improving company culture with Slack

Company culture is crucial to growing a robust and successful team. Understanding the company's mission and its values (and how they come to life through action) places teams into a higher level of alignment for the roller coaster of growth ahead.

There's a reason you hear so much about thriving companies with a great culture, such as Google, and those that combust because of a negative one, such as Away. The bottom line is that company culture makes or breaks your business. In this section, we will look at how we can improve our company culture.

Why Slack is an optimal cultural tool

You don't need to drop everything right now to build out your vision and values, although, in time, it's not a bad idea to get them on paper. Culture can start simply by creating spaces that allow for open communication, entertaining encounters, and honest feedback.

Slack is an amazing and easy way to improve your company culture because it fits into the predominant culture aspect of communication. Connecting team members in a collaborative and efficient environment allows for conversation to occur on a daily basis. When a team can connect with a click of **Send message**, creativity and innovation flourish. You are setting your team up for success by providing an avenue for them to brainstorm and create together.

Slack is a powerful tool that breaks down the barriers a disconnected team feels in communicating with one another. Have you ever been on a team where you were unable to get the help you needed quickly to complete a task? Had a piece of important feedback to share and no channel to do so? How about hosting an impromptu happy hour for team bonding? If your answer to any of these questions is yes, I am excited to tell you that Slack is the answer you've been seeking, as it can help you build strong bonds across team members and break down strict lanes of communication.

Someone in accounting should be able to chat with a technical team member. The CMO should be able to hear of a product team's stellar accomplishment. The co-founders should be able to speak their values every day through inspiring morning messages. Every word that's spoken across a team strengthens the culture that envelops it, which is why communicating is so important to a culture's growth and why Slack is the optimal tool for doing so.

Setting the tone

There are many ways you can go about setting the tone in your Slack workspace. Many of the tools mentioned previously, such as themes and emojis, aid in creating a more personable tone in your work environment.

While work should always be a professional place, it's critical that a workspace owner allows their team members to interact in a casual and social way when appropriate. Digital offices present a barrier with a lack of physical interaction among its employees. Slack works to break that barrier by offering different means of communication that are not presented in a typical formal manner.

We've already talked about themes and emojis being a great way to individualize your Slack experience, but there's a variety of other ways to connect with your channel.

Here are some ways you can create an open company culture in your Slack channel:

- Set the tone of communication in Slack with GIFs, in addition to emojis, that can tell/show more of what you're trying to say.

- Give public shoutouts to team members who are doing great things in your workspace.

- Send out weekly check-ins to monitor people's progress while also letting them know you're available and there to talk if they need to.

- Invite employees to ask questions in identified threads about a particular topic.

If your team can't physically be together, it's imperative to simulate a personable and social environment digitally to avoid disconnect or miscommunication. While messaging serves the overall communication purpose, the rise of video chatting and scheduled meeting times supplements this virtual experience.

Hosting a Slack meeting

There are many ways you can go about hosting a Slack meeting with your team. It doesn't always have to be a Zoom or Google Meets call in which each participant pauses what they're doing to partake. Meetings can be optional and take place throughout the day as reminders and ways for team members to get involved with one another and keep engagement flowing.

Here are some examples of types of Slack meetings:

- **Standups**: Request that team members join a singular thread to update the team on what they worked on yesterday, what they plan to work on today, and any blockers preventing them from completing their work.

- **Designated meeting channels**: Create channels specific to a meeting where people can communicate and ask questions in real time. You can also announce the meeting's details in a channel and pin it for reference later.

- **Automatic check-ins**: Similar to announcing, when you're signing on and off every day, ask your team to check in every morning or night by providing an update regarding their work status.

- **Ask Me Anything sessions (AMAs)**: Encourage leaders to host AMAs frequently to bridge the gap between team members.

- **Video conferencing**: For the easiest way to promote social interaction among your team, the workspace owner should coordinate calls either one-on-one or in group settings so that people have a means of putting a face to a digital profile.

Each of these examples offers something different for your workspace. You, as the workspace owner or team member, have the liberty of expanding these boundaries based on the nature of your company culture. Plan events outside of work, or even host town hall sessions and virtual happy hours. The opportunities are literally endless.

With this ongoing communication taking place, it's hard to ignore a huge factor of this application – storage. Every message, every document – they all find homes in your workspace. These naturally, begin to pile up over time. This is where Slack storage comes into play.

Storage on Slack

Like any application, Slack has its limits when it comes to how much data it can hold. If your company is functioning 100% online, odds are many, if not all, of your documents exist in a digital format as well. And, while it may be created it one place, it must be shared via Slack to make its way to your team members. As a Slack workspace owner or general member, you deserve to know your options regarding how to maintain this.

Here is the breakdown for storage plans on Slack:

- **Free**: 5 GB total for the entire workspace
- **Standard**: 10 GB per member
- **Plus**: 20 GB per member
- **Enterprise Grid**: 1 TB (1,000 GB) per member

The space per member is transferred to the total file storage that's shared across the entire workspace. If 10 members are on the Standard plan, the workspace would have 100 GB of storage.

If your workspace reaches its limit throughout your time using Slack, the application will let you know. No, this does not mean total destruction or elimination of your workspace at this point. But it does mean that at that point, older files will begin to be archived to make room for new ones as they're uploaded.

> **Important note**
>
> You will no longer be able to use archived files in direct messages or channels until you update to a plan that offers larger storage options. You can also delete older files to allow for more storage.

The good news is that if your company already keep their documents and files in another space such as Google Drive, Dropbox, or OneDrive, sharing files via those outlets will not count toward your overall storage.

Saving and sharing documents is a fundamental part of any work setting and, in addition to keeping an eye on your storage count, it's also important to keep an eye on how your team is interacting with those documents and in general. Slack offers tools that allow you to check in on these analytics; essentially, the data of your workspace.

Slack Stats and Analytics

It may seem strange to compare numbers to positive communication habits. However, Slack allows you to simplify this foreign concept and track trends in your channels and monitor how your workspace is being used. This can be something as simple as seeing where people send the most messages and files, whether it's public or private channels, and the overall count of messages being sent between your members.

Slack compiles all this information into its Analytics dashboard, where it offers various filters that can sort the information you're looking for based on what team members most respond to.

Analytics dashboard

Like any dashboard, Slack Analytics uses specific lingo to easily identify types of members using your workspace. Workspace Analytics is only updated once a day and cannot be manually adjusted.

Active members are broken down like so:

- **Weekly active members**: The number of members who have posted/read a message in a public channel, private channel, or direct message in the last 7 days

- **Members who posted**: The number of members who have posted a minimum of one message in the last 7 days

- **Daily active members**: The number of members who have posted/read a message in a public channel, private channel, or direct message in the last 24 hours

- **Daily members posting messages**: The number of members who have posted a minimum of one message in the last 24 hours

> **Important note**
>
> Messages sent in channels or direct messages are only counted if they are sent by team members – not including automated bot messages sent by Slackbot or a third party such as Google Drive when you share a link.

To view your Analytics page on the Free, Standard, and Plus plans, follow these steps:

1. On your desktop, click your workspace name in the upper right-hand corner.

2. Select **Tools** and then **Analytics**.

3. Then, click the **Overview** tab and then **Channels** or **Members**.

4. Select **Edit Columns** to customize the table and choose which areas you'd like to show:

5. To view the data outside of Slack, click **Export CSV**.

All members can view the Analytics page on these plans unless the workspace owner chooses to limit who can view and download.

> **Important note**
>
> Data from messages, files, channels, and members is only available on Slack's paid plans.

On the Enterprise Grid plan, only organization owners and admins can view all the data. While the majority of data is accessible to any member on paid versions of Slack's plans, only Enterprise Grid users may access workspace data from the organization level. This includes features such as the workspace URL, total membership of the workspace, number of apps installed, change in active members, and the number of messages sent in private channels, among other things. The **Analytics** page showcases active members, messages sent, and apps and file storage used, as shown in the following screenshot:

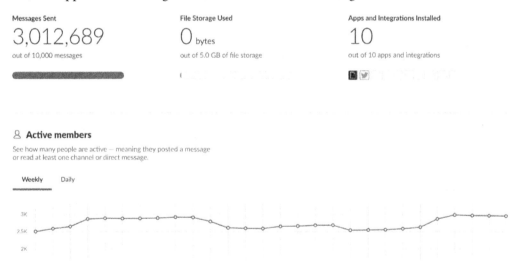

Figure 4.9 – The Analytics page appears like this for a workspace owner/admin

For an easier way to download and understand the data you're viewing, you can also integrate outside applications such as TimeBot, Survey Monkey, and Google Analytics Insights, which will help you pull reports, launch surveys, and discuss critical data in your Slack workspace.

Summary

This chapter brought a lot of technical factors to the plate. In this chapter, we learned how to protect our account with 2FA; customize our workspace both aesthetically and functionally; set the tone with customized features such as GIFs, emojis, and team bonding exercises; as well as how to manage our virtual storage. There are many mechanical features that come into play when working in a digital workspace, all of which are equally as important as the next, whether it's the color coordination of your Slack dashboard or the arrangement of your company's channels. We have come to master some of the basic tools of Slack in these first few chapters, and this will help prep us for what's to come.

In the next chapter, we'll dive deeper into external factors and how they play a role in our workspace. You will learn how to work with workspace guests, create shared channels between multiple organizations, manage your clients and customers, and create live interactive sessions with external guests to further build an advanced and robust workspace.

5
Using Slack Externally with Live Chats, Guests, and Partners

We've established that communication is a key factor and quite literally the basis of Slack's creation, but up until this point, we've only discussed communication within your company. For any organization to succeed, it's crucial that it masters a clear and concise way to streamline conversations between people on a team, as well as with partners and other external organizations.

Chapter 4, Onboarding Your Team to Slack, shared the best practices for onboarding your team members to Slack and building a thriving company culture through the platform. Enthusiastic and enlightened team members are what will make your workspace a hub for team collaboration and connection. Ensuring their deep understanding through proper onboarding is key. Now that you have those details mastered, it is time to continue into another avenue of working with individuals on Slack.

In this chapter, we will cover the following crucial topics:

- Learning how to work with someone who feels like a member of your organization but needs only limited access to Slack

- How to create a shared channel between two unique organizations

- Learning how to invite and manage communication with your clients in Slack

- Creating and managing live interactive sessions with external guests in your Slack workspace

- Learning how your support team can talk to your customers without leaving Slack

This chapter will enlighten you on the best ways to work with external team members and how to make them feel like an essential part of your full-time team. As the day-to-day heart of connection, guests who understand Slack processes and workspace owners who know how to best utilize Slack to work with external teams are crucial to a company's success.

Inviting guests to your workspace

The channels in your workspace are a place for you and your team members to collaborate and communicate with one another. But there comes a time when your company will have a want or need to invite others into this space. These guests may be someone who feels like a member of your organization or who serves a direct purpose for your organization but only requires limited access to Slack. Note that guest accounts are only available on paid plans. You can invite guests to your workspace through the domain menu on the upper left-hand side of your toolbar:

Figure 5.1 – Workspace domain menu

Follow these steps to learn how to invite a guest to a workspace:

1. On the desktop, click on the workspace name in the upper right-hand corner of your sidebar.

2. Select **Invite people to (your workspace name)** from the pop-up menu.

3. Choose between multi- and single-channel guests.

4. Enter the email address of your intended guest(s).

5. If you want to add multiple guests at once, click **Add many at once** and copy and paste the email addresses into the textbox. Then select **Add invitees**.

6. Under **Invite to channel**, choose the proper channels the guests are being invited to. You may set a time limit for the guests to allow them to stay in a channel by selecting Set a time limit and using the drop-down menu to determine a period of time.

7. Lastly, click on **Invite guests**.

While some of these guests may have multiple functions they need to perform, not every member you invite to your workspace will need access to every company channel. The differentiation between these guests is what we call single-channel and multi-channel guests. Let's explore these in detail.

Multi-channel guests versus single-channel guests

Single- and multi-channel guests function in a similar way as any guest you invite to your Slack channel – the main difference being that the former is added to just one channel of the workspace owner/admin's choosing, and the latter can be added to an unlimited number of channels.

Multi-channel guests only have access to the channels you specify and are billed as regular members. On the other hand, single-channel guests are free, but only have access to members within their designated channel. For instance, they can only direct message other members in channels they are a part of.

Guests, either single or multi-channel, are only available on paid plan options. For every paid, active member of your team, you can add up to five guests.

Guests can be invited into a workspace by a workspace owner or admin or they can choose to send a request invitation.

> **Important note**
> Guests *cannot* be added to channels you are not a member of yet; workspace members can invite multi-channel guests to private channels without having workspace invitation permission.

The following screenshot shows what an invitation page looks like:

Request invitations to Online Geniuses   ×

To: Add from: **G** Suite

name@example.com

Reason for request (optional)

Add a note for your admin

Your request will be sent to your admins, and you'll be notified when it's approved or denied.

Send Request

Figure 5.2 – Invitation request form on Slack

Workspace owners and admins can also change any current member's status to guest at any time. The process of changing a full member to a guest is as follows:

1. On the desktop, click on the workspace name in the upper left-hand corner.

2. Select **Settings & administration** and then **Manage members**.

3. Utilizing the three-dot icon next to a member's name, click the dots and select **Change account type**.

4. Identify whether you wish to make the member a single- or multi-channel guest.

5. Enter which channels they can have access to and set a time limit if necessary.

6. Finally, make the defining decision to make the member a guest.

If you want to change a guest's role within your channel, follow the same steps to simply change the title/access of that guest.

Paid plans that have access to the guest sharing feature can share a channel with up to 19 other organizations via Slack Connect instead of directly inviting guests to a workspace. Sharing a channel can be an easier way to work with multiple companies without members having to leave their own workspace.

Slack Connect

Guests are a crucial way of bringing outside perspectives/opinions into your workspace, but sometimes the complications of moving from one workspace to another can become confusing for both ends. Slack Connect is a feature within Slack that allows you to collaborate with external partners while remaining in your respective workspaces.

Designed as a substitute for email, Slack Connect works as a secure and productive means to extend channel-based messaging to anyone and everyone you work with inside and outside of your team. This feature allows you to create channels with multiple organizations at a time, changing the way you communicate with your partners by eliminating email threads and replacing them with real-time communication.

Professions that benefit from using Slack Connect

Any type of organization can find its home within Slack. No matter your company's focus, Slack can be used as your team's communication center for both internal and external members. Some specific professions that benefit from using Slack Connect include the following:

- **Sales**

   a) Receive quick and direct feedback on proposals to build a mutual plan.

   b) Allows you to bring in financial and business experts from outside of your company to help close a deal.

- **Customer success**

   a) Develop personal connections with customers for direct criticism on the company and product.

   b) Respond to comments, concerns, and questions with a faster response rate.

   c) Share important information on product launches.

- **Support**

   a) Offer personalized support through a direct line of access.

   b) Organize customer information and context in a common space for your support team to communicate and resolve matters in a formulated manner.

- **Marketing**

   a) Collaborate on campaigns across multiple teams and organizations.

   b) Work together by sharing ideas and group conceptualizing campaigns.

- **Operations**

  a) Communicate real-time updates and issues within the supply chain.

  b) More easily adjust to changing environments based on customer demand.

- **Business development**

  a) Bring in experts from other areas such as marketing or legal to finalize a partnership.

  b) Correspond at all hours to establish personal connections with partners.

Some companies currently utilizing Slack Connect include Airbnb, Hulu, Wayfair, and TIME.

Sharing a channel with external organizations

There are many benefits of sharing a channel with external organizations. By including your partner organization within your own workspace, you're simplifying work by creating one space with shared information, updates, and files for members from both partner organizations to utilize.

In a shared channel, you can send direct messages to members in an external organization, view their profiles, customize emojis, and utilize apps and workflows, the same as you would in your own company's workspace. When a member from an invited organization messages in your shared channel, their profile photo will appear with their organization's Slack icon in the bottom-right corner of their photo.

With only minor differences from your average channel, sharing a channel accommodates seamless integration for multiple members of one or many organizations to communicate in a singular space familiar to each party. Let's see how to set up a shared channel.

Setting up a shared channel

Shared channels are identified by a diamond icon next to the name of the channel list. In order to share a channel, every participating organization must be utilizing a paid version of one of the Slack plans. As in any of the upgrades from the free plan, sharing a channel opens up a series of new doors for you and your company.

Sharing a channel with an external organization allows that organization access to only that channel within your workspace. Once a channel is shared, you have the ability to send direct messages to members of that organization as long as you yourself share a channel with them. Members from the outside organization can also join the channel on their own or be added by a member already included in the shared channel.

The caveat: #general channels, multi-workspace channels, and org-wide channels cannot be shared.

Here's how to share a channel:

- An organization can follow the steps mentioned earlier to invite a guest but instead invite an organization to its channel. A channel can be shared with up to 19 other organizations.

- Guests that are invited can either accept or decline the invitation.

- If they accept, the request then needs to be approved by one of the owners of the channel. Someone from the shared organization may also need to approve it.

Although the typical way to share a channel is through an invite, you may also allow members to sign up through their email address from an approved domain. Workspace owners on any plan can enable email signup for their members.

Follow these steps to learn how to allow email signups:

1. On your desktop, click the domain name in the upper left-hand corner.
2. Select **Settings & administration** followed by **Workspace settings**.
3. Select **Joining this workspace** and then click **Expand**.
4. Select **Allow invitations and approve invitations for any email address from these domains**.
5. Enter your team's domain(s), then click on **Save** to save your changes.

Once an invitation is sent either via email signup or a traditional invitation, workspace owners and admins have the ability to monitor pending and accepted invitations as they occur. During this process, they can also choose to revoke any invitations or resend an invitation.

Owners/admins would choose to revoke an invitation to prevent an invited member from utilizing the invitation to join the organization's Slack channels. They can also disable any email notifications they may receive from Slack before they accept. Owners/admins would send a new email invitation if the original invitation expired or was lost in an inbox.

To revoke or resend an invitation, do the following:

1. On your desktop, click the domain name in the upper left-hand corner.
2. Select **Invite people to [workspace name]** from the menu.
3. Choose **See past invites**.

4.   Select the **Pending** tab at the top of the page.

5.   Click **Resend invitation** or **Revoke** next to the invitation you'd like to manage.

If you choose to revoke an invitation, the invited member's account will then show that it's deactivated. If you wanted to invite the person again after revoking their invitation, you would need to reactive the account from the **Manage members page** and then select **Resend invitation**.

In some cases, Slack can limit your ability to send invitations if you have sent a lot of invites but only a few have been accepted. A simple way to avoid this is to create an invite link to share with those you wish to add to the workspace rather than sending them a physical invitation.

Integrating workflows with shared channels

As in your own channels, you can also integrate workflows through Slack Connect with shared channels to allow for the seamless transition of ideas and information across the organizations you're working with. Some examples of the use of these workflows include submitting requests, sending customer feedback, and onboarding new accounts.

To set up a shared workflow, follow these steps:

1.   To get started, head to `https://slack.com/slack-tips/coordinate-needs-across-shared-channels` to download the example workflow.

2.   Import the example into Workflow Builder.

3.   Once you've imported it, select a channel for the workflow.

4.   Then, customize the workflow to fit your team's needs and the information you're looking to collect.

5.   Finally, publish it once completed!

After completing the customization of your workflow, it's time to share your work within the shared channel. The following screenshot shows workflow options for your channel:

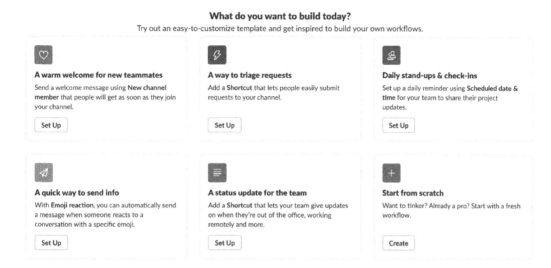

What do you want to build today?
Try out an easy-to-customize template and get inspired to build your own workflows.

A warm welcome for new teammates

Send a welcome message using **New channel member** that people will get as soon as they join your channel.

Set Up

A way to triage requests

Add a **Shortcut** that lets people easily submit requests to your channel.

Set Up

Daily stand-ups & check-ins

Set up a daily reminder using **Scheduled date & time** for your team to share their project updates.

Set Up

A quick way to send info

With **Emoji reaction**, you can automatically send a message when someone reacts to a conversation with a specific emoji.

Set Up

A status update for the team

Add a **Shortcut** that lets your team give updates on when they're out of the office, working remotely and more.

Set Up

Start from scratch

Want to tinker? Already a pro? Start with a fresh workflow.

Create

Figure 5.3 – Workflow options for your channel

To publish your workflow, follow these steps:

1. Following the steps mentioned previously, add a step-by-step message that clarifies which channel(s) to direct the action towards – in this case, your shared channel. The form can be launched by anyone that has access to the shortcut menu.

2. When finished, the request will automatically be posted in the directed channel and will notify the team.

3. When your team approves the request, you can forward it the partner organization to begin a conversation in a thread or to be simply confirmed by them as well.

This quick and easy process saves you and your team's time. It also avoids an unnecessary chain of messages back and forth across different time zones and organizations to accomplish this singular task.

Now that you've mastered the technical background behind working with external partners in a shared Slack workspace, it's time we further understand the *why* – the real importance of why teams integrate their various partners into their company's workspace.

Working with outside partners and freelancers

There are a variety of people that benefit from admission into your organization's workspace. Guests can vary from freelance workers to consultants to partner organizations working on a shared project. No matter the title of your guests, each serves their own purpose and is equally important to the overall success of your team.

If you're a freelance worker or consultant, chances are you don't belong to a singular company and therefore don't fit the mold of the typical Slack user. Freelancers can still be added to shared channels or invited into a workspace for a specified period of time, but once their visit is completed, they could lose all of their messages, files, and information when brought into another workspace. The solution: a single-member team.

Single-member teams

Single-member teams serve as an individual paid Slack "team" so that you as a professional can manage, save, and keep track of all of your work in one convenient place. Slack refuses to penalize freelancers for the traveling nature of their work and provides them with the same tools and access to a workspace as any member of a team. This puts both freelancers and members of your organization on the same playing field when it comes to working together in their common space.

A single-member's Slack channel will look slightly different from a normal Slack space as the majority of their channels will be shared. This means that they will be identified with the diamond symbol of a shared channel on almost every channel they're a guest of, which could potentially change as their work schedule does. In the following screenshot, you can see what the diamond icon looks like:

Figure 5.4 – The diamond icon will appear when you're sharing a channel with a guest or an outside organization

For you and your company inviting these single-member guests into your workspace, it's important, like any guest, that you keep a track of their whereabouts; giving them access to only specified channels or creating their own channel for the purpose of their project. Organization is a key factor when working with freelance/consultant-type professionals, and if done right, can be a great way to collaborate for both sides.

While a guest may enter your workspace with a set goal in mind, there are also a set of unspoken rules that need to be communicated by each party on how to properly interact with one another in a unified channel.

Sharing Slack etiquette and the team knowledge base

Think of your guests as your extended family. Your nuclear family has a set of house rules you maintain to keep the whole place running. When your extended family comes into your home, you share these rules with them so that they can adapt to your family's unspoken code of conduct. This works in a similar style when you invite guests into your Slack workspace.

It may not need to be something said before a person is connected to your workspace, and it may not need to be verbally mentioned at all, but it's crucial that members and guests alike respect and understand each team's communication styles and company culture.

As we discussed in *Chapter 4, Onboarding Your Team to Slack*, each workspace is unique and will therefore have its own way of communicating with one another whether it be a more casual style, emphasis on emojis over messages, or a more formal presentation of ideas. For some teams, colorful language is a regular habit, while for others, formal email etiquette is their traditional messaging format. No matter the differences, the unifying factor is the work both teams are participating in, so it's critical that something as minimal as GIFs over emojis doesn't break your flow of progress.

On the theme of recognizing your partner/partner organization's conversation style, it is equally essential that you don't simply invite outside people into your workspace without an identified purpose or established rules.

Setting rules and expectations

As a guest (either an individual or a partner organization), you should take note of how members of the team you're working with interact with one another so that you can match their style. To avoid a misstep or clash of differing styles/language, establish a list of guidelines for teams both internally and externally in advance so that both teams are clear on what and how things should be discussed on the channel.

Guests invited into a workspace should be conscious of all of the typical expectations and rules mentioned in the previous chapter, from the types of messages they create, the time they send them, to the means by which they communicate one on one with team members. In addition, the organization inviting a guest/partner company into their workspace should establish an identified purpose for a channel, guidelines for communication on the channel, and who is allowed to have access before the merger happens. Once you've established these determinants, create a document including all this information to pin to the channel for continuous access to existing and new members.

By clarifying these factors in advance, you eliminate any confusion that could occur and disrupt the speed and efficiency of your shared project.

Why not email?

The obvious question we've continuously asked over and over throughout this book is why not just email your partners? Traditionally, email is the go-to route when it comes to communicating with external organizations, but, as we've seen, Slack offers so much more. Slack provides a centralized space for all of your work that avoids a long list of email threads that could get lost or deleted over time. While phone calls can also be offered as a substitute, they don't retain files, documents, and conversations between organizations like Slack does.

With that being said, Slack does not by any means completely eliminate the need for email. Sharing channels and direct messages provides a safe and secure place to communicate within and outside of your company, but there are times when an official email to the members included, in addition to those pertinent but not directly working in the channel, can be beneficial. It's important to know when it's appropriate to utilize each tool to match the action you wish to enact.

Team members and partners should always be a priority when it comes to perfecting your communication methods, but they are not the only groups your company will have to correspond with. While not always consistent members of your Slack workspace, customers and clients also serve a purpose in being a part of the conversation.

Slack communication with clients and customers

Customers and clients, while not necessarily direct members of your workspace, are an equally critical cog in the overall machine of your company. They are your product's audience and their input and feedback are imperative to your organization's success. That's why it's important to prioritize speaking to them one on one, even in your Slack workspace. In this section, we will take a look at some tips on how to manage clients in Slack.

Tips for how to manage your clients in Slack

There are many ways you can go about managing your clients, which will vary from business to business. You can choose to respond to clients directly, one on one, or you can set up threads or channels to create a designated space for feedback. To help you find the right process for your team, here are a few tips on how to manage your clients in Slack:

- **Set up a private channel for each customer**: Especially for business-to-business companies (B2B's), setting up a private channel for your customers is a great way to create a space for direct feedback and to encourage conversation. A private channel also stimulates a more personal environment than a response from an email or support hotline.

- **Pick a point of contact**: There are hundreds of tasks being completed in your Slack workspace and it's important not to forget answering your clients. Choose a person to be in charge of checking in on your client/customer channels so no questions go unanswered.

> Tip
> Use the channel topic to declare who your point of contact is so that customers know who to reach out to/who they're talking with.

- **Set ground rules**: The same as for any of your Slack channels, set a list of rules for how the channel should function. Specifically, set a response time. Customers are typically used to slow responses via email. By creating a space with the expectation of real-time conversation, it's necessary to establish a realistic expectation for both parties of when they can expect their questions to be answered.

- **Make a quick response time a priority**: Following the previous tip, by creating a Slack channel for customers, you're already promising a faster response time. Make it a priority of your team, not something that becomes forgotten and completely eliminates the purpose of the channel in the first place.

- **Invite as many reps as possible**: Communicating on a Slack channel is about relationship building. So, when it comes to inviting customers/clients into your workspace through a designated channel, don't be stingy with the guest list. The more feedback, the merrier.

For those invited into a workspace who are unfamiliar with Slack, it's equally important that you provide them with a means to navigate the application and abide by your company standards using pinned comments with helpful docs, files, and alerts as a guideline. All of these factors play into your overall company-customer experience.

While continuous communication is an integral part of any company across the board, it's beneficial to boost communication amongst members from varying teams at varying levels through designated **question and answer (Q&A)** sessions.

Interactive live Q&A in Slack

Q&As prompt all members of your workspace to communicate, no matter what their title or status within the company hierarchy is. Moderating Q&As through this workflow gives the company leadership a chance to answer any impending questions team members or external guests may have in an easy-to-use format.

Q&As can take many forms to adjust to the needs of your team, the most common being **AMA** or **Ask Me Anything** sessions led by an executive of your organization. If you're the workspace owner or admin, this could be you! In this section, we'll discuss how to make your Slack interactive by creating and implementing Q&As, AMAs, and phone and video call conferencing in your workspace.

Prep an Ask me Anything session

AMA works in a panel format. Think of your favorite cast, politicians, or school board answering your questions in a forum. That's how AMA works on Slack, but obviously in a digital layout. AMA is a great way to essentially stick to office hours and remain accessible to employees no matter the size of your organization by simulating an open-door policy. You can frame your Q&A channel to appear similar to the following screenshot:

#q_a_sessions ☆

📌 3 | AMA/Q&A channel - only to be used for scheduled events!

Figure 5.5 – Setting a channel for the purpose of your AMA

To properly run an AMA, follow these steps:

1. Create a new channel designated for the session.

2. Announce the time/place/location of the AMA in a channel with the majority of your organization and encourage them to take part.

3. Post and pin a document outlining the rules and setup of the session to help participants format their questions properly and understand how to use the workflow.

4. Lastly, open up the floor for your team to dive in!

Although designating an entire channel shows you're committed to constant communication amongst your members, sometimes it simply makes more sense to bring the Q&A to an already existing channel. This may be the case for sessions that directly affect a singular team only or invited partner team(s)/guests. In that case, you would set up a workflow to administer your session.

Setting up your workflow

Automating workflows saves both you and your team time, especially when it comes to attending to and answering the questions, comments, and concerns of your consumers. To set up your workflow, follow these steps:

1. Head to `https://slack.com/slack-tips/moderate-live-qa` to download the workflow example.

2. Navigate to Workflow Builder and import the example.

3. Similar to other workflows, once imported, edit the workflow to match your needs for the Q&A session.

4. Publish the workflow and let your channel know the workflow is in place:

This tip uses:

Slack features

Workflow Builder Required

Download example

Figure 5.6 – The downloaded example can be found on Slack's official website

Once you've set up the structure of your workflow as we have in the past, it's time to set your workflow in motion.

Putting your Q&A into action

Your workflow doesn't start working until you tell it to. Now that you've set up your workflow, it's time to put it into action. Follow these steps to set your Q&A workflow gears in motion:

1. Once you've imported the template, assign the channel and shortcut name for your workflow.

   Names can vary from "Submit your questions," to "Ask me anything," to "What do you want to know?" Workflow names are dependent on the host and their channel's style. The name will appear in the menu so it's important to be brief and concise so people know what you're requesting.

   The workflow starts when the member selects it from the shortcut button on the message board on the channel.

2. Select the moderator channel to review and approve incoming questions.

3. Then, customize the message with any text/content you wish in the message box. You can include a button that will move people to the next step of the workflow if you wish.

4. Finally, select the channel where approved questions will be posted for the rest of the channel to see. You can customize your message with text, emojis, and so on to meet your standards.

   The workflow will show a preview of your action before it's sent.

5. Save and you're on your way to a more efficient and transparent team!

The shortcut button can be found at the bottom left of your message bar. You can find the button highlighted in the following screenshot:

Figure 5.7 – The lightning button symbolizes the shortcut tab

In any of these scenarios, it's important to keep your team in the loop of when the sessions are occurring. For a designated channel, you can simply post and tag @here or @ channel to ping members. For existing channels, setting reminders on shared channels is a great way to prep in advance and let all members know when a Q&A is about to occur.

Other than virtual Q&As and AMA, video chats, phone calls, and conferencing are other ways to digitally interact with your team in a more personable fashion, face to face or over the phone.

Video conferencing

Video conferences, phone calls, and screen sharing take your virtual workspace and bring it back into the real world. They show the faces behind the profiles and transport your work into real time as you can instantaneously respond to questions and provide answers with explanations or a visual tutorial. You can see how the phone icon looks in the following screenshot:

Figure 5.8 – Slack phone icon on the upper right-hand side of your direct message screen

Let's first see how to call a person via direct messaging.

How to start a call from a direct message

To start a call, open a DM and click the phone icon in the upper right-hand corner of the page.

The call will begin right away and the person you're calling will immediately receive a pop-up notification. On any of Slack's plans, you can click the camera icon to switch to video. On the Standard, Plus, and Enterprise Grid plans, you can share your screen in 1:1 direct messages in addition to video.

If the person you are trying to reach is currently on **Do Not Disturb**, similar to your phone, they will receive a missed call notification when they open your chat.

How to start a call from a channel

Follow these steps to start a call from a channel:

1. Open the channel you wish to start a call with and click the details icon in the upper right-hand corner.

2. Click the phone icon and confirm that you wish to start the call.

3. Similar to the direct message format, if your workspace is on the Standard, Plus, or Enterprise Grid plans, you can switch the call to video and share your screen once the call begins.

On any of the paid plans of Slack, you also have the ability to invite others into your call directly or through a link, as well as joining an existing call yourself. The following screenshot shows the **Details** menu where you can find the **Call** button:

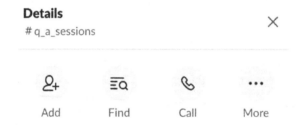

Figure 5.9 – The Call button found in the Details menu on your channel

Next, let's see how to invite members to join a call.

Inviting members to a call

Here, we will see different options for how to invite a member or members to join a particular call:

- Direct invite:

    1. Click the invite icon in the top-left corner of the call window.

    2. Find the member you'd like to add to the call.

    3. Select and click **Invite**.

- Link share:

    1. Click the invite icon in the top-left corner of the call window.

    2. Select **Copy Link** or **Get a link to this call**.

    3. Share the link in either a DM or directly to the channel.

If you're a member that's simply late to the party, you can always join a call once it's already in session. To do so, follow the simple steps mentioned in the next section.

Joining a Slack call

Here, we will see different options for how to join a Slack call:

- Direct message:

  a. A pop-up notification will signal a phone call invitation.

  b. Click the green phone icon to accept and join the call.

- Channel call:

  a. Select **Join call** from the in-channel invite. A window will then open showing everyone on the call and who is currently speaking.

  b. If your workspace is on any of the paid plans, you can share your video and screen after joining the call.

If you're constantly joining large meetings after they've already begun, you can set up your preferences to automatically join a video call with your audio muted. To do this, do the following:

1. Head to **Preferences** from your profile.

2. Click on **Advanced**.

3. You should be able to find the **When joining a Slack call**, option then check the box next to **Mute my microphone**.

While your internal team is meant to be your main focus, as we've learned throughout this chapter, it's vital you never forget your external team. Every person that interacts with your company is a priority and while acknowledging your clients within your Slack workspace is a step in the right direction, it's not enough.

Utilizing Slack for support teams

Support teams vary in every organization, whether it is their entire job description or an additional factor that plays into their day-to-day work. No matter the makeup of the group, your support team is critical to your customer satisfaction and therefore, a critical part of your company. As we've mentioned, for any group that has an effect on your organization, support teams have a right to be a part of the conversation in your workspace, as any customer could. To communicate with your customers without leaving Slack, say it with me, *we create a shared channel.*

Creating a specified support channel is similar to designating a channel for your customer/client interactions. Name the channel appropriately so that members know the purpose and invite your support team and clients to work together in their new collaboration space. After they're included in your workspace, develop a set of guidelines to follow in regards to style, how often to respond, and what would require reaching out to executive members in the company for assistance.

You could even bring in customer reactions/feedback that may not have previously had direct access to Slack from outside applications such as Twitter, HubSpot, or Salesforce. This allows an overall outreach to your customer base while allowing your team to solve issues in one convenient space.

In addition to the verbal conversation taking place on these channels, files, links, and other documents are another significant factor constantly being shared back and forth from customer to team member to workspace owner or admin.

File sharing

Rather than just discussing documents and files critical to the conversations happening on your channels, why not just share them directly and have continuous access to them? We discussed this in *Chapter 3, Slack Features, Tips, and Tricks*, and the ability to share files amongst your team members, but have not specifically gone into the how and why. Add files directly from your computer by selecting the paperclip attach button in your message bar and select **Your computer**, as featured in the following screenshot:

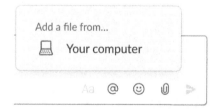

Figure 5.10 – You can find the Add a file button via the paper clip icon on your message board

File sharing directly into a Slack channel provides a more contextual experience compared to searching through endless folders piled up within other applications. You can hyperlink your outsourced link for a cleaner look or include a plugin that shares the title of the document and where the file is coming from before clicking. Especially important and helpful documents can even be pinned to a channel for continual reference. This is what a shared document looks like in Slack:

Figure 5.11 – Sample document shared on a Slack channel

You can share anything from files, photos, documents, to videos from your device into your Slack workspace from any range of outside applications such as Google Docs, Dropbox, or WeTransfer. Simply drag and drop a file or insert the link into your message board on your channel to begin the sharing process. Once a file is shared, only the people within that channel will have access to it, and not any other external, invited participants. It really is that easy.

The ability to share documents in a workspace really expands the opportunities your support team, partners, customers, and guests have by keeping all aspects of the interaction and communication easily secluded to one area everyone has access to.

Summary

In this chapter, we dove further into what it means to work with members outside of your immediate workspace team. We discovered how to incorporate outside guests, partners, clients, and customers into shared channels and interactive sessions. We learned how to set up a call and video through direct messages and channels and how to invite internal and external guests to join. We set up a means to develop manageable communication standards within channels and created expectations for how to respect and respond to customer-based feedback. Having become proficient in communicating verbally with all types of members within your company, we will now dive into the digital mechanics of maintaining your workspace in the most efficient way possible.

In the next chapter, we'll get a better understanding of what Slackbot is and how it functions. We'll focus on the difference between commands, understanding the ways bots can impact your workspace and help run things more efficiently, customizing answers to commonly asked questions, and organizing conversations with Slackbot in threads.

Section 2: How to Use Third-Party Applications and Bots

With a basic understanding of Slack, you're now ready to take on some of the app's more advanced features, such as integrating bots and other applications into your workspace. We'll begin by taking a look at Slack's built-in bot, Slackbot, before addressing how to add other existing third-party bots to help automate your workspace.

In this part, you'll learn how to save time and avoid stress by allowing bots, external applications, and tools such as Zapier to do the work for you. Read on to learn how to automate everyday, tedious tasks, messages, and workflows with Slack.

In this section, we will cover the following chapters:

6
Your Workspace Slackbot

Up until this point, we've discussed how to communicate with all different types of members of your team. From workspace owners, admins, team members, clients, and partners, to guests, we've broken down the varying ways to interact within your workspace through channels, threads, and direct messages. What we're yet to connect is the digital members of your team.

Chapter 5, *Using Slack Externally with Live Chats, Guests, and Partners*, showed us how to better communicate with external members of our team through shared channels while also providing tips on how to call and video chat within your workspace. Now we are going to take a deeper dive into the ways that your mechanical members – bots – can impact your workspace and help things run more efficiently.

In this chapter, we will cover these crucial topics:

- Learning what Slackbot is, what it can do, and the differences between commands
- Understanding the ways that bots can impact your workspace and help things run more efficiently
- Learning how to customize answers to commonly asked questions to save time and avoid covering the same ground
- Organizing your conversation with Slackbot in threads

This chapter will elevate the technical factors in your workspace to a new level. By enlisting Slackbot as, essentially, your own personal assistant, you will save yourself time and energy and create a more productive and competent workspace for you and your team members. Slackbot serves to automate everyday, tedious aspects of your business because, as we've learned more and more in each chapter, *Slack exists to make your company's communication smarter not harder.*

What's Slackbot?

Do you remember Microsoft Office Assistant's infamous paperclip friend Clippy? Slackbot is Slack's very own version of Clippy – only more. Slackbot is your full-time friend, helper, and assistant all in one. Any type of member and guest alike (on any paid or free plan) can utilize the benefits of Slackbot to set reminders, automated messages, responses, and tasks in direct messages, channels, or both across your Slack workspace. Yes, that's a lot. Let's break it down. Once you activate your account, Slackbot will introduce itself to you in a private direct message:

Hi, Slackbot here!

You're here! Hello!

If you're looking for help using Slack, click the question mark in the top right corner of the app, visit our Help Center, or reach out to a human by typing /feedback in the message bar.

I, however, am not a human. Just a bot (a simple bot, with only a few tricks up my metaphorical sleeve). But I'm still happy you're here!

Figure 6.1 – Every Slack account has its own Slackbot direct message

Essentially, Slackbot is a chatbot available to receive and respond to you or any of your members' questions within the Slack interface. Unlike Siri, your verbal Apple support assistant, Slackbot is limited to the range of the Slack Help Center and therefore cannot answer *every* question, but can answer *every* question within Slack's boundaries.

> **Important note**
> It is not possible to turn off all automated notifications from Slackbot.

Like any of your team members, Slackbot also has its own direct message channel for you to communicate with it directly and ask questions or set personal reminders that may not be pertinent to the rest of the channels. You can even view Slackbot's profile photo and information the same way you would any member of your team. Its profile appears like this:

Profile   ✕

Slackbot ♥

Sometime helper, sometime messenger,
always bot.

⊜   ✊   •••

Message   Remind me   More

Display name
Slackbot

Figure 6.2 – Slackbot has its very own profile, like any other member

From Slackbot's profile, you can easily access pinned messages, documents, files, or even have Slackbot search for information within your workspace. While contacting Slackbot through your shared direct message channel is the most simplified route, there are many ways to utilize the bot throughout your workspace without having to go out of your way. Optimize the usefulness of Slackbot to get the most out of the tool's many features, such as responding to mentions and sending automatic messages and reminders.

Getting the most out of Slackbot

Now that you understand what Slackbot is, it's time to implement it in your workspace. Your bot is now programmed to react to you and your team members, but it doesn't yet have anything to do with the selected information it's collecting through the event types. This is where things get tricky.

If you're not a coder yourself or advanced in the technology, we're going to discuss the most basic way to create app code that will help your bot receive and respond to events. In this section, we'll focus on learning how to set your bot up to respond to events and mentions, understand actions, and automate responses, as well as setting personalized reminders and tasks.

For more information on more complex coding for your bots, head to Slack's APIs help page: (`https://api.slack.com/bot-users`).

How to get the most out of Slackbot

Slackbot is a bot of many talents. Depending on the needs of your company, Slackbot can be automated to do many things within your workspace. Here are a few ways to get the most out of Slackbot:

- **Monitor your channel's activity**: A bot can help oversee and process activity on any public or private channel it's invited to, in addition to direct messages.

- **Post messages and reactions to members**: Bots can receive and post their own messages on channels they're a member of.

- **Make messages interactive with buttons**: Bots have the ability to add interactive components such as buttons to messages to promote engagement amongst your team that can later be tracked. These components trigger specified actions on your server so that you can perform certain tasks without monitoring.

Slackbot uses these features to accomplish simplified tasks across your team so that your time and efforts aren't wasted on menial, repetitive assignments.

If you're facing an issue and need Slackbot's assistance, simply ask for help. Slackbot will respond with an answer or redirect you to the Help Center for further advice. Slackbot's response may appear like this in your threads:

Slackbot 12:57 AM
If you're looking for help, visit our very fine Help Center — or if you'd rather ask a human, you can use /feedback to start a help ticket.

Figure 6.3 – The blue text leads to the Help Center through your device's browser

The Help Center is a great resource where all of Slackbot's information is sourced from. If Slackbot redirects you there, it's usually to provide further support through a more detailed explanation or to speak with an actual human on Slack's help desk. The Help Center appears like this in your browser:

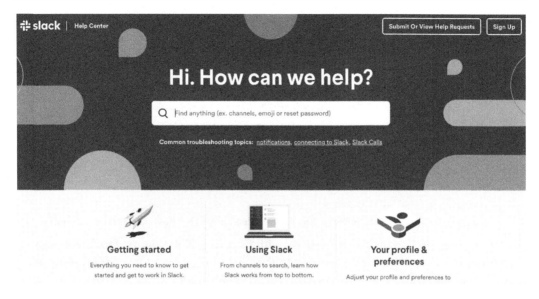

Figure 6.4 – Slack's Help Center offers assistance in every area of Slack

You can find anything in the Help Centre, such as information, articles, and requests, all available at your disposal. While the Help Center is a great resource for topics not necessarily easily explained by Slackbot, there are a lot of amazing features the bot has to offer within its realm of knowledge. Let's break these features down by Slackbot's top functions: replying, notifications, and slash commands.

Responding to mentions

The key triggering event for a bot is when they are mentioned in a conversation, the main trigger for any member that will direct them to a specific channel or direct message. The code you create should utilize the "type" section inside the event payload to spot these app_mention events and differentiate them from other events.

Bots will naturally be triggered by every mention, but should only respond to ones that trigger a specific event with specific phrasing such as "What is the Wifi password?" Use the text field in the payload to personalize the text that your message should contain so that when a bot is mentioned with that specific phrasing, the bot will know exactly how to automatically respond. Otherwise, the bot will remain silent. This process will continue as you continue to update and personalize the coding requests and responses for your bot in varying event type situations.

For instance, if a team member were to import a Google Drive file into a channel, Slackbot would be automated to respond with the following message:

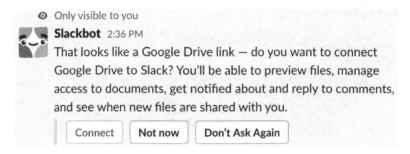

Figure 6.5 – Slackbot's response includes automated buttons for how you'd like to respond

The member could then decide to respond with **Connect**, **Not Now**, or **Don't Ask Again**, whichever way they choose to proceed with their integration of the two applications. We'll discuss more integration options in *Chapter 7, Integrating Your Favorite Tools*.

The Google Drive link included in the text message triggered Slackbot to respond with this programmed message. Should the user choose to connect Google Drive with Slack, they'll then be able to use Slackbot to search for and access that file in the future. And thus, Slackbot's purpose comes full circle!

Setting personalized reminders and tasks

We discussed in *Chapter 3, Slack Features, Tips, and Tricks*, the concept of setting reminders for yourself, whether it's a reminder for a meeting or to go back and re-reference a message. What we haven't yet mentioned is that Slackbot is your very own personal alert messenger for reminders.

To set a reminder, you can utilize the `/remind` command that works on any Slack platform – mobile or desktop. You can also manually set a reminder through the **More actions** sidebar:

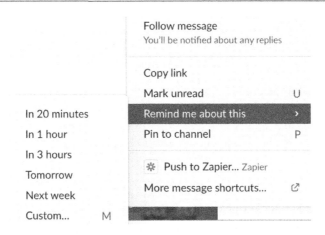

Figure 6.6 – You can choose a variety of time options for reminders

For messages, files, or conversations, choose the **More actions** icon and select **Remind me about this**, to choose a time for Slackbot to remind you. You can also customize the time so that it will send you a reminder if none of the available options meet your needs.

Slackbot communicates with all of your members but works especially well for members you've invited into your workspace: your clients and guests.

If you really want to be straightforward about your reminders, simply type in your direct message with Slackbot to tell it what you would like it to remind you to do. For example, if you were to ask Slackbot to remind you to "Call David tomorrow morning," it should respond something like this:

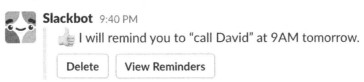

Figure 6.7 – Slackbot responds immediately to your requests

If you've incorrectly asked Slackbot to remind you about something, simply delete the reminder. If you want to view all of your reminders or view the reminder you just created, select **View Reminders**. Slackbot's automated response will then appear similar to this:

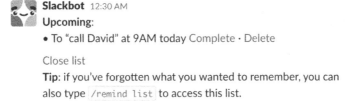

Figure 6.8 – Your reminders can include just a singular reminder or many

If at any point you've forgotten messages or tasks you wanted to remember, just type /
remindlist into your text message bar and send it in a direct message or on a channel
for your reminders to reappear in a new message from Slackbot.

While Slackbot's automated messages and responses are a critical aspect of your
workspace's capabilities, there are instances in which you may want to customize
Slackbot's responses to properly fit terms and phrases personal to your team. In this
section, we'll take a look at how to create custom responses for Slackbot.

Adding automatic responses

Custom responses are one of the most popular features of Slackbot. Having the option to
automate answers to common questions such as those regarding the Wi-Fi password or
to send out customizable intro messages once a member joins a channel saves workspace
owners, admins, and general members an immense amount of time that would have been
taken away from their task at hand.

Slackbot works to answer members that use unique words and phrases in a direct message
or channel by automatically responding with an answer. These custom responses can be
set through the **Customize Your Workspace** page found by clicking on your workspace
name at the upper left of your sidebar:

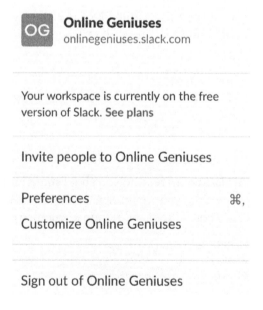

Figure 6.9 – Customize Online Geniuses will bring you to your workspace page

Once you click on the customize option, you'll be brought to your Slack workspace in your device's browser to customize your workspace. In this area, you can set custom emojis as well as creating channel prefixes such as keywords/phrases that Slackbot will respond to with your automated message. Your **Customize Your Workspace** page will appear like this in your browser:

Figure 6.10 – Slack will bring you to your browser's Slack customization page

Any custom Slack response that you create can be sent to any member's personal DMs that works within and has access to the same channel, with the exception of guests of channels that are shared with external organizations. Once you've created your team's customized commands and prefixes, they're good to be set in motion and used by yourself and any of your team members.

You should try to use a command that does not exist within this part of your **Customize Your Workspace** page. Slackbot will even notify you about this rather than keeping you waiting. Slackbot will respond with a distressed bot profile, followed by a message similar to this:

 Slackbot 12:39 AM
/find is not a valid command. In Slack, all messages that start with the "/" character are interpreted as commands.

If you are trying to send a message and not run a command, try preceding the "/" with an empty space.

Figure 6.11 – In this example, /find was the incorrect command used

This response would be automatically sent as well if you were to accidentally send a message as a command when it was meant as a regular message. All of these responses work to make sure you're communicating properly and in the most efficient way possible.

Bringing Slackbot to your threads

Threads are like run-off thoughts. They're conversations within a conversation that allow a seamless string of messages on the same topic to be located in a singular place. Threads can become hidden within your channel and that's why it's important to make sure Slackbot knows how to respond to messages and retrieve the data found in threads as well.

Rather than redirecting common questions to general channels, make sure crucial information is integrated into your threads so that it's easy to find and accessible to members working in that space. For example, if you know your team is going to need access to something such as the WiFi password within that thread, ask Slackbot and then pin the message to the channel so that every member can view it, no matter when they join the thread.

For a more direct impact on members, Slackbot can also be utilized in threads for immediate question and answer responses. In this next section, we'll discuss how to customize your Slackbot responses by setting up FAQ channels, utilizing the workspace language, and creating fun interactions.

Building FAQs with Slackbot

As we mentioned before, any member of your workspace can present a variety of **FAQs**, or **Frequently Asked Questions**, to the channel multiple times as your company continues to grow and expand. To avoid the repetitive nature of tediously responding to each inquiry, create a thread or channel specifically designed for FAQs for Slackbot to answer within these spaces.

Whether it's a shared channel, thread, or direct message, setting aside a specific area for these questions to be answered eliminates the mess and overabundance of messages taking up the main channels. If you choose to incorporate an FAQ section into a thread, make sure you're continuously updating or adding new threads as the weeks pass. Threads can get lost as the conversation progresses forward, so it's important to keep track so that there's always a designated place for questions to be asked and answered.

On top of communicating with your direct company team members, there are instances when Slackbot will have to work with your temporary members as well. Slackbot communicates with all of your members but works especially well for members you've invited into your workspace: your clients and guests.

Utilizing Slackbot for your clients

Chapter 5, *Using Slack Externally with Live Chats, Guests, and Partners*, focused on working with your clients and customers in shared workspaces and channels. Now that you understand what Slackbot is and how to use it, we can discuss how you can utilize bots within these customized channels to your benefit. For example, Slackbot can be used to direct new members or guests to specified channels:

Figure 6.12 – Slackbot offers buttons to get started

As we've learned, Slackbot essentially works as an automated response or action within your workspace. By setting simple commands, you can use Slackbot to respond to members when they answer questions both *internally* and *externally*. For an even easier means of communicating with your support team and clients, you can employ Slackbot to deliver automated responses to consistent questions and actions as they're happening that may seem like a no-brainer to your team members.

For example, answers could include a password to access documents and files, the main point of contact between teams, or even the name of the project. Slackbot can make life easier for outside members by answering their simple FAQs and allowing a smoother transition into the team without the hassle of having an actual member answer repeated queries over and over again.

Customizing your Slackbot responses

Just like your members, Slackbot doesn't have to be all business all the time. Slackbot should reflect you and your team and the type of environment you work in. Bots respond how you want them to, so you can make their responses and keywords as formal or casual as you please.

When selecting your keywords for Slackbot to look out for, it's important to keep the tone and language in mind. Choose phrases your team members would normally use themselves and have Slackbot respond in the same manner to continue the seamless exchange of information without compromising your workspace vibe.

Workspace language

Language is a critical factor of any workspace, especially in today's world. We've grown as a society to adapt and acknowledge wording and titles to better fit the views of ourselves and our peers that should be reflected in every aspect of our company culture.

Slackbot can be used as a tool to promote and monitor the language used amongst your members to keep full-time staff, clients, and guests alike in check with company protocol. For example, if a person were to address the channel with "Hey guys," Slackbot could be programmed to instead suggest "friends," "team," "everyone," or "coworkers," to include the entirety of a group in their statement. This serves as an automatic suggestion for users to get across the same information in a more inclusive manner.

This feature also serves to keep members in check with a specific workspace language when it comes to project or company titles. Without having to call someone out directly, Slackbot simply nudges a person in the right direction when a misstep occurs.

Creating fun interactions

While Slackbot is a unique and profound tool for the technical purposes of your company, it can also be used in a fun and entertaining way, engaging your members through custom responses as well as aiding them in their communication patterns.

Teams have utilized Slack to play games to test their team members for a daily challenge or a weekly reward. Ask Slackbot to flip a coin, pick a card, or roll a die, or even choose a secret word that'll celebrate members when they happen to use it in conversation. Slackbot can be a tool for incentives as well as a tool for efficiency.

Summary

In this chapter, we discovered Slackbot. Bots are a complicated mechanical tool to understand if you're not familiar with the concept. Coding isn't an easy task. While you may not become an expert at creating code for your bots right away, you can now say that you've mastered how to create one, integrate it into your workspace, and understand what it is and how it benefits you and your company while working in Slack. We learned how to answer commonly asked questions, customize replies and exchanges, and integrate bots into your threads. We've laid the groundwork for getting your foot in the door with Slackbot and its endless possibilities. Now, we'll begin to bring in outside apps to further complicate, yet expand, the boundaries and capabilities of your workspace.

In the next chapter, we'll discover how to bring some of your favorite applications such as Google Drive, Dropbox, Trello, and so on directly into your Slack workspace for a more seamless transition. We'll highlight what a Slack directory is and how to use it, creating the perfect app approval process, choosing the right apps for onboarding, and improving the work culture, and how to integrate them into your individual channels.

7
Integrating Your Favorite Tools

Now that we have your team up and running, it's time to get down to business. We've developed communication channels and honed your company culture and language through regular members, guests, partners, and clients as well as mechanical bots. Your team has the backbone for success; now it needs the tools to set it into motion.

In *Chapter 6, Your Workspace Slackbot*, we broke down Slackbot. We learned how to create our own bots, incorporate them into our workspace, and set them into action in an efficient way that automated typical everyday tasks. As we progress through our Slack education, we'll continue to learn new ways to set up our workspace using the most effective tools and tips. Having mastered Slackbot, we'll focus now on how to implement helpful additional applications in our Slack workspace. In this chapter, we will cover these topics:

- Learning what a Slack directory is and how to use it
- Creating the perfect app approval process for your organization
- Getting the best apps that every team needs for onboarding and improving work culture
- Learning how to integrate Google Drive, Outlook, GitHub, Dropbox, Twitter, and dozens of other apps

In this chapter, we'll focus on the benefits of applications outside of your Slack workspace. Slack is designed to be your communication hub but does not claim to have all of the tools your unique workspace needs to succeed. To accommodate this reality, Slack opens its doors to outside tools that work on the general level as well as toward specific niches to bring your existing information into a singular space.

What is the Slack App Directory?

The Slack App Directory is essentially your workspace's version of the App Store found on your smartphone. It's your go-to place for any and all apps you can utilize within your company's Slack workspace. The app directory has over 2,000 apps developed to assist you and your team throughout your Slack experience. By connecting your Slack account to the best tools and services already available on the market, you begin to build the most well-rounded workspace possible.

The Slack App Directory appears as shown in the following figure through your Slack application:

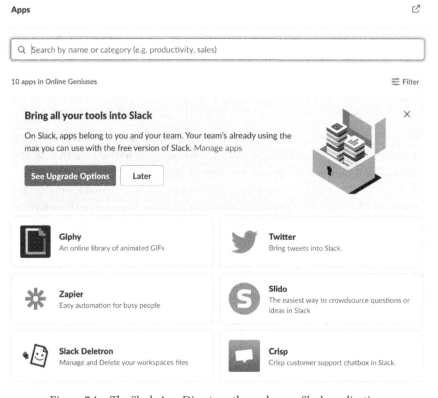

Figure 7.1 – The Slack App Directory through your Slack application

Slack understands that you have existing files, documents, contacts, and information stored elsewhere. So, why work out of multiple outlets when you can simplify the clutter and bring all of your tools into a communal space? Apps can be used for multiple purposes depending on your company's needs.

A few things the assortment of apps within the Slack directory cover include the following:

- Adding Slack messages to Google Sheets

- Syncing your Slack status with your calendar

- Receiving event reminders and notifications

- Running a poll to collect ideas from your teammates

- Using screen sharing to resolve problems collaboratively

- Creating and assigning tasks

- Keeping track of each other's schedules with calendar sharing

If you have a need, the chances are Slack has an app to fill it. When searching for existing and new applications to incorporate into your workspace, you'll find that the way apps appear is sorted in a certain format.

Apps are sorted in your workspace in the following ways:

- **Your top apps**: The apps most frequently used by your team members.

- **Apps in [workspace name]**: Apps already installed in your workspace.

- **Recommended apps**: Popular apps you can choose to install in your workspace. If more than 10 apps have already been added to your workspace, this feature won't appear in the directory.

- **Pre-approved apps for [workspace name]**: Apps the workspace owner has already pre-approved for any member of the team to use. If app installation has not been restricted for your team, this feature won't appear in the directory.

> **Tip**
> Select **Filter** in the upper right-hand corner of the **Apps** page to view apps by type or category.

This sorting format allows you to discover new apps you might not have previously taken advantage of, while also painlessly integrating the apps you're already familiar with. The app directory works to bring external applications directly into your workspace to get more work done without having to leave Slack.

Getting apps into your Slack workspace

Applications are a type of software that works to connect a tool or service, such as Google Drive or Salesforce, to Slack. Apps can be built specifically for Slack or simply adapted and integrated into an existing workspace. Adding apps to Slack creates a centralized working environment. This allows your business to streamline information for all of your internal and external members from a singular source.

The Slack App Directory is the hub for all Slack-reviewed apps built to work through this communication medium. You can view the directory through your internet browser on your desktop or through the Slack application. You can find the directory through the **Apps** icon in the left sidebar on your Slack page, to search for new apps or open existing apps.

To integrate an outside app into your Slack workspace, you first need to create an account with that service. Depending on the app, you may be able to utilize the service for free when paired with Slack, or with a paid plan. If that information is offered by the developer, it will be described in the Slack directory as follows.

Pairing options for outside accounts with Slack are the following:

- **Free**: You can use both the service and Slack for free.
- **Free and paid plans available**: You can use the service and Slack for free, but paid options are available.
- **Paid with free trial**: A paid account is required with the service to use it in Slack, but there is also a free trial option available.
- **Paid**: A paid account with the service is required to use it in Slack.

Any general member can add apps by default to their workspace, but workspace owners/admins have the right to restrict the ability to add apps. If you are not given permission to install an app, you may have to submit an app request for approval.

Now let's see how the Slack app approval process works.

The Slack app approval process

Apps are a critical part of combining the tools that keep your company running with your organization's communication center. With the power of the Slack directory, tools such as your calendar events, company and client contacts, and external file folders and drives can be brought into your very own workspace. The **Apps** tab can be reached through the **More** option shown on the left sidebar of your Slack workspace:

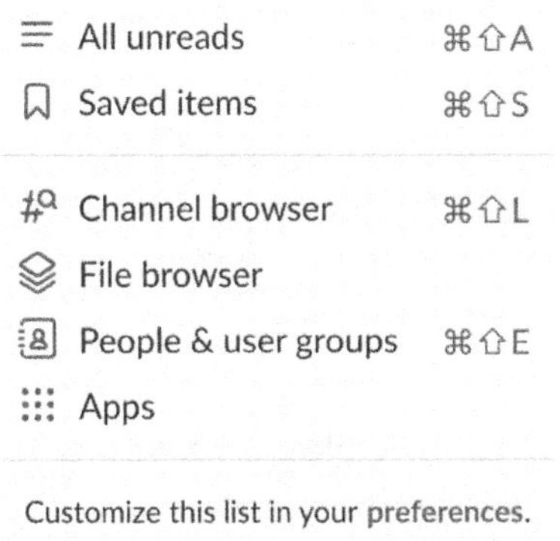

≡	All unreads	⌘⇧A
⊓	Saved items	⌘⇧S
#ᵠ	Channel browser	⌘⇧L
⊗	File browser	
⒜	People & user groups	⌘⇧E
⸬	Apps	

Customize this list in your preferences.

Figure 7.2 – The App tab option as seen in your Slack application

Once you've been directed to the Slack App Directory, take the following steps to add an app to your workspace:

1. Select the **Apps** button from the **More** tab on the left sidebar.

2. Search for the app you're looking for, then click **Add**, and you'll be directed to the Slack App Directory.

3. Click **Add to Slack**.

4. Follow the prompt that appears to install the app. If the application is already installed, it will then request your login information to connect your account.

While many apps will be used by most of the members of your workspace, there are some apps that could be used on a team-to-team basis based on the nature of the service. Because of this, some workspace owners and admins may require a member to request to add an app to the workspace before it's added by the team member. To send an app request, take the following steps:

1. Select the **Apps** button from the **More** tab on the left sidebar.

2. Search for the app you're looking for, then click **Add** and you'll be directed to the Slack App Directory.

3. Click **Add to Slack**.

4. Create a custom message with information regarding your request.

   Depending on your workspace owner, this step could be optional or mandatory.

5. Submit your request.

   After it has been reviewed, Slackbot will deliver a direct message to you.

Any member within your Slack workspace will be allowed to connect to and utilize an app once it's installed. Now that you know how to find and install an app in your workspace, it's time to put them to work.

Using apps in Slack

After an app is officially installed in your workspace, it's ready to hit the ground running right away. As we discussed in *Chapter 6, Your Workspace Slackbot*, apps also have bots that can be directed and used to your advantage. Some apps send a welcome message and directions to get you familiar with tips on how to set it up and get started. Others provide a **Home** tab where you can find general information, configure app settings, and other necessary instructions.

For example, Google Calendar automatically generates a welcome message to connect your account, as you can see in the following screenshot:

Figure 7.3 – Google Calendar is a common app Slack users utilize

Depending on the app, you may also be able to utilize the shortcut feature to take specific actions in Slack. You can use shortcuts to do typical things in your workspace such as setting a reminder or writing a post. But with apps, you can also use shortcuts to set up an event, book a meeting, or even create a document, presentation, or GIF.

You can find the shortcut menu by selecting the lightning bolt icon at the bottom left of the message box:

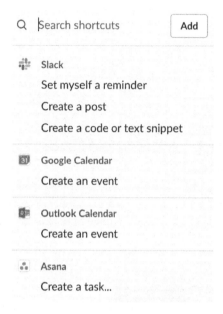

Figure 7.4 – The more apps you have, the more options will be available in your shortcut options

Another way to access your apps is through individual messages sent in a direct message or on a channel or thread. Simply select the **More actions** option on a message to utilize an app's features.

No two apps are built the same way and there is an endless array of apps to choose from in your Slack directory. Utilizing apps to create a more efficient team is a top priority when incorporating them into your workspace, but you should also make an effort to use apps more smartly.

Here are some quick tips for using apps:

- **Avoid clutter**: As we've discussed in each chapter, we always want to avoid unnecessary messages and posts when possible. Pay attention to apps that use a high volume of updates and may require a separate channel to control the flow of constant data.

- **Familiarize yourself with the app's features**: Each app has its own shortcuts and commands. Get familiar with each so that you can employ its tools when the time comes. This includes slash commands that will allow you to take action immediately rather than heading to the **Shortcut** tab from the message board or the **More Actions** option.

- **Pay attention to the logistics**: Keep an eye out for an app's terms and conditions as well as capabilities and permissions, otherwise known as scopes. This is the outline of how an app functions with your workspace. Scopes will be discussed further in *Chapter 10, Building Your Own Bot.*

If you keep these things in mind, your apps should have a smooth transition into the flow of your workspace. Apps have a variety of tools and services to offer you and your team. We've brought apps into Slack and we've learned what to expect and how to familiarize ourselves with them, so now let's learn which tools you and your team should keep an eye out for when it comes to improving your overall Slack experience.

Using Slack apps to improve your work culture and onboarding process

Apps serve many purposes across your team, whether it's importing calendar events or connecting outside documents and files directly into your channels. But apps can also work with your team in other ways than simply bridging the gap from one workspace to another. Many apps are designed to pair well with tools such as Slack to assist you and your team with onboarding and developing a workspace culture through a digital lens.

There are a variety of categories for these types of apps, from **Health & Wellness** to **Working from home**.

The Slack App Directory can be found through your desktop browser, in addition to your Slack app:

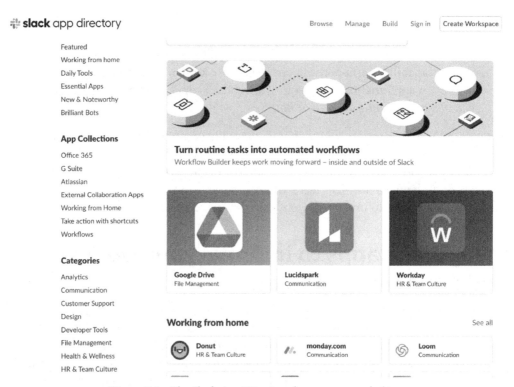

Figure 7.5 – The Slack App Directory home page on desktop

There are over 2,000 apps to choose from when it comes to finding the right fit for your company's vibe, so we'll take a few popular choices that serve a purpose in almost every workspace to make the search a little easier.

We will look at some of the best apps for improving a company's culture in the following sections.

Simple Poll

Simple Poll is quite literally what it's titled – a simple poll. With this app, you can create polls and surveys directly in your Slack workspace to get team members', clients', guests', and partners' feedback immediately, whether it's a big decision about your latest project or simply deciding on a place for lunch.

Simple Poll can be found in the Slack App Directory as shown in the following figure:

Simple Poll

Description   Features   Permissions   Security & Compliance

Simple Poll

Get your colleagues' thoughts in minutes, not in
the next meeting. All right in Slack.

Sign In to install

Learn More

Supported Languages
English

Pricing
Free and paid plans available

Learn more & Support
Get app support
Visit developer website
support@simplepoll.freshd
esk.com
Privacy policy

Categories
Featured   Social & Fun

With Simple Poll you can create native polls and surveys right within Slack.
Get your colleagues' thoughts in minutes; not in the next meeting.

Need to decide on whether to proceed with a candidate? The next step with a customer? A favourite product
design? Or even where to go to lunch on Thursday? Simple Poll provides an effortless and collaborative way
to make these decisions.

Native Polls

Figure 7.6 – Simply Poll is a quick and easy way to get company feedback

Once the app is installed, all you have to do is set the /poll command followed by
the poll information and click **Send**. You'll get feedback within seconds, without going
through the process of outsourcing to an application such as Google Forms.

Donut

Donut Bot is an easy and effective way to build relationships within your team – even
when you don't work physically with one another in the office. Donut is essentially
everyone's mutual friend. The app works to introduce members of your team to one
another in a virtual environment by creating specific events, channels, or direct messages
to introduce themselves and begin a conversation.

Donut can be found in the Slack App Directory as shown in the following figure:

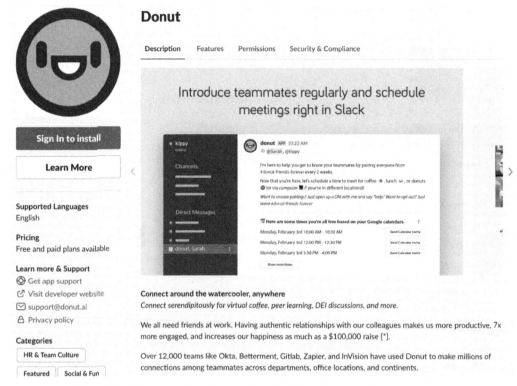

Figure 7.7 – Donut works to fast-track onboarding new members to your team

Donut works like any bot, so you can set it up to interact with your team in specific ways. To quickly introduce new members, guests, clients, or partners that join your workspace after it's set up, use Donut to reach out to groups or pairs of people to set up a time to chat, grab coffee (or donuts) in person, or virtually create a more cohesive working environment.

Giphy

You may recognize Giphy from social media platforms as well as your smartphone messages. Giphy is a fun, interactive way to convey a message to your team members that gives a more personal and casual tone to your conversation.

Giphy can be found in the Slack App Directory as shown in the following figure:

Figure 7.8 – Giphy allows you to take moving images and incorporate them into your images

You can choose from the hundreds of thousands of animated GIFs to use in response to a message by typing /giphy followed by the type of GIF you wish to send to enable Giphy's features.

Zoom

In the age of working from home and digital offices, Zoom is a critical part of any team. Although you can utilize video meetings from your Slack channels, Zoom is an app widely used by companies and workplace professionals that can be easily integrated into Slack and incorporated into your company culture.

Zoom can be found in the Slack App Directory as follows:

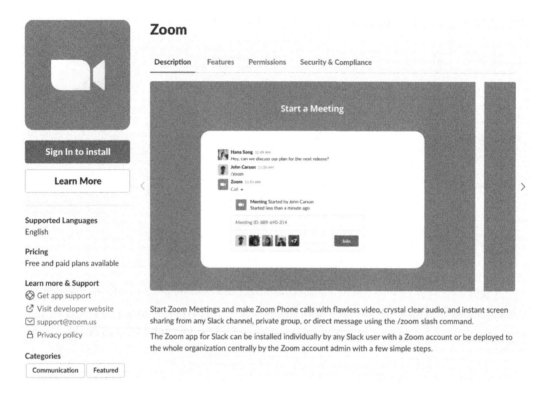

Figure 7.9 – Zoom offers instant video and audio chats through the app's integration with Slack

Zoom allows you to see and hear your team members in real time so it doesn't feel like your computer is your only co-worker. Bring your office space to life with conference meetings as well as company celebrations to personalize your socially distanced workspace.

Troops

For any team utilizing Salesforce as a part of the company structure, Troops is the Slack app for you. Troops offers the easiest means of utilizing Salesforce directly from the Slack interface to keep sales members informed and connected.

Troops can be found in the Slack App Directory as follows:

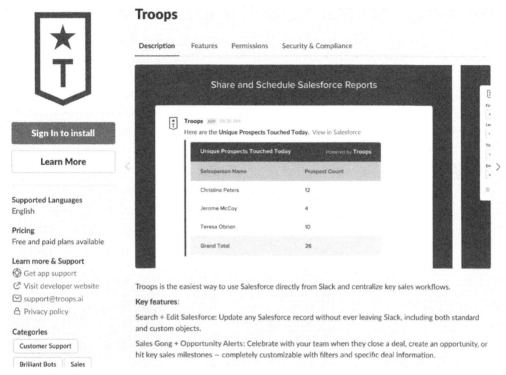

Figure 7.10 – Troops is the bridge that brings Salesforce tools into your Slack workspace

The app allows members to work collaboratively while managing and reporting on sales pipelines and centralizing workflows to celebrate updates and wins together. It also allows your sales members to have a place within your Slack workspace and convey information to all members who might not have previously been aware of or had access to.

All of these apps have something different to offer to the overall strengthening of your workplace as a team. Communication is a key factor in developing and maintaining a bond across the tiers of your company's hierarchy. Apps such as these help to bridge the communication gap in digital workplaces while promoting a fun and inviting place to work.

Now let's see some of the most commonly used Slack apps and integrations.

The most common Slack apps and integrations

There are hundreds of apps to utilize within the Slack workspace. We could literally write a whole other book describing them all. It's difficult to pick and choose which ones to highlight over the others and that's why it's important that you and your members do your own research within the Slack App Directory as well as finding out which apps fit the needs of your team. The Slack App Directory offers **App Collections**, **Slack Picks**, and varying other categories, such as **Daily Tools**, to help narrow your search process:

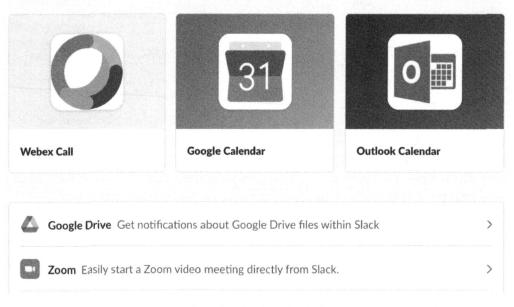

Figure 7.11 – Daily tools offered on the Slack App Directory

To make life simpler, we broke down a few key apps every workspace has a unique use for. In the following sections, we will look at some of the most common Slack apps and integrations.

Google Drive

Google Drive is the basis of many workplaces. With so many critical features, such as Docs, Sheets, Forms, Slides, Gmail, and so on, it's important that Drive finds a home within your Slack workspace. All of the Google Drive applications, as well as Google Drive itself, can be found in the Slack App Directory:

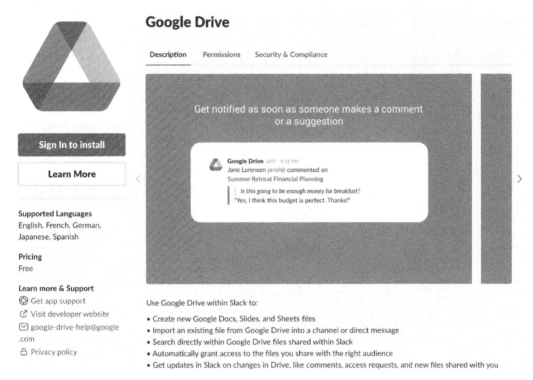

Figure 7.12 – Share Google Drive files and docs directly with your Slack channels

If you're familiar with Google Drive's many functions, bringing the app into your workspace simply becomes an extension of the tools you have already used. Search for Drive files and docs shared within your Slack workspace within the app, as well as automatically granting team members access to shared docs and replying to comment notifications that are then posted directly to the file. Work within Drive, within Slack. It's really that simple and a real time-saver.

Dropbox

Dropbox is the Slack of file hosting services, collecting files, documents, cloud content, and more in a centralized location. Now, with the power of Slack apps, you can bring your already saved and organized files straight into Slack. Dropbox can be found in the Slack App Directory:

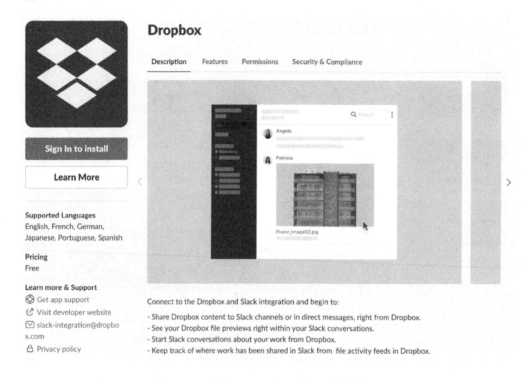

Figure 7.13 – Import and share Dropbox files with Slack team members

Share already existing content from Dropbox in Slack channels or direct messages, view file previews, and keep track of where your work has been shared across your workspace. Combine both of these powerhouse tools for an increasingly efficient distribution of information.

Outlook Calendar

Outlook is another application familiar to many offices for company emails as well as calendars. Outlook Calendar allows you to share your already populated and busy calendar directly in Slack messages and channels to avoid overlapping events and meetings. Outlook Calendar can be found in the Slack App Directory as shown in the following screenshot:

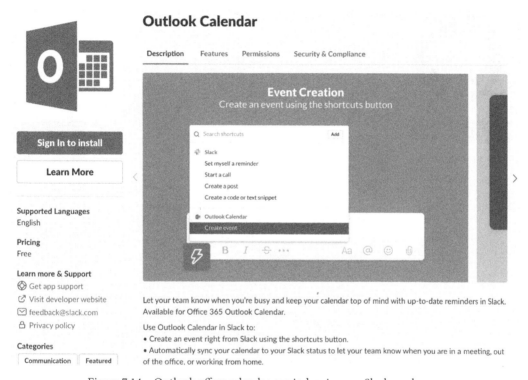

Figure 7.14 – Outlook offers calendar reminders in your Slack workspace

This app is a great way of letting your team members know when you're free, busy, out to lunch, in a meeting, or even just working from home, away from the office. You can even use Outlook Calendar to create your own meetings and events through shortcuts within Slack to immediately share company-wide.

GitHub

GitHub has become a critical part of workspaces as the digital age continues to grow with the advancement of software development. For particularly tech-savvy organizations, the GitHub app is a great way to combine coding software with the communication outlet you use to discuss it. GitHub can be found in the Slack App Directory:

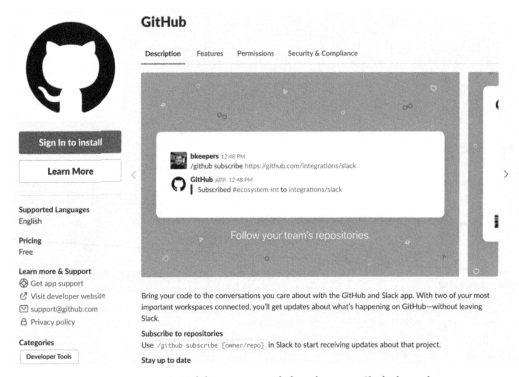

Figure 7.15 – GitHub brings your coded work to your Slack channels

Use the `/github subscribe [owner/repo]` command in Slack to start receiving updates from GitHub about a specific project's commits, pull requests, issues, code reviews, and deployment statuses.

Twitter

A popular social media application, Twitter can also be a useful tool for many organizations using Slack by keeping companies connected to their customer/consumer base. Slack, like social media, exists to keep people connected with one another. With the Twitter app, keep your team members connected with your Slack and Twitter accounts in a combined space. Twitter can be found in the Slack App Directory as shown in the following figure:

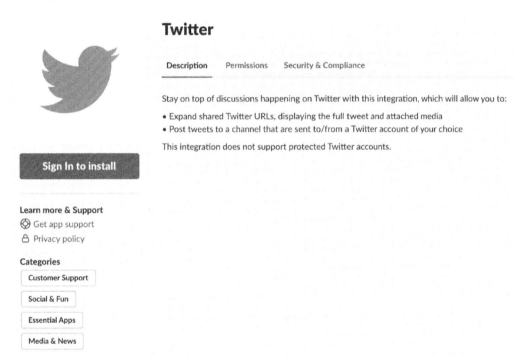

Figure 7.16 – Bring tweets and Twitter threads directly into Slack

Not only does the Twitter app provide a resource for customer feedback and interactions, but it also expands a network for news media organizations utilizing Slack. You can post tweets directly to channels and direct messages as well as expanding tweet URLs to view attached media.

Once your unique assortment of apps is downloaded to your workspace, you can filter through them by category in the Slack App Directory on the Slack app. Some of the category types include **Analytics**, **Design**, **HR & Team Culture**, and **Sales & Marketing**:

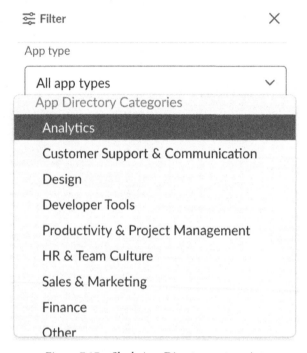

Figure 7.17 – Slack App Directory categories

The options are truly endless when it comes to creating the right assortment of apps, and no two workspaces will have the same collection in operation. We've listed some creative communicative suggestions as well as critical everyday integrations to get you started, but now it's up to you and your team to personalize your app selection to set your company up for all-round success.

Summary

This chapter taught us how to integrate some of our favorite external applications into our Slack workspace. We discovered the Slack App Directory and the thousands of app options and categories it has to offer teams, bettering communication; onboarding; and sharing files, documents, schedules, and even tweets directly in your Slack messages and channels. We discussed some of the best and most popular apps to download and learned how to find the right apps to fit the needs and culture of our workspace. With a wide variety of options at our disposal, we're now going to shift gears to focus on a particular integration to simplify the apps you bring into your workspace.

In the next chapter, we'll take on an even easier way to make this merge possible: Zapier. We'll discover how this integration tool creates workflows, or "Zaps," for your channel, automating them, finding the right plan, and ultimately bringing your outside information and applications into your workspace for the most efficient Slack experience possible.

8
Automate Your Workflow with Zapier

While Slack itself is a unique and useful tool at the fingertips of you and your team, we've learned that there are many other applications that assist in producing the most efficient workspace. Whether it be any of the Google Drive options or a standalone tool such as Dropbox, Slack works to make the sharing process between you and your members as seamless as possible.

But what about the other factors of your company/organization that come into play? What about your email contacts, calendar events, and data collected via other sources? All of these currently have a home in a separate space.

This is where **Zapier** joins the Slack picture!

Chapter 7, Integrating Your Favorite Tools, prepped you for the concept of Slack integrations. *Chapter 6, Your Workplace Slackbot*, introduced you to the world of bots and some of the technical, albeit complex, aspects of coding. Now we're going to show you the one-stop easy tool that allows you to focus on the important stuff – *with no coding required* – while it does all the work for you.

This chapter will cover the following main topics:

- Introduction to Zapier

- Finding the right Zapier plan for you

- Understanding how workflows, called Zaps, work on your Slack channels

- Learning how to integrate Slack and Zapier

- Automating your workflows with Zapier

- Examples of different types of businesses to demonstrate how Zapier and Slack can automate your business

By expanding your boundaries beyond Slack, you invite a different realm of efficiency into your workspace. Zapier works with your company's existing tools to make your life easier by combining the old with the new in a matter of minutes.

What is Zapier?

Zapier is one of the most popular and useful integrations for Slack. In an effort to work *smarter, not harder*, Zapier serves as the middleman between your Slack channel and your existing data on other apps. Without coding or relying on hired developers to create a tool for you, you can connect two or more applications to automate repetitive tasks with the help of Zapier.

By connecting your external applications to Slack – your unified communication platform – you simplify the need for multiple drives, tabs, emails, calendars, applications; you name it. Zapier works to help with organization as much as it does integration, keeping your workspace neat and functional throughout the workday.

You can find the Zapier app's home page through the Slack App Directory or on your desktop. Zapier's description appears as such in the directory:

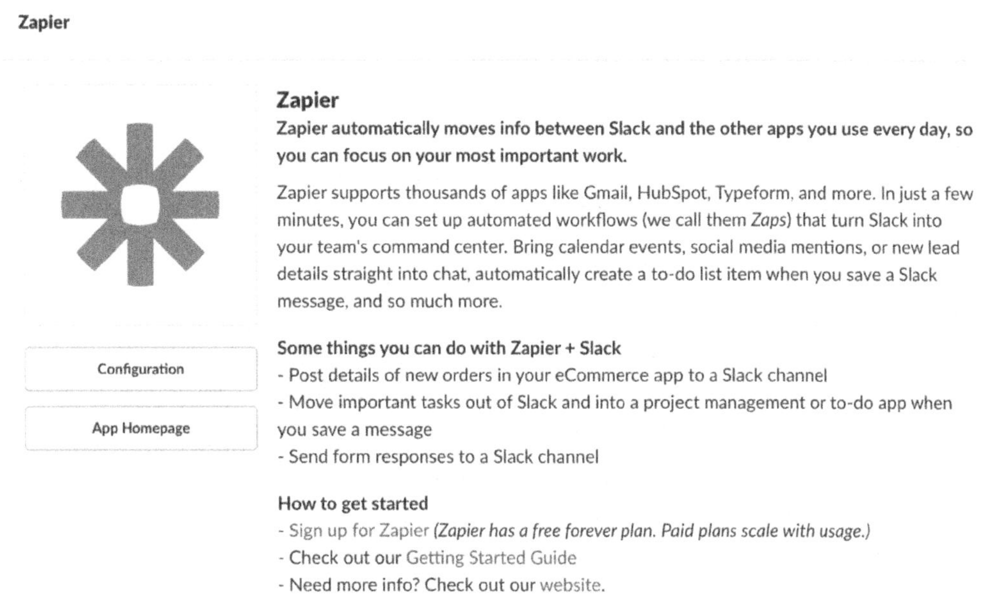

Zapier

Zapier

Zapier automatically moves info between Slack and the other apps you use every day, so you can focus on your most important work.

Zapier supports thousands of apps like Gmail, HubSpot, Typeform, and more. In just a few minutes, you can set up automated workflows (we call them *Zaps*) that turn Slack into your team's command center. Bring calendar events, social media mentions, or new lead details straight into chat, automatically create a to-do list item when you save a Slack message, and so much more.

Configuration

App Homepage

Some things you can do with Zapier + Slack
- Post details of new orders in your eCommerce app to a Slack channel
- Move important tasks out of Slack and into a project management or to-do app when you save a message
- Send form responses to a Slack channel

How to get started
- Sign up for Zapier (*Zapier has a free forever plan. Paid plans scale with usage.*)
- Check out our Getting Started Guide
- Need more info? Check out our website.

Figure 8.1 – The Zapier app's description from the Slack application

Through automation, you can transfer existing information from one database to the communication platform while assigning tasks and actions normally performed manually to be updated and produced on an automatic basis.

Zapier offers a variety of these services depending on the apps you choose to pair the integration with. While some of these features can vary with the skillset of your team, many are created to assist with your company's communication. In the next section, we'll take a closer look at Zapier's communication tools.

Zapier's communication tools

You can utilize a variety of communication methods when using integration with Slack. Some of these key tools include the following:

- Setting your Slack status to specific text or an emoji.

- Updating your team by sending messages to specific channels after people fill out forms on Survey Form, Google Forms, and so on.

- Manage daily tasks by adding starred Slack messages to project management apps such as Trello.

- Archive Slack messages with specific keywords/emoji reactions in Google Sheets/Excel Online for reference later.

Not every single one of these tasks is vital to your workspace, but it aids in simplifying and promoting collaboration.

Now that we know the overall purpose of Zapier and about some of its more common communication tools, we need to know how to bring it into our Slack channels. In this next section, we'll get started with breaking down the options you have when picking the right Zapier plan for you and your team.

Choosing the right plan

To get started with Zapier, you'll first have to set up an account in the application in addition to your Slack workspace. If you sign up for a free account, you'll have access to Zapier's core features forever, and some of the paid options as a trial for up to 14 days.

Zapier offers a range of five different plans to match you and your company's needs, from team size to range and financial status. Each automation, large or small, fits the demands of your team through the number of tasks each plan accounts for.

The Zapier plans and price range are as follows:

1. **Free**: $0/month for 100 tasks/month

    The obvious "free is for me" plan, the basic option offers the standard features that allow anyone to automate their workflow. The Free plan includes the following:

- Five single-step Zaps
- A 15-minute update time
- Single-step Zaps

    A task is counted every time a Zap successfully moves data or takes action for you.

2. **Starter**: $19.99/month for 750 tasks/month

    The Starter plan works well for the beginner company working to build their team with simple tasks and easy-to-adjust data.

    The Starter plan includes the following:

- 20 Zaps
- A 15-minute update time
- Multi-step Zaps that allow a single trigger to perform as many tasks as you want
- Three premium apps that are selectively offered to paying users
- Filters that only let your Zaps run if your data matches a specific criterion

- Formatters that allow you to adjust numbers, dates, and text to meet your needs

- Connections via webhooks to create custom integrations for any app

This plan provides more room to experiment with Zaps and multi-step Zaps to continue to automate your workflow.

3. **Professional**: $49/month for 2,000 tasks/month

As your team grows, so does your plan. The Professional plan allows for more adept Zaps and features.

The Professional plan includes the following:

- Unlimited Zaps

- A 2-minute update time

- Filters, formatters, and connections via webhooks

- Custom logic – paths that build advanced workflows to run different actions based on conditions previously decided upon.

- Auto replay automatically retrying any failed tasks due to technical errors.

The key features of this plan are the significantly quicker update time and advanced workflows.

4. **Team**: $299/month for 50,000 tasks/month

This package covers your basic team needs for building a collaborative workspace.

The Team plan includes the following:

- Unlimited Zaps

- A 1-minute update time

- Filters, formatters, and connections via webhooks; custom logic – paths and auto replay

- Unlimited users added to your account

- Folder permissions to limit who can access shared Zaps and folders

- Premier support prioritized at this plan level

- Shared app connections without needing to share passwords or API keys

- Shared workspace for full access to Zaps across your team

By allowing easy access to shared folders and docs, the Team plan prepares its unlimited members for a smooth, cohesive working experience.

5. **Company**: $599 - $3,599/month for 100,000-2,000,000 tasks/month

   This is the big picture plan. The largest plan, the Company plan covers everything a large-scale organization would need to achieve all of its actions in an efficient manner.

   The Company plan includes the following:

- Unlimited Zaps

- A 1-minute update time

- Filters, formatters, and connections via webhooks; custom logic – paths, auto replay, unlimited users, folder permissions, premier support, shared app connections, and a shared workspace

- Advanced admin permission to add unlimited teams to your account

- User provisioning (SCIM) to monitor, add, change, and delete user accounts

- App restrictions to manage which apps can be added to your account

- SAML **Single Sign-On (SSO)** for **identity and access management (IAM)**

- Custom data retention to meet your company's legal and regulatory requirements

- Account consolidation to implement a single, secure account company-wide

   From better security standards and restrictions to upward of 100,000 task possibilities a month, this final plan has it all with its enterprise features.

The options are seemingly endless as each plan offers itemized features designed for you and your teams' needs on a variety of levels. The more you experiment with Zapier and its tools, the more you can expand your toolbelt to encompass a wider range of data and pre-programmed actions.

Each of these plans notes a collection of options when it comes to Zaps and the number of tasks based on the level of the plan. But what are Zaps and how do they work? Zapier works as an integration tool, so before you break out your wallet to invest in the different options automation has to offer, you first have to understand how it works. We are going to see how to integrate Zapier and Slack with our existing tools in the next section.

How to integrate Slack and Zapier

Zapier is the bridge from the old to the new, transferring all of your past data into one convenient place. The app allows the seamless integration of the applications your company uses every day into your new messaging platform: Slack. Through Zapier, you have the power to instantly connect your Slack channel to 2,000+ web applications within *minutes*.

Now that you understand what Zapier is, it's time to connect the online automation tool to your personalized Slack channel. In the following section, we'll discuss how to connect Zapier with your Slack account as well as learning how to utilize its supported features.

Connecting Zapier with Slack

In this section, we are going to see how to easily connect Zapier with Slack. Follow these steps to connect Zapier with your Slack workspace:

1. First things first, add your Slack account to Zapier. To connect Slack, a user needs to be a Slack "owner" in addition to being an admin. This integration works for both paid *and* free subscriptions.

2. After joining Zapier and proceeding to integrate your Zaps, a page will appear asking you to create a new account or select a Slack account.

3. You will then see a pop-up window from Slack asking which team you'd like to connect to.

4. You must then authorize the connection between the two applications.

5. If all goes smoothly, you will be brought back to Zapier where your accounts will have been fully connected. Save, continue, and you're good to go!

Zapier's automated workflows (AKA **Zaps**) allow Slack to connect and collaborate with other existing apps to become your "command center." Once you've connected the two, you open the door for endless creative opportunities to interact with other members of your Slack community. Similar to Slackbot's direct message channel with users, as we discussed in *Chapter 6, Your Workplace Slackbot*, you can develop a direct message with the Zapier app to access more information:

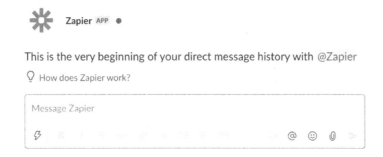

Figure 8.2 – Zapier responds to you the same way an automated bot would

Zapier supports thousands of apps such as Gmail, Airtable, and Trello that allow your existing information such as contacts, calendar events, and social media activity to be brought straight into the chat. You as a user have the ability to control the automatic actions Zapier takes on your behalf to complete tasks, saving you both time and stress.

Utilizing Zapier's tools in Slack

Like many of the other features of Slack, Zapier uses its own language to identify the variety of tools it offers. There are many ways to creatively use Slack and Zapier together through features such as triggers, searches, filters, and actions. For example, you can use Zapier to trigger when a new #channel is created within your workspace. Zapier will notice this event occurring within Slack and notify you of the change through Zapier.

Let's take a look at some examples of these direct services.

Triggers

A trigger is an event that starts a Zap. Once a Zap is set up, Zapier will monitor the app for that event. There are 11 different triggers supported by Zapier. Trigger a message instantly when the following occur:

- A new message is posted to any public #channel.
- A new message is posted to a specific #channel you choose.
- A new #channel is created.
- You save a message.
- A new file is uploaded to your workspace.
- A custom emoji has been added to a team.
- A username or highlighted word is used in a public #channel.
- A new message is posted to a specific #private-channel or multi-dm.
- A reaction is added to a message in a public #channel.
- You click the **Push to Zapier** button from a message in Slack.
- A new Slack user is created or first joins your organization.

Use triggers to signal tasks when a minimal change occurs in your workspace. This way, you can keep track of specific types of events as they're happening in real time.

Actions

An action is an event that completes a Zap. There are nine different actions supported by Zapier. Some of these actions include the following:

- Adding a reminder for yourself or a teammate. This is similar to the remind slash command /remind.
- Sending a direct message to a user or yourself from Slackbot. You can also schedule a message for later.
- Creating a new channel.
- Setting the topic on a selected channel.
- Setting your Slack status to a given text or emoji.
- Posting a new message to a specific #channel you choose. You can also schedule a message for later.
- Inviting an existing user to an existing channel. You must be a member of a channel to invite someone to it.
- Posting a new message to a private channel of your choosing. You can also schedule a message for later.
- Updating basic profile fields such as name or title.

Actions are the key to what Zapier is meant for. Triggers trigger actions, which put your events into play and thus accomplishes the purpose of the integration by automating your workspace.

Searches

There are five different searches supported by Zapier. Search through Zapier to find any of the following in your Slack workspace:

- A Slack message using the Slack search feature
- A user by matching against their email instead of their username
- A user by their username
- A user by matching against their real name, rather than their username
- A user by their ID

Zapier can also keep track of your searches.

> **Important note**
> A full list of tools accessible to Zapier and Slack integration users can be found on Zapier's official site: `https://zapier.com/apps/slack/integrations`.

Now that you've integrated your web apps to share data with Zapier, the next step is to "Zap" your way into automating your Slack workflows with Zapier.

Automating your workflows with Zapier

Zapier automatically moves information between your web apps using workflows called Zaps. A workflow is a process through which a piece of work passes from initiation to completion. Rather than creating individual workflows on your own each time something needs to be done, Zaps help to automatically achieve these tasks.

There are 300+ ways to automate your workspace with Zaps to create a more efficient working environment for you and your team. Zapier supports thousands of applications, from Gmail to Trello to Airtable, to fit the varying needs of your company with Zaps, and continues to grow with the expansion of your knowledge utilizing its tools. In this section, we'll take you through the process of understanding an individual Zap, how to create one both from existing formatting and from scratch, and ultimately, how to add it to your workplace for the magic to really happen.

Zaps

A Zap is an automated workflow that exists between your apps. They consist of two parts: a trigger and an action, working together to achieve a combined task. The trigger sets the desired task into play while the action decides where that task will be implemented. Together, they combine two separate applications to bring all of your company's information into one convenient, shared space. Sounds familiar, right? A brand-new Zap that has yet to be customized may appear as in the following screenshot:

Figure 8.3 – How your Zap appears before you begin to customize it

Zaps are to Zapier what Slackbot is to Slack. They are the bridges between one web app and another that are created and work to serve you. But before you can master the concept of the Zap, you first have to learn how to create one.

How to create a Zap

There are two ways to create a Zap: you can use a Zap template (a pre-built workflow), or you can create your own Zap from scratch depending on how customized your automation needs to be. Now that we've discussed the basics of how Zapier works, it's time to learn how to create your very own Zap. Let's break down each of these ways to create a Zap.

Adding a Zap template to your workspace

Zapier has conveniently created thousands of templates ready to use and customize. You can find these adaptable templates on your dashboard in your Zapier account. Follow these steps to add a Zap from a template:

1. From your dashboard, type in the name of the app you want to create a Zap for in the **Connect this app...** field.

2. Next, type in the name of the app you wish to connect with the first app in the field titled **with this one!**.

3. Select a trigger for your Zap.

4. Choose the action you want to happen whenever the trigger occurs.

5. Scroll down to see popular options for Zaps involving the triggers and actions you've selected.

6. Click **Use Zap** to start editing the template in the Zap editor.

7. Select **Sign in** to connect your account in the app (such as Slack) to Zapier if this is your first time creating a Zap for the application. It should appear as an option from the drop-down menu.

8. After this, steps become customizable for the app you're using with optional and required field options. With Slack, you'll need to select things such as the channel the Zap will send the message to and the picture and username associated with it.

9. Once you're done with customization, click **Finish Editing!** to officially add the Zap to your account and turn it on.

That's it – simple as that! You'll even have the option to test your Zap to see how it'll perform on its own before relying solely on the technology to do its job. And you can always adjust the Zap or add changes later from the Zap page.

When creating a Zap through a template, obviously the easier of the two options, there may come a time when you have to design a specific Zap just for you and your team. You can begin to create a Zap through your Zapier account on the website:

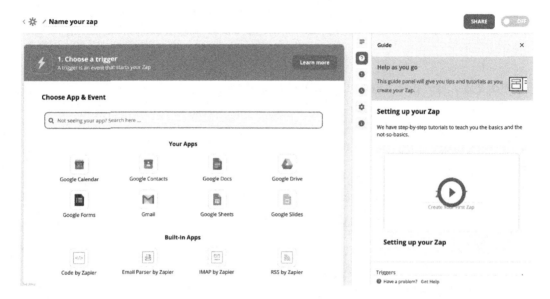

Figure 8.4 – Zapier app and event options

Like baking a cake, creating a Zap becomes more complicated when you decide to make it from scratch. You will choose to create a Zap from beginning to end if you need more customizable features that will create the triggers and actions your team needs.

Creating a Zap from scratch

As we've discussed, Zaps come in two parts, therefore, creating a Zap from scratch involves two parts: trigger and action. First, we'll set up the trigger:

1. To start, select the + button in the upper left-hand corner of the navigation menu. This will bring you to the Zap editor page where you can set up your Zap's triggers and actions.

2. First, choose the trigger app or the app you wish to start the Zap. Enter the app's name into the search box or, if the app has already been connected, select it from the drop-down option.

3. Select the specific trigger for that app from the list of options. For example, options can include a document being updated, a new email being received, or a new thread. Then click **Continue**.

4. Next, you'll have to select your account from the app. A popup will appear asking you to authorize Zapier to connect. Again, click **Continue**.

5. Similar to the steps in the template setup, fill out any of the required or optional options as needed when they appear. Click **Continue**.

6. Now you'll have to test your trigger to make sure it works. Select **Test & Continue** and wait for a success message before proceeding.

Once the test has proved to be a success, it's time to set up the action. The action is what tells the Zap what to do. Follow these steps to set up your Zap's action:

1. First, you must choose your action app. Again, type the name of the app into the search box or select it from the drop-down options.

2. Next, you'll decide how the app should act in response to the trigger. For example, the action could be sending an email or updating a calendar event.

3. It's time to connect your account. Choose which account, through the app, you wish to connect with and then a popup will appear to verify it. Click **Continue**.

4. Now is where the real ingredients come into play. You can begin to customize exactly what you want your Zap to do with the data it collects by filling in the blank fields. From the drop-down menu, you can choose from a list of data from the trigger app to find which most closely aligns with what you're trying to automate. Click **Continue**.

5. Again, you'll have to test the action. It'll show what information from the trigger app will be sent to the action app for further clarification. Select **Create & Continue** to test it out.

6. Lastly, click the **Done Editing** button and be sure to give your Zap a name. Click the Zap from on to off and it will automatically run until you tell it to do otherwise.

Like the template format, you can revisit your Zap and adjust or restructure it at any time. When your Zap requires permission from your trigger application and your Slack action, the request may appear as in the following example:

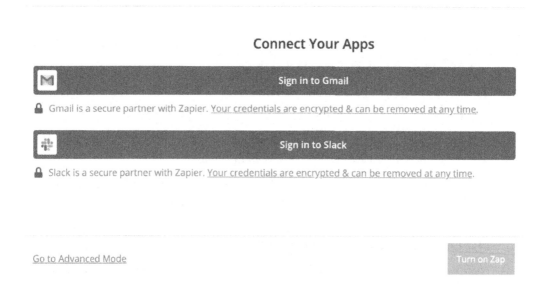

Figure 8.5 – You need an account with both applications you wish to utilize with Zapier

By creating it through a template or building the Zap from bare bones, you've now created the tools to automate your workspace for you and your team. Speaking of your team, Zaps are meant to be shared and, once created, should be dispersed amongst your Slack members to be used by everyone as needed.

Using Zapier for teams

Zapier acknowledges that your Zaps may be conveniently utilized more than once and in more than one place. So, Zapier provides the option to create a team account that allows you to share Zaps with the rest of your company.

Team accounts allow shared folders that let anyone on your team update, view, or copy Zaps. Slack is based on collaborative working and working through a team account in Zapier lets your team connect and communicate by creating workflows together and tweaking existing ones to fit each teammate's needs. Take advantage of team accounts and folders by trying out some of these commonly used Zaps together.

Popular Zaps

Let's take a look at some popular Zaps that can be utilized by almost any member of your team:

- Sharing a blog post to your channels
- Keeping your notes with your tasks
- Collecting feedback and other info through form/survey sources
- Creating an email list
- Receiving notifications and reminders about everything in Slack
- Tracking events and tasks with a calendar
- Starting automated workflows with a push

Zaps are multipurpose tools meant to be conveniently recycled by all members of your organization after they're created and implemented in your workspace. For even easier access to existing Zaps, push content, documents, files, or messages to Zapier directly from your Slack channels.

Exploring Push by Zapier

As if it couldn't get any simpler, Push by Zapier allows you to push content directly to Zapier from your Slack direct messages, threads, and channels. For specific messages you wish to bring directly to the integration tool, utilize the **Push to Zapier** option through the **More Actions** tab on an individual message. The **Push to Zapier** button appears as in the following screenshot in your Slack channels:

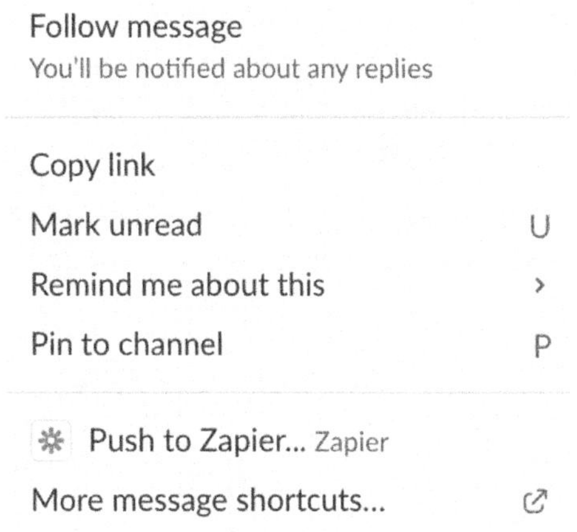

Figure 8.6 – Push to Zapier is a shortcut to your Zapier/Slack integration

Pushing items to Zapier brings an already created workflow that's only clicks away for an even more straightforward interaction. This shortcut easily combines information from an external application with Slack and brings your company one step closer to automating its workspace.

Setting up Push by Zapier

Follow these steps to set up Push by Zapier within your Slack workspace:

1. Authenticate Push by Zapier and Slack.

2. Select one of the apps as a trigger, which will set off the automation.

3. Choose an action the trigger will result in from the other app.

4. Pick the data you wish to transport from one app to the other.

Once you've allowed your Slack account to accept Push to Zapier features, you can then begin to push information directly to your Zaps and set the process in motion as it's occurring in your feeds. For instance, if a notification of a product being sold appears, push that data to Salesforce where it can be stored for further use.

Many parts of your team will benefit from automating tedious aspects of their job description that would more traditionally be performed manually. By utilizing Zaps, you modernize your company and industry by moving the focus from mechanical tasks to focus on communication and relationships among all facets of your organization.

Zapier based on your business

Zapier can be utilized in any Slack workspace for any part of your organization. But, although your company may exist as a singular unit, there are a variety of teams that work together to achieve a final product. For these teams and types of organizations, Zapier has specific Zaps and functions that exist to make communicating and working simpler and more efficient for every member of your team.

In this section, we'll focus on the project management, customer support, social, and e-commerce aspects of your organization and how to automate them through Zapier's integration tool, Zaps.

Project management

Every company has some form of project management involvement across their teams. Whether it's a specific team designated for it or a role every member takes on in some form, there's never been a job that's needed the help of Zapier more. For example, when your project management team sends out a form, use the following template to receive a notification when someone new responds:

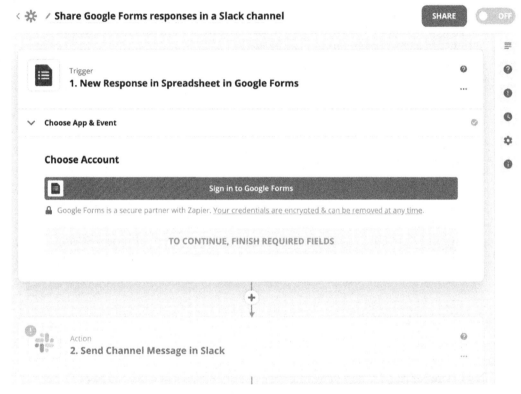

Figure 8.7 – This is a template Zap example

Project management requires a wide range of applications to choose from, so why worry about managing them all when you can simply automate them to work together? Zapier works to integrate tools from each app together so you don't have to. Let's take a look at some ways to utilize Zaps for your project management team.

Here are some Zaps for project management-based companies:

- **Put tasks, events, and goals into a universal calendar**: Many task-related apps come with their own calendar – so do most of your team members. To avoid scattering events and important information across many platforms, consolidate everything into a universal calendar for convenience and efficiency.

- **Schedule events or create projects using a form**: Forms and surveys are the best way to get immediate feedback from your team regarding any and all subjects. Use the responses from these surveys on apps such as Google Forms to automatically input data into another app such as Trello.

- **Share project activity with your team**: Many teams, especially digital teams, work around the clock in all parts of the world. That's why it's important you have a plan in place to keep everyone in the loop by sharing project updates from outside applications directly into Slack.

- **Automatically archive projects**: Projects come and go as your company progresses, but that doesn't mean they lose their relevancy. Keep past projects in a singular space by archiving them in organized spreadsheets/documents.

Some of the best apps for project management include Asana, Monday, and Insightly.

The opportunities for your project management team are endless with over 50 apps many teams use every day. Simplify your data and communication by creating Zaps to organize your information.

Customer support

As we discussed in *Chapter 5, Using Slack Externally with Live Chats, Guests, and Partners,* customers are an equally important subset of your team as any other. While they may not be a hired member of your company, they are possibly the most active and vocal. Zaps exist to make dealing with your ever-present customer feedback that much simpler. Let's take a look at some ways to utilize Zaps for customer service.

Here are the best Zaps for customer support teams:

- **Support on social media**: In the age of the internet, social media has become an immense tool for customers to interact directly with the companies they utilize and purchase from. Use Zaps to track these interactions and reply directly.

- **Add customers to email newsletters**: Newsletters have taken the world by storm in the way they can – daily, weekly, or monthly – interact with your customers to present new information and encourage interaction. With Zaps, add new customers automatically to your subscription.

- **Notifications**: If you have a smartphone, chances are you've been susceptible to the phenomenon of notifications. And you know that they come from a variety of applications. Simplify the important ones to make sure you never miss a notification with Zapier.

- **Log stats**: Customer support information is crucial to your company's success. Stream data into a spreadsheet with Zaps.

Customer support is no easy feat. Stop losing sleep and time stressing over logistics and take more time to build better relationships with your customer base.

Social media

Social media applications have created a unique marketing, advertising, and engaging platform for thousands of companies. Yet, managing social accounts with day-to-day tasks can become overwhelming. For instance, sharing a specific mention of your team on Twitter may be formatted something like the following example:

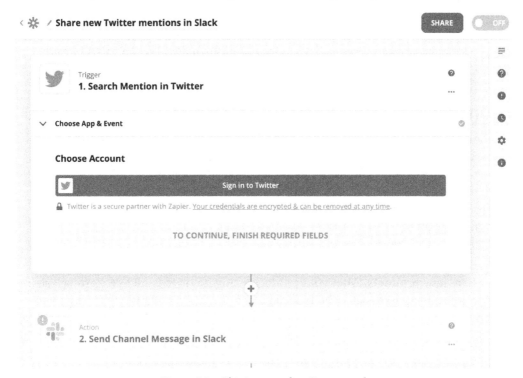

Figure 8.8 – This is a template Zap example

Zaps work to manage and monitor your social feeds so you don't have to. Let's take a look at some ways to utilize Zaps in conjunction with social channels.

Here are the best Zaps for your social team:

- **Share new content**: Schedule and post content automatically to keep your social media presence current.

- **Promote upcoming events**: Use social accounts to spread awareness and promote upcoming in-person or virtual events for your organization.

- **Monitor online branding**: Social mentions, whether they be from customers, clients, or shared partners, can become extremely tedious to manually keep track of in full. Tools such as Mention in coherence with Zapier's social media integrations help monitor social networks automatically.

- **Cross-post information**: The beauty of social media is the ability to reach multiple audiences across multiple platforms. Rather than wasting time posting the same content on each individual platform, automate Zaps to cross-post for you.

Social media adds complexity to any organization that may not have previously had a virtual component to interact with their customers. While inviting customers into your Slack workspace is a great way to interact with them one on one directly, you'll also want to keep an active presence to communicate with them on a general basis. Let Zaps take away the unnecessary step of organizing and individually posting, sharing, and monitoring your content.

E-commerce

E-commerce encompasses many facets under one category: marketing products, shipping orders, communicating with customers, and overall, keeping things running smoothly. As your company grows in size, your e-commerce store will grow with it, and therefore so will the time spent managing it. Avoid micromanaging shipping and handling and let Zaps do the work for you. Let's take a look at some ways to bring Zaps to your e-commerce team.

Here are the best Zaps for your e-commerce team:

- **Share new products**: After your product listing is created and live, Zaps will share your products across all of your social media and virtual platforms to avoid you doing it manually.

- **Get updates when you make a sale**: Placing an order is just the first step your customer takes to get a product directly sent to them. Receive notifications when orders are placed so your team knows to get to work. For example, if products are sold through Shopify, share paid orders directly to Slack channels.

- **Ship products**: For smaller companies or companies selling/sharing a virtual product, shipping could be a task overseen by members of your team. To transfer this burden to Zapier, set up Zaps to watch your online store or a payment processing application and link it to your shipping tool to send out orders automatically.

- **Track customer information**: If your company is successful, chances are your customers will return to your business more than once. Similar to logging customer stats, track your customer information by directing data to a spreadsheet or data platform such as Salesforce as leads for the future.

E-commerce is different for every company depending on the service or product they're attempting to sell. No matter whether it's a physical, virtual, or social tool, each commodity should have a plan in place to organize the influx of information as needed. Employ Zapier to deal with this inflow of content with simpler and more efficient means.

While these four teams may not encompass every aspect of your organization, they scratch the surface of the possibilities Zapier offers to automate your workflow by bringing external applications into your workspace.

Summary

In this chapter, we focused heavily on an integration tool that can heavily automate your workspace and alleviate many of the menial tasks your team takes an immeasurable amount of time out of their day to complete. Essentially dissecting a new application, we learned what Zapier is and how to find the right plan for your team. We broke down Zapier's workflows, AKA Zaps, and learned how to integrate our Slack workspace while automating Zaps to meet our needs. We even focused on specific teams within our organization and how automating Zaps could benefit their everyday tasks, to-dos, and the ultimate collection of data and information. Overall, we learned how useful a tool Zapier is and how even more integral it becomes when combined with Slack.

In the next chapter, we'll get a closer look at what the Slack API is. *Chapter 6, Your Workspace Slackbot*, briefly touched upon the uses of the Slack API when it comes to incorporating Slackbot into your workspace channels, direct messages, and threads. Now we'll attain a greater understanding of what the Slack API is and how to use it, the difference between a Slack API and the Webhook API, how to build apps using the Slack API, using a UI framework, and how to configure the Slack API sandbox. If you thought we'd discussed all of Slack's mechanical features, then you're in for a surprise in the next chapter.

9

Slack API, Webhooks, Block Kit, and Sandboxes

We've discussed a lot of complex concepts on the road to understanding the best and most efficient ways to use Slack. In *Chapter 6, Your Workplace Slackbot*, we learned what Slackbot is, how to bring outside applications into Slack, and even how to integrate features of other apps directly into our channels, all different stepping stones toward your total understanding of how to best understand and use Slack for you and your team.

Chapter 8, Automate Your Workflow with Zapier, introduced us to Zapier and the concept of automating workflows by integrating external applications into your workspace through Zaps. Now, we're going to take a look at what a Slack API is and how to take advantage of its features and tools such as Webhooks, Block Kit, and sandboxes to automate these tasks within the Slack app itself.

This chapter will cover these main topics:

- What a Slack API is and how to use it
- Learn what a Webhook API is and the difference versus a Slack API

- Using the Block Kit UI framework for Slack

- Understanding Block Kit's element fields

- Configuring a Slack API sandbox

In learning these critical tools, we'll be able to understand how Slack works cohesively with other apps to simplify your entire workspace both within and outside of your Slack app. By using a Slack API in conjunction with Webhooks, Block Kit, and sandboxes, you allow yourself to have complete knowledge and appreciation of the basic and more advanced configurations of your apps within Slack.

What is a Slack API?

For starters, what is any kind of API? An **application programming interface**, or **API** for short, is the way in which multiple applications can interact and obtain data from one another. Slack uses APIs for a broad range of niche apps across its platform to promote interaction and communication between all of your applications.

Slack APIs allow you to merge complex services with the communication platform to go beyond the integration Slack provides to customize your own. *Chapter 6, Your Workplace Slackbot*, began this understanding process by introducing us to Event API access, but what about the other features of Slack API? And what about the other types of API? There are many ways to use a Slack API within your workspace that we'll discuss throughout this chapter. To start, let's break down some of Slack API's key features.

Slack API's main features include the following:

- Sending messages

- Creating shortcuts for users

- Automating with workflows

- Creating simplified interactions

- Setting up internal tools

- Publishing your application

In the following sections, we'll learn how each type of API utilizes these features to set up and pair your apps with your workspace. The terminology, such as API, may be heavy, but we'll break things down in the simplest of terms so anyone from beginners to advanced users can understand how to bring these tools to their team.

Types of APIs

Slack is composed of several different types of APIs that allow you and your team to create apps of varying sizes and shapes. There are over 100 methods to choose from that all serve varying purposes through your APIs.

While we couldn't possibly discuss every one of these methods, we can break down a few examples in each section to give you a preview of the opportunities available to you through Slack API. Let's take a look at a couple of API methods:

admin.analytics

This contains the following method:

`admin.analytics.getFile`: Retrieves analytics data for a specified date, presented as a **JavaScript Object Notation (JSON)** file.

admin.apps

This contains the following methods:

`admin.apps.approve`: Approve an app for workspace installation.

`admin.apps.restrict`: Restrict an app for workspace installation.

admin.conversations

This contains the following methods:

`admin.conversations.invite`: Invite a user to a public or private channel.

`admin.conversations.convertToPrivate`: Convert a public channel to a private channel.

`admin.conversations.search`: Search for a public or private channel in an enterprise organization.

admin.emoji

This contains the following methods:

`admin.emoji.addAlias`: Add an emoji alias.

`admin.emoji.rename`: Rename an emoji.

admin.inviteRequests

This contains the following methods:

`admin.inviteRequests.approve`: Approve a workspace invite request.

`admin.inviteRequests.list`: List all pending workspace invite requests.

chat

This contains the following methods:

`chat.deleteScheduledMessage`: Deletes a scheduled pending message from the queue.

`chat.postMessage`: Sends a message to a channel.

`chat.scheduleMessage`: Schedules a message to be sent to a channel.

reminders

This contains the following methods:

`reminders.complete`: Marks a reminder as complete.

`reminders.list`: Lists all reminders created by or for a given user.

These are only a taste of the many, many features Slack APIs can help perform within your Slack workspace. From specified searches, reactions, actions, and reminders, the tasks your APIs can be automated to perform are endless.

Often, these APIs work together to achieve a unified task within your workspace. Yet, on occasion, APIs' capabilities can overlap with one another. Let's take a look at Slack's API types to gather a better understanding of how to incorporate each one into your workspace.

The RTM API

The **Real Time Messaging (RTM)** API is the most basic way to connect an outside application to Slack. An RTM API connects your app to Slack's infrastructure through a WebSocket, to create an on-going, always-on connection between the two. Any and all activity that occurs within your Slack workspace, that is, messages, emojis, reactions, and so on will be pushed through this channel.

While this API is one of the simpler ones to use, it can become overwhelming and difficult to keep track of WebSocket connections as your company continues to grow and expand. To avoid the stress and eliminate room for error, utilize one of the other types of API to build your apps within Slack. These types of APIs are explained in the following sections.

The Events API

An Event API is a pickier version of the RTM API. Rather than sending all of your information through a singular channel, the Event APIs allow you to choose which events you want to receive for Slack to send directly to the endpoint you specify via HTTP.

Avoid the constant influx of any and all data by clarifying which events, such as when a person joins or leaves a channel, are relevant to you. Subscribe to an event and the API will do the rest!

The Web API

The Web API is a follow-up reaction to your Event API, bringing an action or message back into the Slack workspace. These actions could include things such as creating a message or developing a new channel through HTTP methods. The Web API is an interface for asking for information from something, thus enacting change in a channel or workspace.

The Conversations API

A subset of the Web API, the Conversations API is a set of functions used to call on Slack directly. Described in the name itself, the Conversations API focuses on all of the channel-like objects that occur within your workspace, such as public and private channels, direct messages, multi-party direct messages, and external shared channels.

The Web and Event APIs are the more popular and common of Slack's APIs since they encompass a majority of the actions you'll want to take within an app. The other types of APIs serve a more niche basis for very specific types of applications.

In addition to these types of APIs is the Webhook API. In comparison to the types previously listed, the Webhook API works as a basic means of posting messages from an app into Slack without the overcomplicated use of coding.

What is the Webhook API?

The Webhook API is a simplified way of posting messages from external apps into Slack. When you create an incoming Webhook, you're provided with a unique URL. You then send that URL a JSON payload with the message text in addition to other personalized options.

Similar to other APIs and blocks, you can use all the usual formatting and layout blocks to create individualized messages that stand out amongst your team. The **Incoming WebHooks** application appears as in the following figure in the Slack App Directory:

Figure 9.1 – Incoming WebHooks

Incoming WebHooks can be found in the Slack App Directory in the app or on your desktop.

Getting started with setting up and creating your own Webhooks is easy – especially with the setup each chapter has already prepped you for. At this point, you already have a Slack account and have a basic understanding of how Slack apps and integrations work. Now let's take a look at how to set up your own Webhooks.

Setting up and creating incoming Webhooks

The first part of setting up your incoming Webhooks is to enable them within your Slack workspace. To do this, you'll first have to create a Slack app or use an already existing one previously assigned to a workspace. Follow these steps to set up your incoming Webhooks:

1. Once the app is created or if it has already been set up, load your app settings from the app's management dashboard.

2. From the dashboard, select the **Incoming Webhooks** feature, followed by **Activate Incoming Webhook**. Switch that toggle to on to officially enable your Webhook.

   Once you've enabled your Webhook, your settings page should refresh to include new options for your Webhook.

3. From the options, select the **Add New Webhook to Workspace** button to begin the process of creating your incoming Webhook.

   This button will trigger a shortcut version of the installation flow for Slack apps that allows you to avoid building code to generate the incoming Webhook URL. After selecting the button, something like the following figure should appear:

On Hatch Street, Yogi would like to:

Confirm your identity on Hatch Street

Post to   #general

Cancel   Authorize

Figure 9.2 – Example courtesy of https://api.slack.com/messaging/webhooks

4. Use the dropdown to choose which channel from your workspace you want the Webhook to post to.

5. Then click **Authorize** to verify your app's action.

Clicking the button should send you back to your app settings where you will see a new entry under the **Webhook URLs for Your Workspace** section with your very own Webhook URL. Your customized URL should look something like this figure:

```
https://hooks.slack.com/services/T00000000/B00000000/XXXXXXXXXXXXXXX
```

Figure 9.3 – Webhook URL example

Every URL you create for your Webhook will be individualized for you as a user and the singular channel you chose for it to be directed toward. You've enabled and created the Webhook, now it's time to put it into action. We briefly discussed that Webhooks use your unique URL to send text messages to your channels, so let's take a step-by-step look into how that works.

Sending messages using Webhooks

The purpose of the Webhook API is to be able to simply forward messages from an app directly into your Slack workspace. We've set up the outline for the Webhook, now we'll create the message it'll push into your channels.

Your message can be anything you want to say. To create the text for the message, simply use an HTTP POST request. Your POST request may appear like this:

```
POST https://hooks.slack.com/services/T00000000/B00000000/XXXXXXXXXXXXXXXXXXXXXXXX
Content-type: application/json
{
    "text": "Good morning team!"
}
```

Figure 9.4 – HTTP POST request example

You'll replace the URL link in this example with your Webhook URL and the text "Good morning team!" with whatever message you want pushed to your team members in your specified channel. Once you've created the HTTP POST, you're done!

That's really all there is to it. You can see the result of your work by heading to the channel the message was posted to and seeing your message. In this case, "Good morning team!" has been posted by your app. You can use this same formatting with any of your Webhooks for any of your apps as you see fit. While this format of simply using a text message is useful for almost any app and almost any desired task, there are also ways to spruce up your Webhook messages with elements that allow your team to participate in your automated content.

Interacting with your Webhooks

There are many ways to make your Webhooks interactive in addition to the text feature we sampled above. Setting these Webhooks up is as simple as setting up your URL and HTTP POST request, but also including other fields in addition to text such as an image, buttons, or voting features. An HTTP POST request with some of these added elements may appear like this example:

```
POST https://hooks.slack.com/services/T00000000/B00000000/XXXXXXXXXXXXXXXXXXXXXXXX
Content-type: application/json
{
    "text": "Check out Online Geniuses' job board for new openings available every day!",
    "blocks": [
        {
            "type": "section",
            "text": {
                "type": "mrkdwn",
                "text": "Find hundreds of job openings on our job board: "
            }
        },
        {
            "accessory": {
                "type": "image",
                "image_url": "https://drive.google.com/file/d/1GqgGffIaKh1Vq6N05BFF0q2ZuKN0j3gi/view?usp=sharing",
                "alt_text": "Online Geniuses Job Board"

            }
        ]
    }
    ]
}
```

Figure 9.5 – This HTTP POST request includes Block Kit elements

Elements such as the image field used in this example, can be found and built through Block Kit. Block Kit works as a framework you can utilize to find and input these types of visual components into your JSON payload.

In this section, we learned what the Webhook API is, how to create one, and how to utilize it as a tool to post messages that range from simple text to expanded features such as images and buttons. Now that we have an understanding of APIs and Webhooks, we can take the leap into customizing our automated app-pairing messages with the types of blocks and fields provided through Block Kit.

How to use Block Kit

Block Kit is a UI framework for Slack. A UI framework is the set of interfaces that define elements and the behavior of a user; essentially, the supporting structure of the visual elements of an application. For Slack, this includes things such as buttons and icons that allow your members to interact with a product. Blocks allow you to customize the order and appearance of this information by guiding users through designed blocks: reusable components that can be utilized almost anywhere in Slack.

Blocks are visual components that can be stacked or rearranged any way you like across your Slack workspace to create app layouts. Block Kit is the compilation of these tools by composing layouts for modals, messages, or tabs to design specially structured JSON to express features of an application. JSON uses understandable text to store and transmit data. We know that's a large influx of technical terms. Let's break down the many facets of Block Kit, starting with building blocks.

Building blocks

There's no one true way or special setup required to begin building a block. Yet, with any kind of coded feature, it helps to follow an example for reference. Let's take a look at the following generic sample payload. The payload preview can be found in Block Kit Builder:

Figure 9.6 – The left showcases what the message will preview, the right showcases the coding

The JSON in this example featured on the right in the **Payload** section of Block Kit describes a simple "section" block. It also highlights the structure of the blocks. Each contains a "type" to choose which of the different blocks to use followed by fields that describe what's in the blocks. Some different types of fields include the following:

- type: The exact type of block.
- text: The text for the block, in the form of a plain_text text object.
- label: A label that appears above an input element.
- element: A plain_text input element, a checkbox element, a select menu element, a multi-select menu element, or a datepicker.
- block_id: A string acting as a unique identifier for a block. If not previously specified, one will be generated for you.
- hint: An optional hint that appears below an input element in a lighter grey. It must be a text object with a type of plain_text.

- `optional`: Indicates whether the input element may be empty when a user submits the modal.

The `mrkdwn` type is the default formatting method for a top-level text field in a message when using the Web API to publish a message.

You can also stack blocks together within a JSON in visual order. These stacked blocks can appear as in the following screenshot in the coding payload format:

```
Payload    Actions Preview

 1 {
 2      "blocks": [
 3          {
 4              "type": "section",
 5              "text": {
 6                  "type": "mrkdwn",
 7                  "text": "Check out new openings on our job board:"
 8              }
 9          },
10          {
11              "type": "section",
12              "block_id": "section567",
13              "text": {
14                  "type": "mrkdwn",
15                  "text": "<https://jobs.onlinegeniuses.com> \n
    :star: \n Join 1000's of agencies & companies that recruit from
    Online Geniuses. Companies like, CNN, Amazon, Lyft, Ziprecruiter
    and many more."
16              },
17              "accessory": {
18                  "type": "image",
19                  "image_url": "https://scontent-lga3-
    2.xx.fbcdn.net/v/t1.0-
    9/69104661_3135335423149996_8386470313172402176_n.png?
    _nc_cat=105&ccb=2&_nc_sid=e3f864&_nc_ohc=TBpFl6Ch5SgAX8ZiMa0&_nc_ht
    =scontent-lga3-
    2.xx&oh=67cef532b026e8a29aa36b12dbfe1f3a&oe=5FDA204E",
20                  "alt_text": "Online Geniuses' homepage"
21              }
22          },
23          {
24              "type": "section",
25              "block_id": "section789",
26              "fields": [
27                  {
28                      "type": "mrkdwn",
```

Figure 9.7 – Block Kit example code

An example similar to this can be found in the Block Kit section of Slack API's website.

Each block allows you to personalize a different part of the message. For instance, `"text"` on row seven shows the leading line of your message: `"Check out new openings on our job board."` Row 15 produces the text of your link as well as an emoji insert of a star, and row 17 allows for an insert of an image with your link to showcase the Online Geniuses brand. This coding will transfer to your actual message once you fill in the blanks to suit your needs. The final product from the coding in the preceding figure will result in the following message:

 Your App APP 1:37 PM
Check out new openings on our job board:

https://jobs.onlinegeniuses.com

Join 1000's of agencies & companies that recruit from Online Geniuses.
Companies like, CNN, Amazon, Lyft, Ziprecruiter and many more.

New jobs listed at:
Mad Fish Digital, Interaction Design
Foundation & Mindful Marketing

Figure 9.8 – The final product of your coded message

> **Important note**
>
> You can find these pre-designed templates at `https://api.slack.com/block-kit/building`.

The process is essentially translating what you wish to be conveyed in a technical format, to automatically produce your ultimate message product. Like anything, with practice comes perfection, so while the templates are a good place to start, there are ways to progress beyond a simple text message with block elements that create different ways to make your blocks interactive.

Block elements

Block elements can be used inside of section, context, and action layout blocks and include 10 different ways to make your blocks interactive. Use buttons to make options interactive for your members, a date picker to clarify a unanimously available day for an event, a time picker to set a meeting, or checkboxes to create a team list.

The options are endless as you begin to customize, stack, and develop blocks of your very own either through templates or of your very own creation. In this section, we'll break down some of the more popular elements to help elevate your block setup in your workspace.

Button elements

This button element works with the section and action block types. The description is in the name – it's a button. This interactive component can be a trigger for anything from opening a link or starting a workflow. The features vary based on your capabilities. Buttons will appear in your workspace as in the following figure:

Figure 9.9 – Buttons can be customized to say/ask what you need them to

Fields that you can use to create a button element include type, text, action_id, url, value, style, and confirm.

> **Important note**
>
> Limitations on these fields for this block element can be found at https://api.slack.com/reference/block-kit/block-elements.

Use the style field to decorate buttons with visual color schemes that match the nature of your message. The default style appears in black text with a black outline; the primary style gives a button a green outline with green text to encourage affirmation; and the danger style gives a button a red outline with red text to signal caution.

Now that you know about the variations for the aesthetic of your button, let's break down the mechanics behind it. Coding for your typical button may appear like this:

```
{
  "type": "button",
  "text": {
    "type": "plain_text",
    "text": "Click Me"
  },
  "value": "click_me_123",
  "action_id": "button"
}
```

Templates for buttons can be found at https://api.slack.com/reference/block-kit/block-elements.

While this template may service your typical default button, there are many ways to stack buttons to create a variety of options, and as mentioned earlier, they can be customized with the style element according to your needs.

Checkbox groups

This button element works with section, action, and input block types. Checkbox group elements allow users to choose from a list of possible options. A checkbox group will appear similar to this example through section blocks:

Figure 9.10 – Your code appearing in your Block Kit payload

Customize your proposed question and options in the **Payload** section of your Block Kit. Fields that you can use to create a date picker element include `type`, `action_id`, `options`, `initial_options`, and `confirm`.

> **Important note**
>
> Limitations on these fields for this block element can be found at `https://api.slack.com/reference/block-kit/block-elements`.

Use the code on the right side of Block Kit Builder to customize the question you're posing to your team as well as the options for them to choose from. You can add up to 10 different options to this element.

Date picker elements

This button element works with section, action, and input block types. The date picker element is the solution to avoiding overlapping schedules, events, meetings, and plans by allowing users to easily select a date from a calendar-style UI. A sample date picker element may appear like this figure:

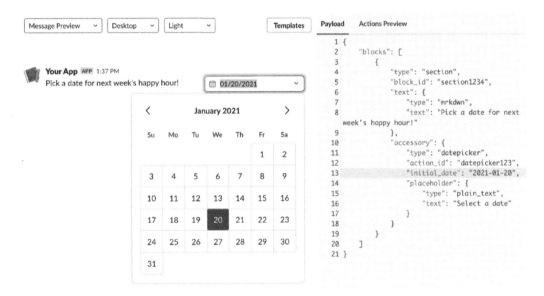

Figure 9.11 – Customize the exact date and message to your needs

The left of the figure showcases how your message will appear. The right of the figure is the sample coding for that message. Fields that you can use to create a date picker element include `type`, `action_id`, `placeholder`, `initial_date`, and `confirm`.

> **Important note**
>
> Limitations on these fields for this block element can be found at `https://api.slack.com/reference/block-kit/block-elements`.

Use these fields to customize the initial date you want the options to start and the text with the reason you're asking your team to respond with a specified date.

Image element

This button element works with section and context block types. As simple as its name, the image element allows you to insert an image into your larger block of content. If you wish to create a block with *only* an image, you'll want to use the image block. Let's take a look at a section block with an accessory image:

Figure 9.12 – Your image block can be customized to fit your needs

Fields that you can use to create an image element include type, image_url, and alt_text.

> **Important note**
>
> Limitations on these fields for this block element can be found at https://api.slack.com/reference/block-kit/block-elements.

Image blocks allow for a range of customization depending on the message you wish to convey and the image you want to portray. Using the template, simply change out image_url for your accessory image to change the image for your own.

Time pickers

This button element works with section, action, and input block types. Similar to many of the other elements, the time picker element works to simplify communication within your team by supplying options that are easy to use and respond to. A time picker serves, as stated, to pick a time for whatever the purpose may be. A time picker element may appear like this figure in your Slack messages:

Figure 9.13 – Choose the time range options and message for your element

Fields that you can use to create an image element include `type`, `action_id`, `placeholder`, `initial_time`, and `confirm`.

> **Important note**
>
> Limitations on these fields for this block element can be found at `https://api.slack.com/reference/block-kit/block-elements`.

Use a time picker to arrange more efficient responses to meeting and event times. On the desktop Slack application, a time picker will appear as a drop-down list with precise options to choose. On the mobile version of the app, the element will use native time picker UIs.

Now that we have an understanding of some of the more popular elements used within blocks, let's dive into the actual types of blocks and how these elements can be used within them.

Types of blocks

As we previously mentioned, blocks are a series of components that can be used individually or stacked to create visually compelling and interactive messages within your Slack channels. You can utilize up to 50 blocks in a singular message and up to 100 blocks in modals or home tabs.

While we've extensively demonstrated the types of elements used within blocks, we've yet to discuss the variation of block types the elements would be used with. Block types vary from action-based to visual design with image and header blocks to cater to the directed message you wish to portray. To get a better idea of how these blocks work, let's take a look at some of the different types of blocks and the elements they include:

- **Action Block**: Designed to hold interactive elements in available spaces such as modals, messages, and home tabs.
- **File Block**: Displays a remote file available in messages. You can't add this block to app surfaces directly, but it will appear when receiving messages that contain remote files.
- **Header Block**: A plain-text block that is displayed in a larger bold font than the regular font used in your messages. Use header blocks to differentiate between different types of text, such as important, highlighted information.
- **Image Block**: Essentially, a message designed specifically for your image to be front and center. Your image must have a URL in order to be linked within the code of this block.
- **Context Block**: Displays message context that can include text *and* an image(s).
- **Section Block**: One of the more flexible blocks, section blocks allow you to place an image and simple text side by side with any of the block element types `text`, `block_id`, `fields`, and `accessory`.

Each of these blocks achieves a different designated task by producing a message with a variety of features. The type of block, combined with an element designed to work with it, continues to build on the advanced features and allows you to offer more to your team through each automated message.

Now that you've chosen an API and arranged your type of Block Kit with its variety of elements, such as anything we've created for our workspace, it's time to test it out to make sure it works. Block Kit offers an app preview to show how your coded message will transfer over visually, but it's equally as important to make sure it will send properly to the right channel with the right features. That's where sandboxes come in.

Configuring a Slack API sandbox

While all of these APIs and Webhooks and Block Kit are amazing tools to utilize to help automate your workspace, sometimes it's hard to test them out on an already established Slack team. For many of these features, we've encouraged you to make sure the Zaps are connecting with the apps properly or the APIs are properly sending your desired text message into the right channel.

But, for the user, workspace owner, or admin that is trying to expand their knowledge in an already existing space, they may not have the leniency or availability to experiment with these tools before they need to be executed properly.

Enter sandbox

Sandbox is your playground and safe space to experiment and test your app against a Slack Enterprise Grid instance without fear of it messing up in production. Enterprise Grids exist for larger organizations and therefore can simulate multiple workspaces to appear like your actual enterprise company Slack account. Let's break down how your Slack sandbox works step by step.

Setting up your sandbox

To get started with using a sandbox, you'll first have to submit a request form for a Slack Enterprise Grid Developer Sandbox. The request form is available as a Google Forms link on Slack API's official site: `https://api.slack.com/enterprise/grid/testing`. Some of the fields on the form include your company's name, website, email, and the purpose of the app to be built.

The request form can be found directly at this link: `https://docs.google.com/forms/d/e/1FAIpQLSe9tIHOq1bZVq5xlzymvPGFbqsv2aLFgg04SOi5KfzKbJYBAA/viewform`. The explanation for the form appears as in the following figure:

Slack Enterprise Grid Developer Sandbox Request

We encourage all developers to make sure that their Slack apps are Enterprise Grid ready. Use this form to request Grid sandboxes so that you can be sure. We'll provide you with two separate Grid sandboxes that you can use to test shared channels and other Grid features.

If you are interested in building a security or compliance solution like eDiscovery or Data Loss Prevention, you'll need access to our Discovery API. To get that access, you'll first need to complete our partner onboarding. You can start that process at https://slack.com/partners/contact. We review those requests on a quarterly basis, based on customer interest.

* Required

Figure 9.14 – The request form can also be found at https://api.slack.com/enterprise/grid/testing

The request, once confirmed, will provide you with two separate Grid sandboxes to test shared channels and other Grid features. You'll receive a separate email for each sandbox, sent to your Enterprise Organization's primary owner, which is specified on the Google form. Once you have the emails, you can then proceed to setting up your sandbox by getting it configured and ready to use in your workspace.

Completing your organization's setup

To complete the setup procedure for your organization, follow these steps:

1. From your email invitation, select the **Finish Setup** link.

2. Begin setting up your primary organization owner's account by entering your name and creating a password.

3. Give your organization a name. This name can be adjusted at a later date should you wish to change it. You will not be able to change your organization's sandbox URL.

4. Select to agree to the general terms of service.

Now that your account is set up and ready to go, it's time to officially create your sandbox workspace. To create a workspace(s) for your team, the primary owner should follow these steps:

1. Select **Manage Workspaces**. This will guide you through the process of setting up a new workspace.

2. For your part, you'll need to provide a name and subdomain for each workspace you create.

Once you've completed the guided process of setting up your new workspace in the sandbox, you'll then want to authenticate the workspace you just created.

Grid requires that all of its users use **single sign-on** (**SSO**), a centralized session and user authentication service that provides one set of login credentials to be used across multiple applications. To do this within Slack, admins must set up an **IdP**, or **Identity Provider**, that offers identity authentication for SSO.

If you do not have access to your own IdP, Slack offers its own app, Simple IdP, which mimics the use of an IdP to allow easy creation and management across your accounts. To use Simple IdP, you'll first have to install it to your workspace.

Installing Simple IdP

IdP is crucial to your Slack account because it adds another layer of security to the content created within your workspace. In addition to SSO, IdP creates an extra buffer between your team's private information. Simple IdP is simply Slack's own version of the security tool.

Follow these steps to set up Simple IdP through Slack:

1. To install Simple IdP, you'll first need to head to the website at `https://slack-test-idp-for-sandboxes.herokuapp.com/` to begin the installation process.

Make sure to install the app for your organization, *not* your workspace. The website for Simple IdP will appear like this:

Simple IdP

Click the Add to Slack button below and select your **Enterprise Grid organization** to install or manage IdP. Make sure to check the menu in the upper right corner of your authentication page to see that your **org** is selected, and not one of your workspaces.

Figure 9.15 – Simple IdP through desktop Slack

2. Select **Add to Slack** to begin the installation process.

    Once the installation is complete, you'll need to copy over some required information into your organization's SSO configuration. The set-pp instructions will provide the exact URLs and coded text for you to copy and paste into your configuration.

3. When you've finished, select the button reading **Ok, I'm done configuring the auth**.

Now that Simple IdP is set up and ready to go, it's time to start adding users. You can add as many autogenerated users as your heart desires through Simple IdP to test out your app, but should you want to add more than one real person to be signed in at a time, there are a few extra steps to take.

Each person that you want to be able to sign into the sandbox must sign in with the primary owner's information, essentially as if they are the primary owner themselves. Then they'll have to authenticate the Simple IdP app, sign out, and then sign in again as themselves. As the primary organization owner, you'll then head to **Create a custom user** to provision an account for them in Simple IdP. In the **Organization Members** list, their usernames will then appear like this: `http://[org-domain].enterprise.slack.com/manage/organization/members`.

When their names appear similar to the preceding example, you'll then add them to a workspace where they'll have to follow these steps to remain logged into the sandbox:

1. Head to the sign-in page for the workspace the user has been added to (`http://[workspace-domain].slack.com/`).

2. Click on the **Sign in with SAML** button.

3. On the following page, select **Sign in with Slack**.

4. Sign in with the primary owner's email and password.

5. Authorize the Simple IdP app.

6. Enter your email address on the resulting page and click the **Sign In** button.

7. This will bring you to the **Org** control panel, where you can then launch the team.

After completing these steps, both the primary owner and the authorized users will be able to remain logged into the sandbox at the same time. Because the sandbox serves as only an imitation of your actual workspace, especially for Enterprise Grid companies working on a much larger scale, the tool comes with some limitations. These limitations include data retention and user account creation as the sandbox is for testing purposes only. Slack will only retain messages and files shared in your sandbox for 3 days after they're created.

That's it! You're now ready to experiment with the APIs we discussed earlier and Block Kit in a safe and controlled space that won't affect any of the real-time work and communication going on in your actual workspace. You can now sample different types of APIs, test out elements, and even reconfigure your own code to truly learn and practice everything this chapter had to offer.

Summary

This chapter included a lot of technical terms, but also a lot of great tools you now have the ability to test out at your leisure in your very own workspace outside of your Slack workspace. In this chapter, we re-discovered Slack APIs with a more detailed explanation of what it is and how to use it. We learned specifically what the Webhook API is and how to create basic and advanced versions with text as well as other elements. We discovered Block Kit and how to customize and create individual and stacked blocks with a variety of types and fields. And we compiled that knowledge into the test station of sandbox by understanding how to set up and invite users to a mock workspace to test out these advanced features.

In the next chapter, we'll take a step further into the technical realm of Slack. *Chapter 6, Your Workplace Slackbot*, taught us the importance of Slackbot and the basics of how to build your very own bot. Now, we're going to take a deeper look into what a regular bot is and how to build and frame one to fit the needs of your company's workspace.

Section 3:
How to Build Your
Own Bots

For our last section, we'll dive into the most technically advanced features of Slack. We'll discuss how to build your own bot from the ground up, how to know when it's easier to buy or outsource your bot rather than starting from scratch, and how to ultimately distribute the product to the Slack App Directory.

Each of the skills you've mastered will be used to create your own tools that personalize your team's workspace. All of the knowledge you've collected in the past two sections comes together for the final piece in completing your Slack experience.

In this section, we will cover the following chapters:

- *Chapter 10, Building Your Own Bot*
- *Chapter 11, Buying, Building, and Outsourcing Your Bot*
- *Chapter 12, Distributing Your App in the Slack App Directory*

10
Building Your Own Bot

Anything team members can do, bots can do better. Bots are like your average team member but they never take a lunch break, vacation day, or sick leave. They work around the clock to answer commands and tasks you set for them to do to make your life easier. In *Chapter 6, Your Workspace Slackbot*, we discovered Slackbot – the most basic and beginner understanding of a bot and its many capabilities. Now, with the skills we've learned through *Chapter 7, Integrating Your Favorite Tools*, *Chapter 8, Automate Your Workflow with Zapier* and *Chapter 9, Slack API, Webhooks, Block Kit, and Sandbox*, you're ready to tackle building your own bot yourself.

Chapter 9, Slack API, Webhooks, Block Kit, and Sandbox, set us up with the many aspects of a bot that you can customize through API elements and fields, webhooks, individual and stacked blocks in Block Kit, and the experimental workspace that is the sandbox. But to utilize any of these tools, you need one common factor: a bot. Without a bot, the whole system fails to automate itself. With an understanding of the role a bot plays in Slack's structure, it's time to learn how to create your very own.

In this chapter, we will break down these factors of bots:

- The difference between Slackbot and regular bots

- How to set up and build your own bot

- Knowing where to start building and hosting your bot

- Using existing frameworks to build a bot

- Testing and pushing your completed bot live

Up until this point, we've focused on basic, beginner-level type strategies for tackling these concepts of coding, building, and designing our own technology for Slack. Now that we have an understanding of APIs and how to identify elements and fields of code, it's time to learn how to build our own bots from existing frameworks to starting from the bare bones and the process for testing and pushing the completed product.

Slackbot versus regular bots

As we discussed in *Chapter 6, Your Workspace Slackbot*, Slackbot is an extremely useful and beneficial tool to your workspace. Working as essentially your digital assistant, Slackbot serves as a quick and easy helper for automated tasks within your Slack channels and direct messages. While Slackbot's skills are varied, they are limited in design. This is where your regular bots come into play.

Bots can range from a simple notifier to interactive, button-based bots that execute programmed commands. The extent to which you can cultivate your bot is limited only by your own capabilities with coding and the advanced nature of this level of technology.

Some of the many features of bots include the following:

- Have names, profile pictures, and can be found in your directory

- Are mentioned with the @ symbol in channels and direct messages

- Post their own messages and upload files

- Are invited or removed from private and public channels as needed

While all of these features may be true, bots can only do these functions if you program them to. Bots don't wake up in the morning and sign in to Slack the same way your other team members do, and team members cannot take advantage of a bot as their own account.

In this chapter, we'll break down how to create your bot as a standalone user, as well as through app building, to recognize the progressive step up a regular bot requires from your traditional Slackbot.

Creating a bot user

There are two ways to go about creating your workplace Slackbot: as a standalone bot or a Slack app. Bots start off universal and are made to fit the app, niche, company, team, or member you choose to pair them with. Standalone bots serve individual purposes within your Slack instance and aren't necessarily connected to an app. In this section, we'll take a look at how to start this building process by creating a standalone bot user. Bots are unique to every workspace and that's why it takes a member, Workspace Owner or Admin to set up the bot and the specified channel(s) they'll work in for the magic to really begin. Let's see how to create one.

Building your bot user

A bot is the key to automating your workspace, and like anything in Slack, your bot should be personalized to you and your team. Follow these steps to create your own bot user:

1. Begin on your app's settings page by selecting the **App Home** feature. It will appear as in the following screenshot in your app settings:

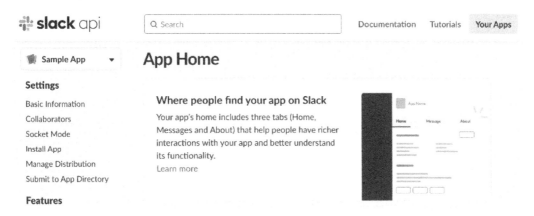

Figure 10.1 – Slack's new App Home feature replaces Slack's Bot User tab

2. Once you've allocated the proper bot token(s) needed for your app, you'll be allowed to access your app's Home tab. The Home tab is a non-message-based surface that uses Block Kit for deeper interactions with your users, utilizing features such as the following:

    a) **Home**: A completely customizable tab individual to your app. You can add Block Kit components to this tab to allow your team to easily interact with your app's features.

    b) **Messages**: The direct conversation between a member and the app.

    c) **About**: Where descriptive information about your app can be found, such as credentials and display information.

3. To access all of these features, simply switch the toggle to *on* to display the surfaces to users when they view the app in Slack. It will appear as in the following screenshot in your app settings:

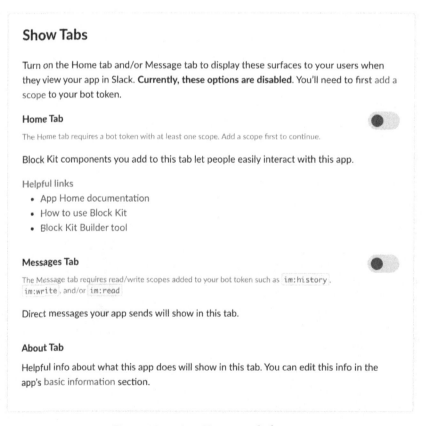

Figure 10.2 – App Home toggle features

Congrats, your bot is created! You're halfway there. Now it's time to set up the Events API. We have already learned about the API types, elements, and fields that help to create what ultimately becomes your individualized bot in *Chapter 9, Slack API, Webhooks, Block Kit, and Sandbox*. Event APIs specifically allow your bot to react to "events" or changes occurring across your workspace.

When something like this happens, a data payload is sent to your bot so that it can use the data to develop a response. Essentially, it's your bot's eyes and ears. These steps will set you up to develop your own Events API. In the next section, we will see how to set up Events API access.

Setting up Events API access

Events are a crucial part of setting up your app. Without them, your app has nothing to react to and essentially, no purpose. Follow these steps to set up your Events API access:

1. Again, in your app's settings, select **Event Subscriptions** from the **Navigation** menu. A toggle will appear to enable events. Switch the toggle to **On**. It will appear as in the following screenshot in your app settings:

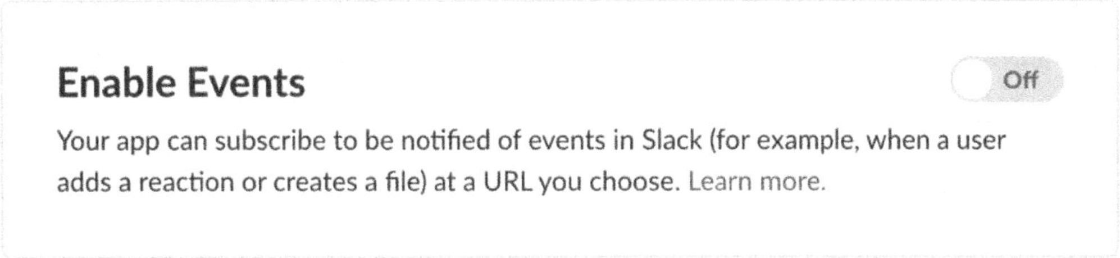

Enable Events

Off

Your app can subscribe to be notified of events in Slack (for example, when a user adds a reaction or creates a file) at a URL you choose. Learn more.

Figure 10.3 – Events API toggle

Once you've switched **Enable Events** to **On**, a screen will appear.

2. You will need to create the request URL, a public URL where Slack can send HTTP POST requests that describes where the payloads will be sent to.

3. Then you can customize your bot with unique individual event subscriptions.

4. Click **Save** and your bot is set up with its event types.

Before we move on to the next step of the process—creating an app for your bot—let's take a minute to dive further into your event type options. Some event types are basic to every channel, while others vary based on the type of business you and your company are in.

Here are some event type examples:

- `app_home_opened`: A user clicked on the app's Home tab.
- `channel_created`: A channel was created.
- `channel_left`: You left a channel.
- `dnd_updated`: Do not disturb settings changed for the current user.
- `emoji_changed`: A custom emoji was added or changed.
- `file_public`: A file was made public.
- `group_open`: You created a group DM.
- `invite_requested`: A user requested an invite to a workspace/channel.
- `pin_removed`: A pin was removed from a channel.
- `team_rename`: A workspace's name has been changed.
- `scope_denied`: OAuth scopes were denied to your app.

Based on the needs of your team, you can select the event types specific to your bot. The Events APIs are not the only APIs you can use to create your bot, but they are one of the most common and easiest to showcase. Once you've added the event types to your bot, you can move on to installing it into your workspace.

Bringing the bot to your workspace

Now that the bot is created, it's time to bring it into the channel(s) where it'll be doing its magic. Follow these steps to bring the bot into your workspace:

1. Still on your app settings page, select the **Install App** settings item.
2. Then, click **Install App to your Workspace**. If the app is already installed, you can select **Reinstall App**.
3. An authorization page will appear—click **Authorize**. The app is now installed, but you'll still need to invite your channels to it.

4. In addition to these channels, your bot should be included in a public channel within your workspace.

5. Now, your bot is happily existing within the channel you chose during the installation process!

Once your bot is officially installed, you will have generated a bot token that you will store for later use when you want to utilize your bot for certain requests. You'll be able to find these tokens by heading to your app's settings | **Install App** | **Bot User OAuth Access Token**. We'll further explain bot tokens and OAuth in the next section when we discuss creating a bot through Slack apps.

As we know, designing a standalone bot from scratch is only one of two ways of going about creating your bot. The more preferred and common way to set up a bot for your workspace is doing so through creating an app.

Creating an app

The latter of the two ways for constructing your bot, utilizing building through Slack apps, allows a wider range of functionality in your bot's future uses. This means of setting up your bot is often recommended by Slack. For these reasons, we'll explore this route in more detail for setting up your bot.

To start, you'll first want to head to `https://api.slack.com/apps`, where you'll be presented with the option of creating your very own app. Using the APIs we discussed in detail in *Chapter 9, Slack API, Webhooks, Block Kit, and Sandbox*, you'll begin the process of setting up your bot by creating an app through the Slack API. Use the button shown in the following screenshot to start:

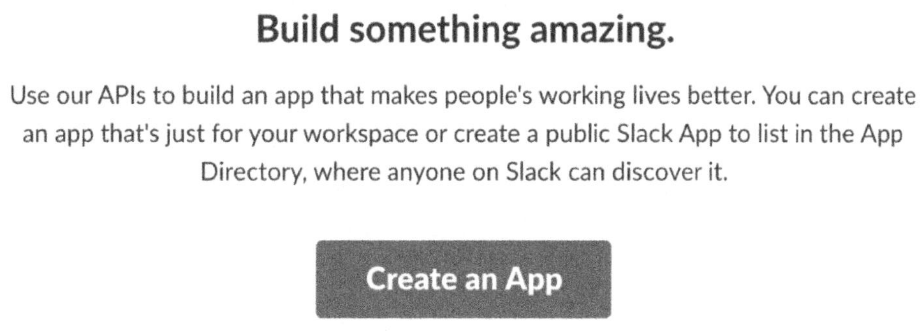

Build something amazing.

Use our APIs to build an app that makes people's working lives better. You can create an app that's just for your workspace or create a public Slack App to list in the App Directory, where anyone on Slack can discover it.

Create an App

Figure 10.4 – Use the "Create an App" button to create a public or private app

Once you select **Create an App**, a popup will appear and you have to enter your app's name and the development Slack workspace you want the app to work in. This process is for creating a Web API application. The **Create a Slack App** window should appear like this:

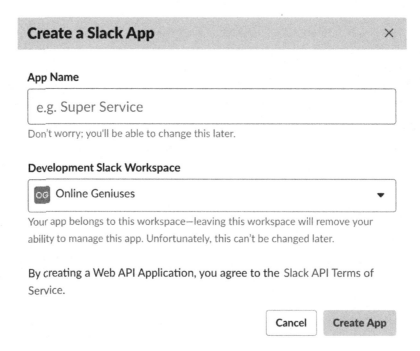

Figure 10.5 – Insert your app's name and workspace to finalize creating your app

The name you input for your app can be changed later, but the workspace you choose cannot be changed, so make sure you select the proper workspace before proceeding. Once you've filled out the designated fields, click **Create App** to complete the process.

Now that your app has been created, you have the freedom to customize it by adding different features and functionalities, such as bots, commands, webhooks, and permissions. We've discussed a few of these features in previous chapters already, but for now, we're going to switch gears and focus on how to build bots through our newly created Slack app.

Building and hosting your bot

When building your app, and therefore your bot, for Slack, you can choose to either create an app specifically for you and your workspace or one that can be made public through the Slack App Directory. Public apps become available to any user that wishes to download them to their workspace, whereas apps specifically designed for you and your team remain private to just you, the creator, or for you and any member within your workspace.

No matter the ultimate distribution of your app, creating your app requires a little more than simply inputting a name and workspace for it to act in. Your app will need elements such as APIs, webhooks, and Block Kit, but before adding all of those extra features, you first have to start with the basics: bot tokens, scopes, and OAuth.

Setting up bot tokens

After you've clicked the **Create App** button shown in the previous screenshot, you'll be redirected to the **Building Apps for Slack** page, where you'll have the ability to add different features and functionalities to your app. The page will appear like this through your desktop browser:

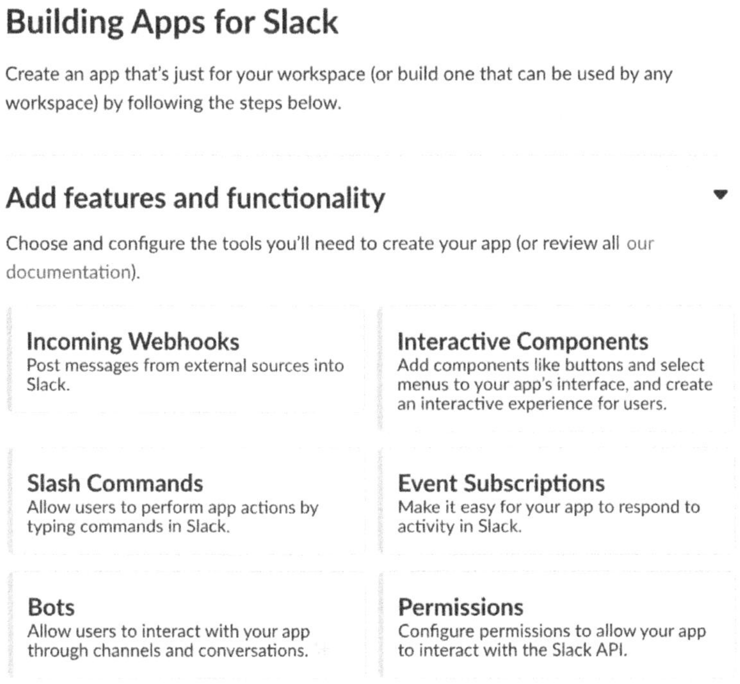

Building Apps for Slack

Create an app that's just for your workspace (or build one that can be used by any workspace) by following the steps below.

Add features and functionality   ▼

Choose and configure the tools you'll need to create your app (or review all our documentation).

Incoming Webhooks
Post messages from external sources into Slack.

Interactive Components
Add components like buttons and select menus to your app's interface, and create an interactive experience for users.

Slash Commands
Allow users to perform app actions by typing commands in Slack.

Event Subscriptions
Make it easy for your app to respond to activity in Slack.

Bots
Allow users to interact with your app through channels and conversations.

Permissions
Configure permissions to allow your app to interact with the Slack API.

Figure 10.6 – These building features can be found at https://api.slack.com/apps

The first part of building your bot is to get your bot token. Bot tokens make it possible for users to interact with your app by using @ mentions for your bot and adding it to channels and direct messages. To access your token(s), select the **Bots** section shown in the preceding screenshot. This may redirect you to another page, where you'll be introduced to scopes.

Finding the right scope(s)

Scopes are in charge of an app's capabilities and permissions. At least one scope needs to be added to your bot token in order to show the Home or Message tab on your app's home page. Let's take a look at some basic scopes you could add to your bot token.

chat:write scope

This scope allows an app to post messages in approved channels and conversations. It's compatible with the following Web API methods:

- `chat.delete`: Deletes a message
- `chat.postMessage`: Sends a message to a channel
- `chat.scheduleMessage`: Schedules a message to be sent to a channel
- `chat.update`: Updates a message

im.write scope

This scope allows an app to start direct messages with users. It's compatible with the following Web API methods:

- `conversations.close`: Closes a direct message or multi-person direct message
- `conversations.mark`: Sets the read cursor in a channel
- `im.open`: Opens a direct message channel
- `im.close`: Closes a direct message channel

You can find more scope options at `https://api.slack.com/scopes`.

These two scope options are your most basic forms and the most commonly used when creating an app. Once you've selected the scopes you want to add, you'll then head to **OAuth & Permissions** to actually get the tokens.

Authorizing OAuth permissions

OAuth, or **Open Authorization**, allows you to exchange information without having to provide your password and lets any user in any Slack workspace install your app. It allows a safer exchange of allowing authorization to private details.

This page can be accessed through the tab by the same name on the left sidebar of your screen. Your chosen scope(s) should appear under the **Scopes** section on this page:

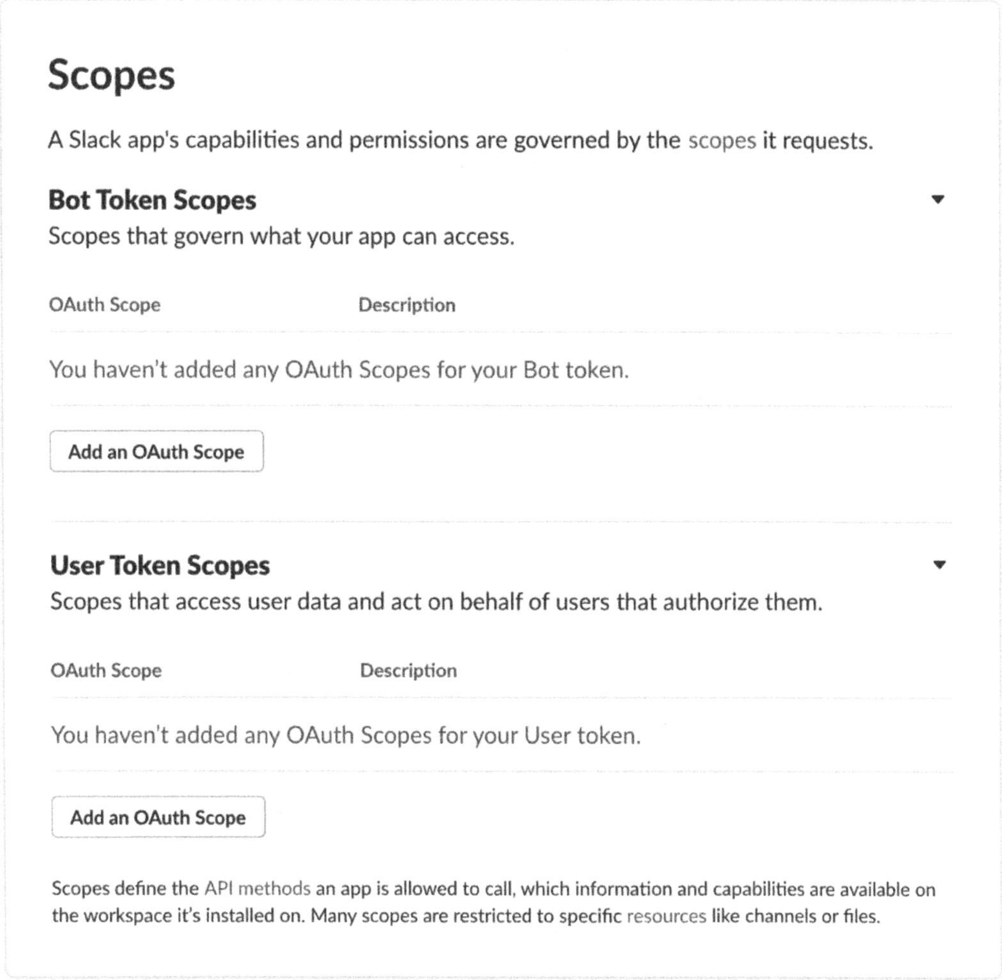

Scopes

A Slack app's capabilities and permissions are governed by the scopes it requests.

Bot Token Scopes   ▼

Scopes that govern what your app can access.

OAuth Scope   Description

You haven't added any OAuth Scopes for your Bot token.

[Add an OAuth Scope]

User Token Scopes   ▼

Scopes that access user data and act on behalf of users that authorize them.

OAuth Scope   Description

You haven't added any OAuth Scopes for your User token.

[Add an OAuth Scope]

Scopes define the API methods an app is allowed to call, which information and capabilities are available on the workspace it's installed on. Many scopes are restricted to specific resources like channels or files.

Figure 10.7 – "Bot Token Scopes" is the area we're focused on for this section

OAuth tokens will be automatically generated when you finish connecting the app to your workspace. You'll use these tokens to authenticate your app.

> **Important note**
> Bot tokens typically start with `xoxb-` when they appear in your code.

On this page, you'll be able to install the app to your workspace and generate the necessary tokens. Depending on your position in your workspace, you may need to request approval in order to install. If you're not a Workspace Owner or Admin, select the **Request to Install** button on the **OAuth & Permissions** page:

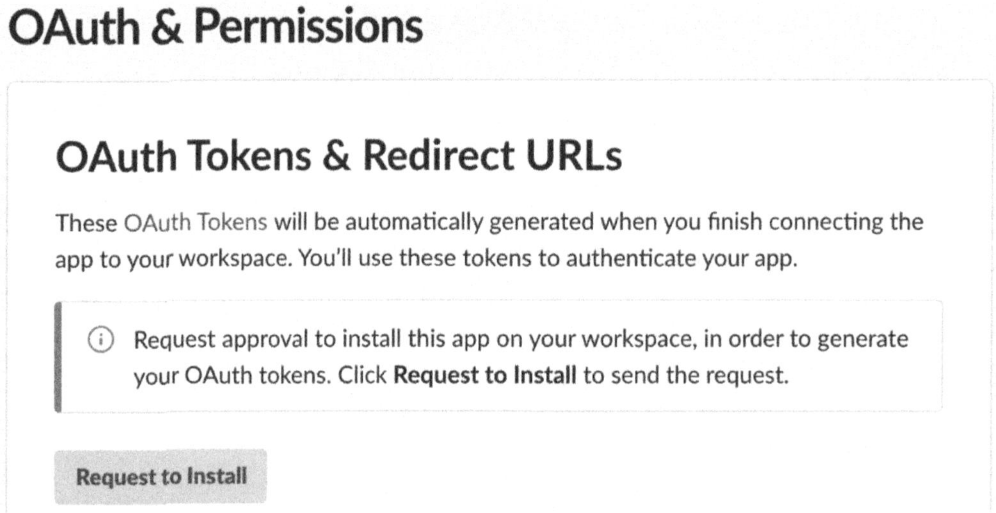

OAuth & Permissions

OAuth Tokens & Redirect URLs

These OAuth Tokens will be automatically generated when you finish connecting the app to your workspace. You'll use these tokens to authenticate your app.

ⓘ Request approval to install this app on your workspace, in order to generate your OAuth tokens. Click **Request to Install** to send the request.

Request to Install

Figure 10.8 – OAuth tokens are needed to authenticate your app

After your request is approved, you can then proceed with installing the app to your workspace. For this, you'll also want to have your signing secret handy. You can find this information under the **Basic Information** tab in the left sidebar, followed by **App Credentials**. The page will appear as in the following screenshot:

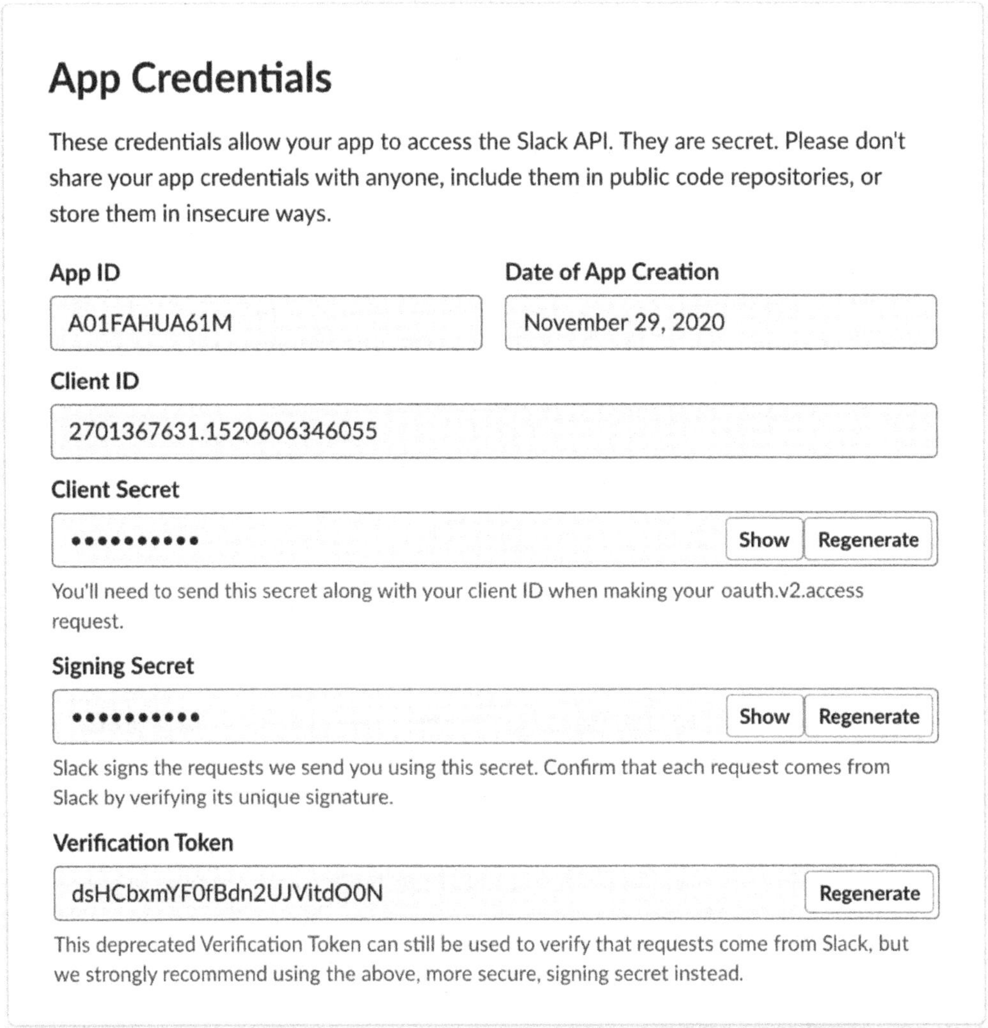

App Credentials

These credentials allow your app to access the Slack API. They are secret. Please don't share your app credentials with anyone, include them in public code repositories, or store them in insecure ways.

App ID

A01FAHUA61M

Date of App Creation

November 29, 2020

Client ID

2701367631.1520606346055

Client Secret

•••••••••   Show   Regenerate

You'll need to send this secret along with your client ID when making your oauth.v2.access request.

Signing Secret

•••••••••   Show   Regenerate

Slack signs the requests we send you using this secret. Confirm that each request comes from Slack by verifying its unique signature.

Verification Token

dsHCbxmYF0fBdn2UJVitdO0N   Regenerate

This deprecated Verification Token can still be used to verify that requests come from Slack, but we strongly recommend using the above, more secure, signing secret instead.

Figure 10.9 – Use the "Show" button to view the configuration of your signing secret

Your signing secret is unique and individual to your app. Use the designated code to allow Slack to sign requests using your "secret" and confirm that each request is coming directly from Slack. Should you need to change over permissions from time to time, you can regenerate your signing secret, which would then invalidate your existing one.

Once these steps are completed, you're finally ready to put your homemade bot into action! You've finalized the credentials needed to set up your app for your bot; now let's create the commands for the bot to follow.

Putting your bot into action

Having created and added your bot to your workspace, you now need to begin to set it into action to get the most out of your bot by having it respond to what it hears. In *Chapter 9*, *Slack API, Webhooks, Block Kit, and Sandbox*, we learned what an HTTP POST request is. Now, we're going to use that skill set to run our own request with the proper channel and—now—token to match to interact with the Slack API! Let's take a look at an example with a sample token and `Hello, team!` text message:

```
curl -X POST \
    -H 'Authorization: Bearer xoxb-your-token' \
    -H 'Content-type: application/json;charset=utf-8' \
    --data '{"channel":"#testchannel","text":"Hello, team!"}' \
https://slack.com/api/chat.postMessage
```

Figure 10.10 – The channel being used is "testchannel" and the text is "Hello, team!"

Once you've sent your coded command, head to that channel, in this case, **#testchannel**, to see your desired message appear. While this did in fact achieve the requested task, we want this process to be achieved programmatically to promote a more efficient workspace.

You can't be expected as a Workspace Owner, Admin, or even regular user to be able to set up specific coding for each message you want your bot to send throughout the average workday. That's why Slack offers simple methods to trigger these actions for you. Let's take a look at some of these mechanisms, such as scheduling and commands.

Scheduled messages

Scheduling messages is a great feature for any workspace. It allows you to plan set messages to send to your team in advance, whether it be a reminder for a weekly meeting, a set motivational booster, or a monthly survey response. Whatever your workspace needs, scheduled messages remove the fuss attached to menial tasks that could otherwise be handled automatically.

To utilize the scheduled message feature in HTTP, add a `post_at` parameter to your JSON request. Then, pass your JSON to `chat.scheduleMessage` instead of `chat.postMessage`. Your scheduled message may appear something like this:

```
POST https://slack.com/api/chat.scheduledMessage
Content-type: application/json
Authorization: Bearer xoxb-your-token
{
  "channel": "all-company",
  "text": "Hey, team! Reminder to attend our weekly meeting this afternoon.",
  "post_at": 1551891428,
}
```

Figure 10.11 – The channel being used is "all-company" and the text is the reminder

Once you've entered the code into your bot, you can sit back and watch as your message appears at the exact time you entered for `post_at` using UNIX, a system for describing a point in time using the number of seconds that have elapsed since 00:00:00, minus leap seconds, for the timestamp.

> **Tip**
> Messages can only be scheduled up to 120 days in advance.

You can always delete a scheduled message if it no longer serves its original purpose. Simply take `scheduled_message_id` and use `chat.deleteScheduledMessage` to delete. You'll receive a response once your message has been successfully removed.

Slash commands

One of the most difficult bots to create, Slash commands bots are any type of command beginning with a slash. For example, `/giphy` is a command that would trigger a bot for finding animated gifs from the Giphy app. Based on the apps you have connected to your workspace and the actions you're trying to accomplish, slash commands can include a variety of commands.

To set up your own slash command, take the following steps:

1. Head to your app's settings.

2. Once there, select the **Slash Commands** button or the tab by the same name from the left sidebar.

    From there, you're given the option to create a new command or copy an existing one.

3. Click on **Create New Command** to get to the following pop-up page:

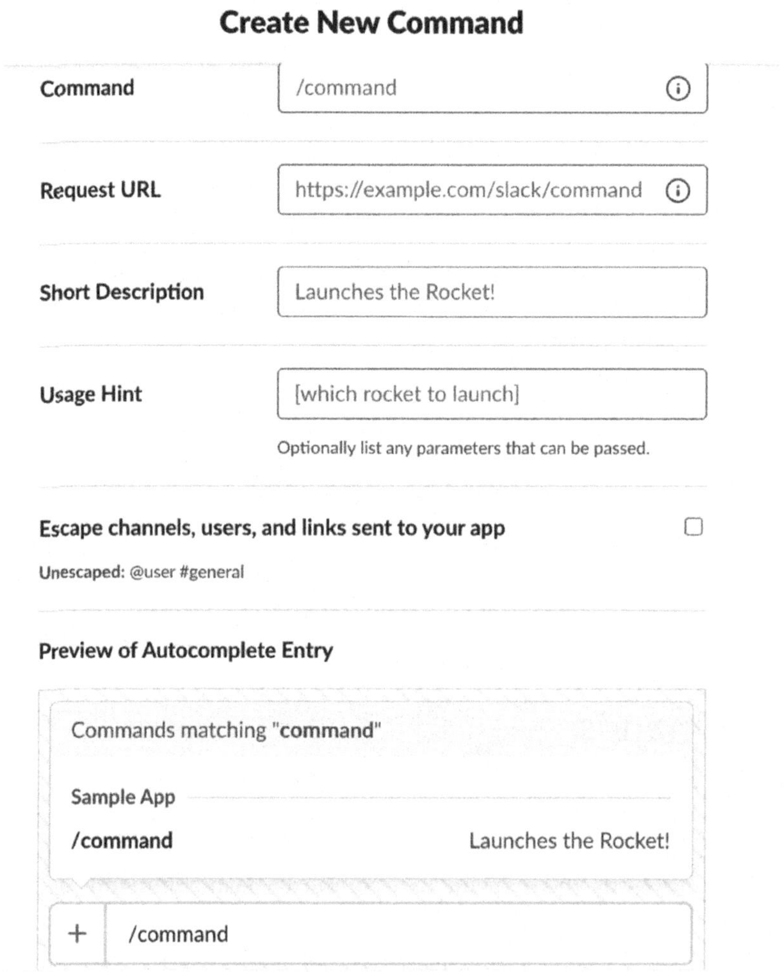

Create New Command

Command	/command ⓘ

Request URL	https://example.com/slack/command ⓘ

Short Description	Launches the Rocket!

Usage Hint	[which rocket to launch]

Optionally list any parameters that can be passed.

Escape channels, users, and links sent to your app   ☐

Unescaped: @user #general

Preview of Autocomplete Entry

Commands matching "**command**"

Sample App

/command   Launches the Rocket!

+   /command

Figure 10.12 – Adding a slash command requires having a bot

There are a few categories to fill out before your slash command can be put into motion. To start, you'll first have to create the actual command you want to use to enact the action. For instance, /assignments could be used to access the upcoming assignments for the day. The actual command text can be customized to whatever command you need.

4. Next, add a short description of what the command should be intended to do.

    In this case, access today's assignments would fit the /assignments command.

5. Lastly, you'll want to add in the request URL.

    If you remember from *Chapter 9, Slack API, Webhooks, Block Kit, and Sandbox*, your request URL can be found through your webhook.

6. Simply copy over the URL and paste it into this field.

7. Click **Save** in the bottom right-hand corner and you've created your slash command!

As we learned in *Chapter 3, Slack Features, Tips, and Tricks*, you can utilize slash commands for almost any kind of situation that may occur in your workspace. Now, rather than using commands for simple tasks, you can create your own to have your slash commands trigger actions internally as well as externally.

While creating your bot from scratch has many benefits for customization, there are instances where utilizing an existing outline can make more sense for time and capability purposes. That's where Slack frameworks come into play.

Using existing frameworks

Creating your bots from scratch can be a difficult process. There's a lot of technical factors that come into play that can be jumbled or inputted incorrectly, which can affect the entirety of the final message/action product.

Frameworks exist to make your life easier.

Slack's frameworks serve as a kind of guideline for your bots. You have the option to pick and choose the outline you want to use and then customize it to your needs. Change a text message to read the announcement you're trying to make. Alternate the time and date in your date picker to match your meeting details. All of these options are available to you more quickly and easily when you choose to utilize frameworks.

To do this, it helps to know where you can access these pre-existing frameworks. In this section, we'll discuss the two most common outlets for finding existing code to alter: Block Kit and Bolt.

Block Kit

In *Chapter 9, Slack API, Webhooks, Block Kit, and Sandbox*, we were introduced to the concept of Block Kit. As we know, Block Kit allows you to build and stack blocks through a variety of elements, such as images, text options, actions, headers, and buttons. The beautiful thing about Block Kit is that for each of these elements, Block Kit provides you with a framework block for you to then customize and make your own.

Block Kit is your most basic framework tool to utilize for most any of your bots. The coding for each block is already generated; all you have to do is go in and adjust the text, emoji, image, or any other elements as you see fit.

For example, let's revisit the common issue of *what's the Wi-Fi password?* An example of the code you would set up to receive that question may look like this:

```
router.post("/", function(req, res, next) {

let payload = req.body;

res.sendStatus(200);

if (payload.event.type === "app_mention") {

if (payload.event.text.includes("what is the WIFI password"))

// Make call to chat.postMessage using bot's token

    }

  }

}
```

Figure 10.13 – The text portion of this code can be personalized to fit your needs

When a text message mentions the bot and includes the words `What is the WIFI password?`, your bot will automatically respond with the designated password. For example, the response may look something like this:

The WIFI password is OnlineGeniuses1234.

Figure 10.14 – A bot will respond with your organization's Wi-Fi password

Through the Slack API, your app will then use the token you generated to send the request. An example of the request may appear like this:

```
POST https://slack.com/api/chat.post
Message Content-type: application/json
Authorization: Bearer YOUR_BOTS_TOKEN
{
"text": "Hello <@USER>! The WIFI password is
OnlineGeniuses1234.",
"channel": "GENERAL"
}
```

Wi-Fi requests are only one of the many redundant questions that most likely occur in your channels more often than you think. Rather than going through the effort of building this code from scratch, take advantage of the framework to request and respond to the more commonly asked questions in your workspace.

The Bolt framework

Bolt is a framework available in JavaScript, Python, and Java that allows you to quickly build Slack apps. Bolt includes things such as token validation, server support, a simplified OAuth interface, and automatic retry and rate-limiting logic.

Each version of Bolt works to help you build apps and integrations without the hassle of creating your own code. Bolt for each programming server appears like this:

Bolt for JavaScript

- TypeScript bindings available
- Nifty support for Workflow builder: steps from apps
- Built on top of node-slack-sdk
- Getting started guide

Bolt for Python

- Asynchronous request handling
- Examples for deploying to cloud providers
- Built on top of python-slack-sdk
- Getting started guide

Bolt for Java

- Rapidly develop with Kotlin bindings
- Works with Servlet containers out-of-the-box, including Spring Boot
- Built on top of and included as part of java-slack-sdk
- Getting started guide

Figure 10.15 – Programming servers (https://api.slack.com/tools/bolt)

You can utilize almost any of Bolt's features no matter your chosen version of the formatting tool. Similar to the steps mentioned throughout this chapter, Bolt works with you to help you create your app, install it, and then go through the steps of building your bot.

Some of Bolt's most commonly used features include the following:

- Installing your app using OAuth 2.0
- Receiving events and messages in real time with the Events API
- Composing interactive messages with Block Kit
- Responding to slash commands, shortcuts, and interactive messages
- Utilizing a web library of Web API methods

In action, Bolt works the same as you would on your own, but with a little added guided help. To see how a code appears when sending a message with the API using Bolt, visit `https://api.slack.com/tools/bolt`.

The import of the Bolt package appears as `@slack/bolt` in your code. The coded example as seen on the website also includes features we've learned about throughout this chapter, such as bot tokens and your signing secret.

There are many different things you can code with Bolt. Depending on the event you're looking to achieve, Bolt can offer various options of sample code to achieve these measures.

Here are a few sample codes you can use on any of Bolt's server options:

- Calling `chat.delete`
- Calling `chat.postMessage`
- Calling `files.upload`
- Calling `users.info`
- Fetching conversation history
- Retrieving a message
- Scheduling a message

Most of the code samples for Bolt are available on all three of these tools, with the exception of Python, on occasion. Depending on the programming platform that is easiest for you to use, some of the features vary. For instance, JavaScript utilizes Glitch for setting up your app. Glitch works similarly to a sandbox as a testing platform for your apps and bots.

Testing is a key part of completing and publishing your work. For large and small organizations, it's important that you ensure your app and bot will work properly once they're set into action. In the next section, we'll take a look at the procedures needed to test and push your bot live.

Testing and pushing your bot live

Once your app is published and your bot is designed to your standards, the next step is to publish your work for your Slack world to see, right? Seemingly, yes, this would be the proper next step. But, as we've learned in previous chapters, there are many instances in which your bot may not have been coded or built properly, especially when being built from scratch, and could not function as it's supposed to.

Everybody makes mistakes, and that's why we want to prep for these mistakes in advance so that they don't have a negative effect on work happening in real time in our workspaces. We do this through testing.

Testing

Slack recommends that you always test out your app before putting it into action. From *Chapter 9, Slack API, Webhooks, Block Kit, and Sandbox*, we know that a sandbox is the ultimate one-stop shop for testing out your apps and bots. A sandbox works effectively for big organizations as a workspace to see how your automation will react and appear in your Slack channels and direct messages.

Yet, while a sandbox is always an option for larger grid enterprise workspaces, what about for smaller companies or simply members that don't want to go through the hassle of working with an outside application to test out their work? The solution: a designated #test channel.

Members can simply set up designated #test channels the same way you create any kind of channel. Instead, this channel will be used with the purpose of being integrated with apps and bots before they're ready to be brought into your actual workspace. This provides a safe space within your Slack to test out your apps and bots for any kinks without the stress.

If your team has an already-existing channel with a few members that wouldn't mind becoming a test space, you could also choose to use that as well. This prevents the clutter of adding a channel for this sole reasoning and allows you to utilize an already-existing space. Once you feel that your app/bot are performing properly, you're ready to finally publish and push it into the live space.

Updating

After your app has been published and made available in the App Directory, you may realize there's some tweaks or improvements you want to make. Over time, updates may be necessary or even a change in name could require a makeover. Thankfully, Slack allows you to edit this in your app in a similarly safe way to testing your work.

When you want to update your app, it will be sent to the review team before you can publish your new changes to the live version. But to make the actual changes, you'll first have to create a development copy of your app using the **Edit App** option. This allows you to make changes to test and submit without affecting your current app in the live directory.

Your development copy supplies you with all your app's background from your basic information to your event subscriptions, which are all up for editing. Similar to any time you create an app, you should also test out the updated version of your app once it's completed.

Summary

In this chapter, we again learned about bots, but on an advanced level. We can now appreciate the difference between these types of bots and our beloved assistant Slackbot and know how to set up and create our very own version. We were introduced to existing frameworks to avoid the ultimate code creation and know the importance of testing our bots before we push them live into our workspaces. Now that we have an appreciation for both the basic and advanced levels of learning what Slack has to offer, it's time to learn how to spot when the right moments are to utilize each.

In the next chapter, we'll learn how to identify when it's best to buy or build your bots. We know the difference between Slackbot and a regular bot and how to build our own. Yet, in some instances, for the not-so-technically-inclined, it may make more sense to purchase a pre-designed bot or completely outsource some of the more labor-intensive and detailed work. We'll go into detail about finding the right kind of talent and what you need to prepare before contracting out your workspace to external organizations as we proceed to the next step of our Slack journey.

11
Buying, Building, and Outsourcing Your Bot

We have achieved the hard part, that is, we have learned how to build apps and bots from the ground up. We have brought external applications into our workspace to integrate multiple aspects of our organization into one communal place. We have utilized frameworks with Zapier, APIs, and webhooks. Now, we're going to take all that knowledge, everything we have learned, and hire someone else to do the work instead. Well, not always, but occasionally.

Building is a great skill to have, but is an even greater time consumer for the average busy Workspace Owner, Admin, or even general team member. *Chapter 10, Building Your Own Bot*, taught us the ins and outs of achieving this more difficult route from setting up to pushing a bot live, through the original coding, to framework assistance. Now, we're going to explore a different course of direction completely that may make the bot-creating experience more accessible and enjoyable for the average Slack user.

Slack understands that you have a lot on your plate already and is constantly working to make your job *smarter, not harder*. That's why it's critical to know when it's best to build your own material, buy it, or even outsource it.

In this chapter, we'll cover the following topics:

- Benefits of building your own Slack bot

- How purchasing frameworks can assist in building your bot

- Benefits of buying your own Slack bot

- Where to buy your bot and knowing what bot to buy

- Understand what's needed to outsource a bot

- Where to find the talent to outsource a bot

There are scenarios where building internally is the best option to create the right material for your workspace, but there are other ways to retrieve the content you're searching for. In this chapter, we'll discuss how to optimize your time and Slack content by recognizing when it makes the most sense to buy, build, or outsource your bots.

Benefits of building your own Slack bot

In many ways, building your own bot is the easiest way to go when it comes to customization. When you build an app or a bot, you hold the reins. You decide how the bot is framed, what it says, where it reacts, how it appears, and whether it includes an image, or text, or text with bulleted lists, or questions. You are totally and completely in charge of the result of your product.

In addition to customization, there are many other reasons why you would choose to create a Slack bot of your own. Let's revisit some of these basic advantages.

The following are the benefits to building your own bot:

- **Around-the-clock shifts**: Bots are constantly active, that is, 24/7, unless you choose to turn them off.

- **Instant responses**: Bots respond immediately to you and your team's questions and requests.

- **Patience**: Bots, unlike human members, have all the time and patience in the world to respond to repetitive questions and consistent needs.

- **Automated responses**: Bots are programmed to respond to keywords and terms with your specified message or action.

- **Personalization**: Bots can be individualized to fit the language and necessities of you and your team.

As we learned in *Chapter 10, Building Your Own Bot*, there are many upsides to creating your own app and bot from the ground up.

Yet, building a bot may not always be that simple. There are a lot of technical factors that come into play and although you have the options to utilize available frameworks to assist in the building process, a lot of the customization still falls on you.

While building a bot from the bare bones up may not be your cup of tea, frameworks allow you to have the tweaking power you desire without the intense amount of labor. There are some free options available to do this, but with set limitations. Using a paid framework to assist in the making of your bot, without fully contracting out the project, could prove to be the better option.

Using external and paid frameworks

If building your bot yourself is still a priority for you and your team, it may make more sense to purchase a framework rather than the actual bot or app itself. We learned in *Chapter 10, Building Your Own Bot*, that there are existing frameworks within Slack, such as Block Kit and Bolt, but we have yet to discuss using them as a paid or external option.

In this section, we'll focus on different types of frameworks outside of Slack, both free and paid, such as Botkit, Microsoft Bot Framework, and Amazon Lex.

Botkit

When it comes to free, for me, Botkit is the go-to framework option. This open source developing tool aids in building bots for Slack such as chatbots as well as apps and custom integrations. Open source essentially means a type of software where the code is released under a license in which the owner has the right to use, change, and distribute to others. Botkit provides a built-in source for hundreds of already-existing frameworks that you as the user can employ for your own bots within your Slack workspace.

Botkit utilizes Node.js to create bots through Node.js made up of the Botkit core library. The library lives on GitHub, where these frameworks are hosted. Botkit's website looks as in the following screenshot:

Figure 11.1 – Botkit's home page (https://botkit.ai/)

Botkit even offers its own `#botkit` Slack community channel where you can join and interact with other developers building bots and messaging apps. Once you install Botkit, you're ready to get to work and start making your bot, as well as exploring the many open source framework options.

If Botkit's frameworks aren't meeting your standards or you're looking for something more advanced, there are also paid framework options, such as Microsoft Bot Framework and Amazon Lex, which provide free trials but are ultimately paid framework options.

Microsoft Bot Framework

An extension of Botkit, Microsoft Bot Framework is a more advanced framework option for larger, Enterprise Grid-level companies/organizations. Similar to Botkit, Microsoft Bot Framework is an open source resource for developers and teams to design and build their apps and bots.

The framework uses Azure Cognitive Services to help you create bots with the ability to listen, speak, understand, and learn from you and your users. Microsoft Bot Framework's website, where you can go to sign up for a free or paid plan, looks as in the following screenshot:

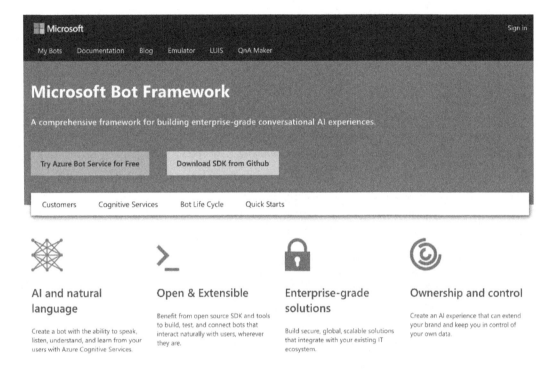

Figure 11.2 – Microsoft Bot Framework's features page (https://dev.botframework.com/)

Microsoft Bot Framework offers a free tier in addition to an S1 tier. Their options are broken down by price as well as limitations. Let's take a look at the key differences between the two.

The following is a summary of the Microsoft Bot Framework plans:

- **Free tier:**

   a) Unlimited messages on standard channels

   b) 10,000 messages per month on premium channels

- **S1 tier:**

   a) Unlimited messages on standard channels

   b) $0.50 per 1,000 messages on premium channels

Like Slack and Zapier's paid plans, Microsoft Bot Framework's paid option and the platform itself exist for larger and more established companies that require resources and mass distribution of their bots across their vast Slack workspace.

Botkit and Microsoft Bot Framework resemble existing frameworks we discussed working with in *Chapter 10, Building Your Own Bot*, on larger or smaller scales. Yet, there are also framework options, such as Amazon Lex, that add enhanced framework features, such as voice recognition, to your bots.

Amazon Lex

Amazon Lex is like Amazon's Alexa for your bots. Like the common household tool, Amazon Lex frameworks work on device control through advanced functions that recognize voice as well as text in their responses and actions.

The framework utilizes **automatic speech recognition** (ASR) for converting speech into text, as well as **natural language understanding** (NLU) to recognize the intent of text. Essentially, Amazon Lex creates highly progressive versions of Slackbot. You can find more information about the framework's details on its website, featured in this figure:

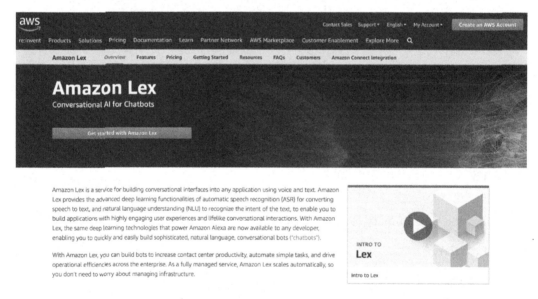

Figure 11.3 – Amazon Lex's information overview (https://aws.amazon.com/lex/)

Amazon Lex is a free service to start, and only charges you monthly fees per each request that is actually processed. Currently, its fees are $0.004 per speech request and $0.00075 per text request. For example, if you were to send 4,000 speech requests and 1,000 text requests, your monthly fee would be $16.75.

This sophisticated framework powers Amazon's Alexa and, should you choose, can also be used to power your bots to act and exist in a similar automated fashion.

When even assisted frameworks are too time-heavy a project for you or your team members, the next step in utilizing bots without building one would be to purchase an existing bot for your own use. In the next section, we will cover the benefits of buying your own Slack bot.

Benefits of buying your own Slack bot

Creating your own bot is an individual and rewarding experience as you are building something specifically for you and your team. But there comes a time when constantly building bots becomes a labor-intensive process that many companies just don't have the time or energy to do. That's when you have to ask yourself, why build when you can buy?

There are hundreds of bots already on the market available for you within the Slack App Directory. While it may seem like your bot and app needs are unique and exclusive to your company, chances are some developer out there has faced the same issue, created the bot, and made it available for you to use via purchase. You can find these bots on the Slack App Directory, featured in the following screenshot:

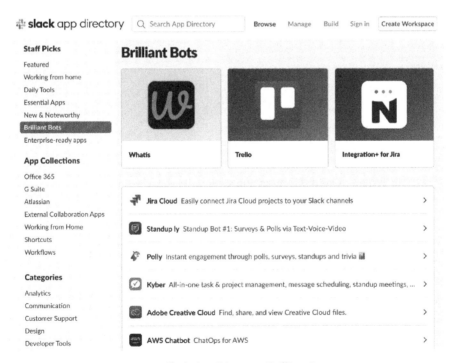

Figure 11.4 – Slack App Directory Brilliant Bots page

We'll discuss the directory and how to deliver the app you create to the resource further in *Chapter 12, Distributing Your App in the Slack App Directory.*

You can find a wide variety of apps as well as bots throughout the Slack App Directory. These range from existing applications, such as Google Drive and Dropbox, to tools created by fellow developers that then chose to put their bot on the market for the general public.

You can also access the directory from within your Slack desktop and mobile app. From your apps page, you can also find which bots are currently being used within your workspace. The bots featured in your Slack app will appear something similar to the following:

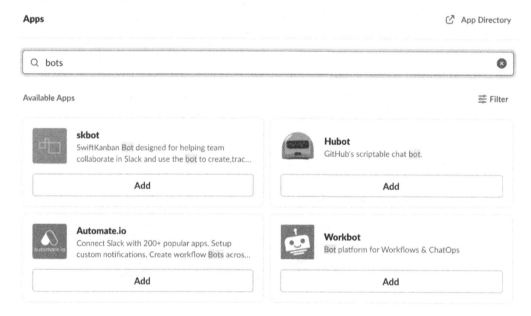

Figure 11.5 – Online Geniuses utilizes the following bots in their workspace

There are many bot options to choose from throughout the directory that can assist your workspace in a variety of ways that you would normally customize your own bot to do. From recording company terminology to scheduling to taking care of stats, why go through the struggle of creating an app that already exists? So, in this section, we'll focus on a few key existing bots you can integrate into your workspace.

Brilliant bots for your workspace

In *Chapter 7*, *Integrating Your Favorite Tools*, we discussed some basic apps available in the directory, specifically focusing on the onboarding process and team communication. Now, with advanced knowledge of bots, bot building, and customization, we have a better understanding of the proper components we're looking for a bot to accomplish.

With these things in mind, it's time to search for the perfect bot that'll fit the mold we would have originally used to build our own. While you may not find a bot that meets your criteria specifically, chances are you can hit the mark pretty close, especially with some of the more general bots. Let's take a look at some useful, available bots already on the market.

Whatis

The Whatis bot is Dictionary.com for your organization's terminology. Whatis literally answers the question of "What is [blank]" within your Slack instance when your team members need a constant refresher or when outside guests, clients, and partners join your workspace for the first time.

By simply asking through the /whatis (insert term) command, Whatis is put into action to search the app for the term, a definition, and any notes or links attached to it. This bot can be used not only for company slang but also for projects or files kept within your designated channels so that key information can be accessed at any point in time. Whatis looks as in the following screenshot on the Slack App Directory browser page:

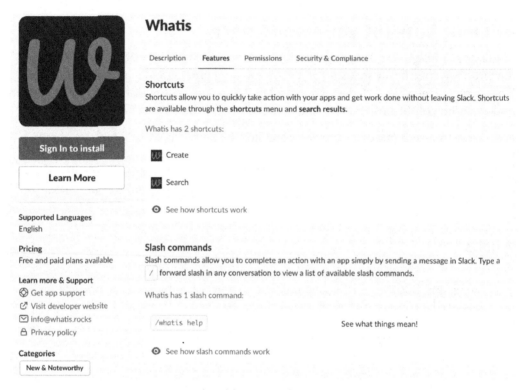

Figure 11.6 – Whatis' features in the Slack App Directory

While you can use Whatis for free, there are advanced, paid options that don't limit your capabilities with the bot and allow you to have a greater outreach. Let's take a look at some of Whatis' different free and paid plan options for Slack users.

Whatis' pricing options

There are free and paid plans available for the Whatis bot. Each plan is broken down into the following features:

- **Hobby**: $0/month:

  a) Create unlimited Whatises.

  b) Migrate in your team's existing terms.

    c) Update Whatises.

    d) 50 searches per month.

    e) 1 administrator.

    f) 250 max users on a team.

- **Standard**: $65/month:

    a) Create unlimited Whatises.

    b) Migrate in your team's existing terms.

    c) Update Whatises.

    d) Role-based access control.

    e) Unlimited searches per month.

    f) 10 administrators max.

    g) 250 max users on a team.

- **Enterprise**: $139/month:

    a) Create unlimited Whatises.

    b) Migrate in your team's existing terms.

    c) Update Whatises.

    d) Role-based access control.

    e) Unlimited searches per month.

    f) 10 or more administrators.

    g) Unlimited users on a team.

    h) Custom features request.

As suitably named by the pricing tiers, the size and expansion of your company play a big factor in finding which option is right for you. For smaller teams, the free "Hobby" plan could be all you need, while larger enterprise companies may require the "Enterprise" plan straight out of the gate. No matter which pricing option you choose, Whatis is a great bot to utilize within your company to easily share company knowledge in an interactive and automated format.

Statsbot

Statsbot is essentially a bot in charge of the stats of your workspace. The bot is designed to work with raw data to store, read, and transform the charts, reports, dashboards, and so on within your Slack workspace. It can be utilized by tech-savvy and non-technically-advanced members of your team alike since there's no need to learn coding or complex interfaces to integrate into your Slack instance.

The bot pre-aggregates information in the background of your channels to put together insights and data queries for you to view. To access this data from Slack, use the / statsbot slash command to view your saved metrics and reports in a dashboard and the /statsbot-goals slash command to view all your team's goals in one place.

Statsbot looks as in the following screenshot on the Slack App Directory browser page:

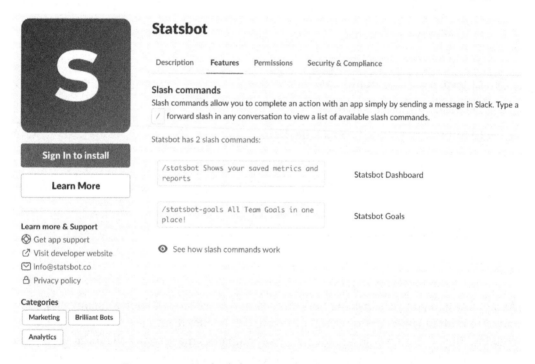

Figure 11.7 – Statsbot's features in the Slack App Directory

Statsbot can be used entirely as a free app if you choose to do so, but, like most apps, there are additional paid options that allow you to utilize the app on a larger scale. Let's break down Statsbot's features by its pricing plans.

Statsbot pricing plan options

Statsbot offers a free option as well as customizable paid plans for you and your team. Each plan varies by size and capabilities that are broken down into the following features:

- **Free**: $0/month, forever:

  a) 5 users

  b) 50 scheduled report messages per month

  c) Unlimited number of GA profiles and SQL databases

  d) 100k database rows

  e) Unlimited dashboards

  f) Slack integration

- **Pay As You Go**: $45/month:

  a) 10 users included, up to 200 users

  b) 100 scheduled report messages per month included

  c) 150k database rows included, up to 10 million

  d) Unlimited number of GA profiles and SQL databases

  e) Public dashboard

  f) Roles and permissions

- **Enterprise**: Price unique to your company:

  a) Dedicated data analyst

  b) Unlimited users

  c) Unlimited number of GA profiles and SQL databases

  d) Public dashboard

  e) Roles and permissions

Statsbot understands that they can't necessarily price out plans that will fit the mold of every company out there, and that's why the customizability of the larger plans is a unique feature that allows anyone to use the bot to match the exact needs they're looking for.

TimeBot

TimeBot is your go-to helper for anything to do with the attendance of your team. The bot works to automate managing time off requests, vacations, work from home hours, and absences so that you don't have to do it by yourself. By storing your team's log of vacation and time off requests, TimeBot keeps your team informed of each other's calendars and who will be available when.

The bot also allows you to request time off by submitting a request with all of the information, such as the type of time off, the date(s) you'll need off, and whether it'll be for a full or half day(s). You use the /ooo slash command to request new time off, /summary to view time-off history, and /later [your message] to send a scheduled message to arrive in the morning.

TimeBot looks as in the following screenshot on the Slack App Directory browser page:

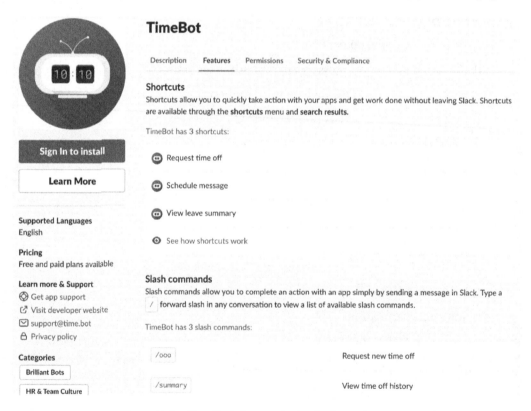

Figure 11.8 – TimeBot's features in the Slack App Directory

Similar to the Whatis and Statbot bots, TimeBot offers free and paid options to use the app. The free plan offers 20 time off requests per month, but requires you to upgrade for advanced features and unlimited time requests. Let's take a look at TimeBot's upgraded plan options.

TimeBot's price plan options

In addition to the free plan, TimeBot offers a Starter, Premium, or Custom plan for its users. Each option provides different features that add on to the larger plan you purchase. Timebot's plans are broken down into the following:

- **Starter**: $1.00 per active user per month:

  a) Try free for 14 days.

  b) Unlimited time off requests.

  c) Sync with calendars.

  d) Custom time off types.

- **Premium**: $2.50 per active user per month:

  a) Try free for 14 days.

  b) Unlimited time off requests.

  c) Sync with calendars.

  d) Custom time off types.

  e) Arrival tracking.

  f) Priority support.

- **Custom**: Special pricing:

  a) For unique and customized pricing, for enterprise, annual, non-profit, or student teams, you can contact TimeBot.

Each of these plans offers a free trial option that allows users to try out the plan before deciding to fully commit to it. The Custom option pertains to particular teams that may require their own specialized pricing or discount.

We couldn't possibly break down every available bot on the market. In addition to these three, there are hundreds of available bots to purchase that each offer unique tools and skills that can be critical to you and your team's automated success. Before setting out to create your own, search the Slack App Directory for an already-existing bot, which could save you both time and energy in building a bot from scratch.

Now that we've thoroughly examined our first two options, constructing from the ground up and purchasing our bots from the directory, it's time to dive into our last resource for bringing a bot into our workspace: outsourcing.

Understanding the cost and time to outsource a bot

You can build your own, as well as buy your own, but what happens when you need a combination of both, when you don't have the time to build, but you can't find exactly what you're looking for already on the market?

This is where the concept of *outsourcing* comes into play.

Outsourcing is a unique tool that allows you to utilize external resources to essentially do the work for you. There are hundreds of thousands of professionals selling their time and skills online for this very purpose. But, before you go ahead and contract out your bot to an external freelancer or company, it's important to understand how to prep yourself to discover the right outlet to outsource to. In this section, we'll walk you through how to find freelancers, consultants, or agencies that focus on building Slack apps and bots for you.

Finding freelancers

Freelancing has become a popular way of outsourcing work by hiring a self-employed worker(s) for a specified task or project. If you or a team member is too busy or not overly skilled in a subject—such as building bots—your next resource is to outsource for someone who has the availability and knowledge to do so.

In this day and age, there are endless options to hire freelancers in these areas, from writing to programming to tech, that it can be hard not to get lost in the clutter. A simple search could result in thousands of options that leave you wondering who and what qualifies for the work you're looking to have completed.

That's why we're breaking down a few of the most popular options, especially for Slack, that'll make your search process that much easier. Let's take a look at some of the top freelancing websites.

Freelancer

As basic as the name, Freelancer is a broader version of a freelancing website that doesn't meet a specific niche, but rather any kind of topic you could be looking for. Fill in a form as shown in the following screenshot to lay out a project you're looking to be completed or, if you're the freelancer yourself, browse the existing projects to find the right fit for you:

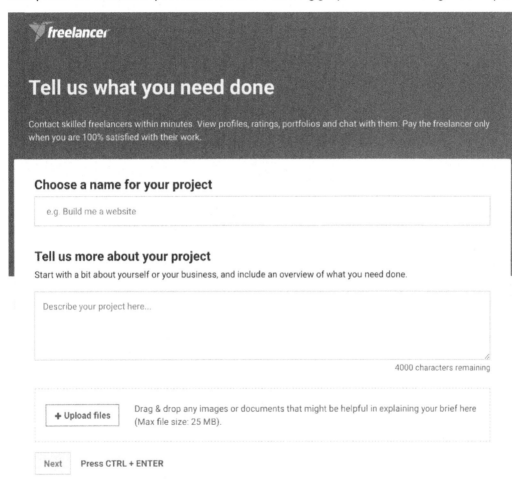

Figure 11.9 – Freelancer's project form (https://www.freelancer.com/)

Freelancer leaves you, the freelancer-seeker, at the mercy of finding the right person since they'll be reaching out to you, rather than you browsing a person's skillset and pitching a concept to them. The website also gives you the option of choosing between the freelancers that respond to your project by viewing a person's profile, ratings, and portfolio, and even chatting with them one on one beforehand. You can also overview your project entirely before the person signs on for the work so that there's no confusion about what needs to be done.

This option is great for team members or organizations that are unsure of the type of skillset or person they're looking for and just want to lay out their project and see the options available that come to them.

Fiverr

No matter what you're trying to create or build, Fiverr has the right professional freelancer for the project. Fiverr is one of the most popular freelancing sites that offer a variety of niche-based freelancers that offer their skill set for you to peruse at your liking.

Search among hundreds of freelancers selling their expertise to find exactly what you're looking for by category, service, or keyword. Fiverr's search page looks as in the following screenshot:

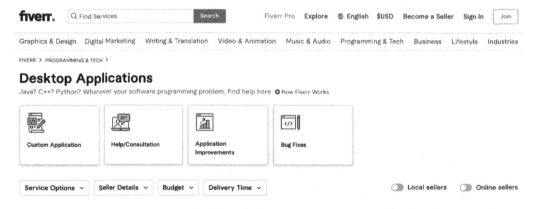

Figure 11.10 – Fiverr's service options (https://www.fiverr.com)

For instance, if you were searching for someone to create a desktop application, you could break down your service options by programming language (such as Java or Python), operating system (such as Windows or macOS), and expertise (such as performance, security, or development). These added features make it easier for you to find the perfect professional for your project that can check off every box on your list.

We could go on forever listing dozens of dozens of freelancing websites, but these two fit the bill for some of the top professional websites with people qualified for application and bot building. If scouring these types of websites still seems like too much work, you can always turn to the freelancing website designated for Slack-related projects: Upwork.

Using Upwork to hire Slack professionals

Upwork is freelancing for Slack—that is, it has everything you're looking for when outsourcing, creating, or building apps or bots for you and your team. While any kind of freelancing website can potentially achieve the same goal of finding and hiring for, and then completing, a desired project for Slack, Upwork can guarantee that the pool of people you're looking through not only has experience but also has expertise working with the Slack platform.

Upwork has the largest selection of proven, remote Slack professionals that can be used to assist with building aspects of your Slack workspace. Upwork's website looks as in the following screenshot:

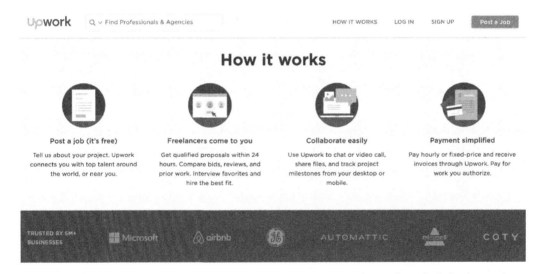

Figure 11.11 – Upwork's step-by-step process (https://www.upwork.com/hire/slack-freelancers/)

Every freelancer listed through Upwork is titled as a Slack freelancer and specializes in different areas of the application that are listed on their profile. Similar to Freelancer, Upwork asks you, the person looking to hire a freelancer, to post your desired job and then let the freelancers come to you.

You can post your project for free and choose from the freelancers that respond to your proposal within 24 hours. Let's break down how to hire a Slack professional using Upwork.

How to hire through Upwork

Slack specialists are skilled in all types of areas of Slack, from building bots to creating workflows and managing files. That's why it's important to break down the needs you're specifically looking for when hiring a Slack professional to narrow your search and identify the right kind of freelancer for your project. Filter out what you're searching for by going through the following short list:

- **Business role**: Business professionals fit the mold for jobs such as developer, project manager, or office assistant. Is this the type of role you're looking for?

- **Project experience**: Evaluate profiles by specified skills and experience to find the qualities needed to accomplish your project.

- **Feedback**: Similar to purchasing a product or renting an apartment, check the reviews of a Slack professional to see the feedback others have given their past work.

Creating a list can help define the exact type of person you're looking for as well as filter out any red flags or issues you could potentially face when working with a freelancer.

But before you can view your freelancer pool options, you first have to create the most optimal post that will guarantee you get the right freelancers to choose from. Follow these tips to write the most effective job post for you and your team:

- **Scope of work**: This is where you define the requirements. You need to fill in whether it's building a bot, setting up workflows, and so on. Make sure all of your expectations are laid out for the freelancer to view.

- **Project length**: Arguably the most important aspect of your project, identify how long the project should be expected to last, that is, whether it's a smaller or larger job.

- **Background**: If you have experience working with freelancers with a certain background/qualifications, list this so that the freelancer is aware beforehand.

- **Budget**: Set your price for the project and specify whether you prefer to pay by hourly rates or fixed-price contracts.

Your job post doesn't need to be as detailed as a typical job description would be, but it should check off all the basics of your project so that there's enough transparency on both ends of what's being asked of the hired and hirer.

Depending on the type of work you're looking for, the next part of this process can vary heavily in the length and effort needed to complete the job. This is where the cost factor of hiring an outsourced Slack professional comes into play.

Cost for hiring a Slack professional

While building your bot is always a free option, it's typically a labor-intensive one. So, while you or your team members may choose to outsource for that same labor, you must always be conscious of the compensation that kind of work warrants.

With that being said, there is no exact cost for hiring any kind of freelancer for your work. Each project can range from basic tasks to complicated coding and therefore the pricing can vary just as much. Rates for freelancers, especially Slack professionals, vary based on many factors, from expertise and experience to location and market conditions.

An experienced professional with good ratings can also have a quicker and higher turnaround time that makes them worth the extra cost they may have per hour. A newer contractor in the process of building their clientele may price their skillset at a lower rate to contract companies searching for a more reasonably priced option. Which of the two is right for you will be determined by the amount you're willing to spend on your freelancer and the qualities you're looking for in a working partner.

Summary

In this chapter, we discussed what comes after the hard work. After learning the basics of being able to recognize the tools needed to create and interact within your workspace, we took our knowledge to the market to understand when it's appropriate to extend the effort to build our bots and when it simply makes more sense to allow someone else to do the work for you.

We revisited the concept of frameworks to introduce paid options that assist in creating a bot from the bare bones. We returned to the Slack App Directory to find bots already available on the market to purchase through a variety of plans and immediately integrate into our workspace. We even considered outsourcing our bots to external freelancers and companies to build the type of bot we needed for us.

We've touched on a variety of topics all across the Slack platform throughout the last 11 chapters. Next, in our concluding chapter, we'll head back to the Slack App Directory to discuss how to bring your app or bot public once it's been created.

In our final chapter, we'll discuss the last step in the production of your app: submitting to the Slack App Directory. As we learned in *Chapter 7, Integrating Your Favorite Tools*, the Slack App Directory is an extremely useful tool to access applications other Slack teams or members have created as well as existing applications adapted especially for Slack. We'll discuss how to prepare the app you've created throughout this process for distribution, completing the submission checklist, and maintaining your app once it's officially published. We've made it this far in our Slack journey; let's take the last step together to make your work public.

12
Distributing Your App in the Slack App Directory

This is it. Whether you chose to build, buy, or outsource, through some means, you've reached the point where you have an app or bot and need something to do with it. The tool works well for you, but understandably, you want to be able to share your creation with the world. A lot of skill and effort goes into creating something as complex as a bot or app, so the ultimate product should be spread across every and any workspace that may benefit from its resource. If your bot could be useful to others, you can list it on the Slack App Directory.

In *Chapter 7*, *Integrating Your Favorite Tools*, we discovered what the Slack App Directory is and how it functions similar to your smartphone's App Store. But we've yet to learn how to make your content a part of it. Similar to any public distribution platform, your app needs to undergo a process before it can be accepted and widely spread among other users. In *Chapter 11*, *Buying, Building, and Outsourcing Your Bot*, we talked about the many routes you can take to create your bot. Now we'll take a look at the step-by-step procedure of making your work, and any others you may create, available to the public.

In this chapter, we'll cover the following topics:

- Preparing your Slack app for the App Directory submission
- Knowing whether your app is fit or unsuitable for the directory
- Completing the submission checklist
- Submitting your Slack app
- Maintaining your published Slack app
- Updating your published Slack app
- Removing or discontinuing your app from the directory

The Slack App Directory is a familiar concept to us. We've utilized its features in many aspects throughout our exploration of the platform. This is simply the final step in coming full circle from the Slack workspace creation, development, building of tools, and ultimate distribution for the mutual enjoyment of others. In this chapter, we'll revisit the App Directory to learn how to prepare your app for submission, actually submitting it, and then maintaining and updating it once it's published.

Preparing your Slack app for submission

Let's start with a refresher course. As we learned in *Chapter 7, Integrating Your Favorite Tools*, the Slack App Directory is a hub for all of the existing apps available for public use within the Slack platform. The directory has over 2,000 applications for you to browse, buy, and test out by integrating into your workspace.

Apps can range from functional to just plain fun and each has a different means of assisting the efficiency and enjoyability of communication in your channels. The Slack App Directory looks as in the following screenshot on your desktop browser:

Figure 12.1 – The Slack App Directory can be found at https://slack.com/apps

The directory's main purpose is to help users discover apps. If you've created an app you think will be useful if discovered by others, you would then decide to submit it to the App Directory. Your app can only be used by your team in your workspace if it is not shared in the directory.

> **Important note**
>
> Submitting your app to the App Directory is not necessary for the app to work for you and your team's Slack workspace.

Once you've decided you'd like to make your app public, there are a few steps you need to take before the actual submission. There are a lot of things to consider about the technical and social factors of your app that will then be reviewed by the App Directory team for final consideration. They are the people in power who can officially approve your app and give you the green light for publication.

The review is manual and exists to ensure your app meets Slack's standard for quality and utility by complying with the platform's API Terms of Service, Developer Policy, and Brand Guidelines. Let's walk through some of these preparation steps by understanding which apps are suitable for review and making sure your app completes the submission checklist.

Apps unsuitable for the App Directory

While the App Directory accepts many applications to be featured and shared with the rest of the Slack world, there are some aspects of an app that would make it unsuitable. Apps that would not be accepted to the App Directory include apps with the following features:

- Export or back up message data.
- Are built for the sole purpose of searching Slack messages outside of Slack.
- Use legacy scopes or methods.
- Allow possibly destructive behavior such as deleting files.
- Embed Slack into another site.
- Only use **Sign in with Slack** functionality.
- Replicate Slack client functionality or are third-party Slack clients.
- Request a large number of scopes for simple, non-work-related functionality.

- Share sensitive information in Slack.

- Circumvent admin features in Slack.

- Do not provide any functionality that the App Directory team deems valuable to Slack.

These are the general guidelines to follow, but it's important to note that the App Directory team has the right to deny any app submitted with a request based on their own judgment.

After you've ensured your app doesn't violate any of these rules, you're then ready to proceed to the app submission checklist. This is where you can mark off everything required for you and your app before its submission.

App submission checklist

Checklists are great for a multitude of reasons. You use them at the grocery store, during your daily work tasks, and even to outline many of your projects. They're important not just because you feel great every time you get to mark something off as done, but mainly because they help you not to forget things. The app submission checklist serves this purpose for your app to ensure that not only is your app suitable but it also meets all the proper points of a great app to be distributed on a wide scale.

When you physically go to submit your app, this checklist should appear before you. The checklist covers the most common failure points throughout the review process and will help your app be approved in a quick and efficient manner.

To better understand the submission checklist, we'll use Google Drive as a sample app to help you visualize the different aspects of the process. The exact checklist can be viewed in full (with the exception of the provided examples) at `https://api.slack.com/reference/slack-apps/directory-submission-checklist`.

The app submission checklist is broken down into the following checkpoints:

1. Reviewing your permission scopes:

- Confirm that your new or previously listed app uses granular permissions.

- Confirm your app runs within the user context, that is, it should not ask permission to read or post the organization data and should not pass on any sensitive information outside Slack.

- Confirm all the requested scopes in every step of the OAuth flow are listed in the app configuration list, and detailed reasons are provided on how each scope is used.

2. Reviewing your user experience:

- An excellent Slack experience, for a suitable workplace, is provided by the app.

- Before the submission of the app, installation in a new workspace is done to confirm that its installation, onboarding, and functionality are proper.

- Once your app is listed in the App Directory, it is ready to support a number of users and is open to everyone; that is, the app should not be in private beta.

- Clear and consistent formatting is used by the app when messages from the app are received.

- There are no typos and grammatical errors in the messages received from the app.

- Only direct messages are sent by the app or @channel or @here notifications are used by the app whenever applicable.

- Default messages are not sent to the #general channel by the app.

- No user is contacted by the app using the information obtained from Slack without their permission.

- When a slash command is used by the app, the user can either ask for help or send feedback.

- When the App Home **Messages** tab is used, the bot responds to the direct messages from the users. The app also uses the app_home_opened event for sending a welcome message when the user opens this view for the first time. A welcome message may appear something like this in your direct message:

This is the very beginning of your direct message history with @Google Drive

♀ How does Google Drive work?

Figure 12.2 – Google Drive's bot

- The content displayed on the **Home** tab (the app's home page) is helpful and appropriate for the users when they view it.

- Only domain events are requested by the app that are needed to function.

- No financial transactions are facilitated by the app in Slack.

- All API tokens will be revoked from the app when it is no longer maintained. The app should explicitly convey its deprecation plans to the users as well as the App Directory team prior to the app's removal.

3. Preparing your App Directory listing:

- The app complies with Slack's Brand Guidelines.

- Any copyright, trademark, and other intellectual property rights are not violated by the app.

- The name of the app is different from the others that are listed.

- Your app should not use the name "Slack" in its name or domain. It should refer itself only as a third-party integration.

- Your app has a unique and high-quality icon that is different from the Slackbot and Slack icons. Your app's icon may look something like the following figure:

Figure 12.3 – Google Drive's icon

- The app has a brief description of 10 words or fewer explaining how it works and what it does. Your app's short description may look something like the following:

 Google Drive
Get notifications about Google Drive files within Slack

Figure 12.4 – Google Drive's app description

- The app has a long description detailing clearly what it does. The long description of your app may look something like this:

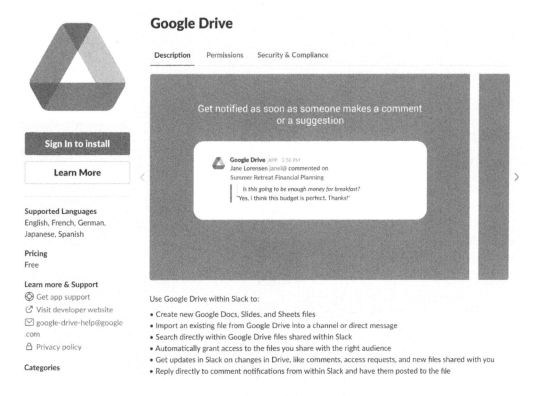

Google Drive

Description   Permissions   Security & Compliance

Get notified as soon as someone makes a comment or a suggestion

> **Google Drive** APP 5:56 PM
> Jane Lorensen janel@ commented on
> Summer Retreat Financial Planning
>
> > *Is this going to be enough money for breakfast?*
> > "Yes, I think this budget is perfect. Thanks!"

Sign In to install

Learn More

Supported Languages
English, French, German,
Japanese, Spanish

Pricing
Free

Learn more & Support
◎ Get app support
↗ Visit developer website
✉ google-drive-help@google
.com
🔒 Privacy policy

Categories

Use Google Drive within Slack to:

- Create new Google Docs, Slides, and Sheets files
- Import an existing file from Google Drive into a channel or direct message
- Search directly within Google Drive files shared within Slack
- Automatically grant access to the files you share with the right audience
- Get updates in Slack on changes in Drive, like comments, access requests, and new files shared with you
- Reply directly to comment notifications from within Slack and have them posted to the file

Figure 12.5 – Google Drive's long app description

- If a YouTube link is provided, a video explanation on how to use the app in Slack is demonstrated.

- If included, images clearly explaining how to use the app are high quality.

- All the languages selected by you are supported by the app.

- Proper pricing information is provided for the app.

4. Reviewing your installation landing page:

- Domain names for its privacy policy, landing page URLs, and support are owned by the app.

- The landing page of the app includes a summary, which details what the app does and how the app integrates within Slack. Your app's landing page may look something like the following:

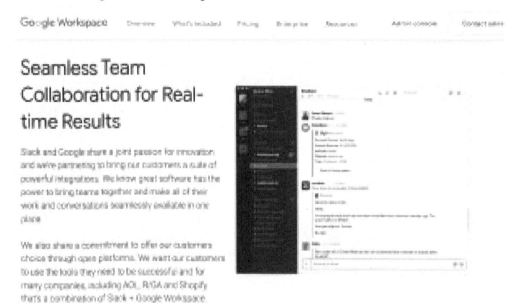

Figure 12.6 – Google Drive's landing page

- Explicit instructions for configuring and using the app are present on the landing page of the app.

- The **Add To Slack** button is clearly displayed on the landing page of the app so that the users can install the app. If not displayed on the landing page, the app has detailed instructions so that users can access this button.

5. Reviewing your direct installation URL:

- If a direct installation URL is provided, the URL should respond with a 302 redirect back to Slack's authorization URL.

- The OAuth flow of the app uses a state parameter if you connect Slack with private customer data.

6. Preparing your customer support:

-   If users face any problems or need any help, the app is linked to a page where it has clear instructions for contacting the team. Your app's support features may look something as in the following screenshot on the left-hand side of your app's directory page:

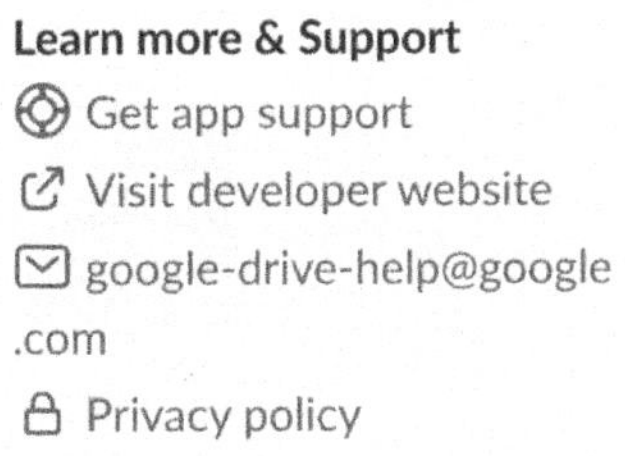

Learn more & Support

⊚ Get app support

⬀ Visit developer website

✉ google-drive-help@google
.com

🔒 Privacy policy

Figure 12.7 – Google Drive's app support links

-   There is no need for users to create a new account if they want to get in touch with the support team.

-   The app must be kept up to date as well as being backed by an active support channel.

7. Reviewing and agreeing to Slack policies:

-   All the Slack guidelines and API Terms of Service are met by the app.

-   Your app should agree to Slack's App Developer Policy and App Directory Agreement.

8. Preparing your privacy policy:

- An accessible link on the landing page is provided where information is available explaining how the app will be collecting, managing, and storing third-party data. Your app's privacy policy may appear as in the following figure:

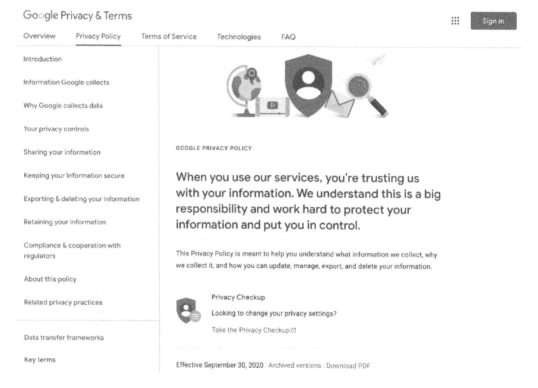

Figure 12.8 – Google Drive's privacy policy page

- A procedure for deleting, accessing, and transferring an individual's data is provided for the users.

- The personal data collected and processed by the app is not held or used in the future unless for the stated reasons or agreed to in advance.

- Personal data is gathered for specific and genuine reasons and is not kept unnecessarily.

- The owner or the creator of the app should be able to exhibit adherence to all the privacy regulations and laws that are applicable if a customer requests it.

9. Preparing for a security review:

- The app should agree to go through Slack's security review by considering the terms mentioned in the Slack App Directory Agreement (`https://api.slack.com/slack-app-directory-agreement`) as well as the Security Review Guide (`https://api.slack.com/security-review`).

- The security and compliance details, if mentioned, are correct and truthful.

- Slack's security guidelines (`https://api.slack.com/start/distributing/guidelines#security`) are followed by the app.

- TLS 1.2 or higher is used for redirect URIs, web pages, and endpoints by the app.

10. Helping the Slack App Directory team review your app:

- A test account information is provided for the Slack App Directory team if accessing the app requires an account or paid plan. Providing this information will help the App Directory team test more quickly.

- If submitting changes to the app, briefly describe them in the new submission.

Although seemingly lengthy, these 10 points are the key to creating the perfect Slack app. If your app meets the directory team's suitability and passes the checklist with flying colors, you should be well on your way to approval and ultimately publicly publishing your work.

You've now completely prepped your app for a seamless submission by following Slack's detailed guidelines of acceptable physical and mechanical features. The next step in this process is to actually submit your app for review. In this next section, we'll focus on how to present your application for a proper review.

Submitting your Slack app for review

This is the simplest part of the process. Your app meets all the criteria: it is designed well, but simple; accessible, but not invasive; unique, but useful to the average user; and overall, a productive asset to any workspace. You've created and prepped; now it's time to submit.

The purpose of the App Directory team is to monitor the kinds of applications that are shared across the Slack platform. Slack users expect a standard of innovative, communicative, and collaborative apps that the App Directory team works to maintain. If your app meets the preparatory requirements, you'll be admitted into the exclusive group that is the Slack App Directory. The App Directory appears as in the following screenshot on your desktop browser:

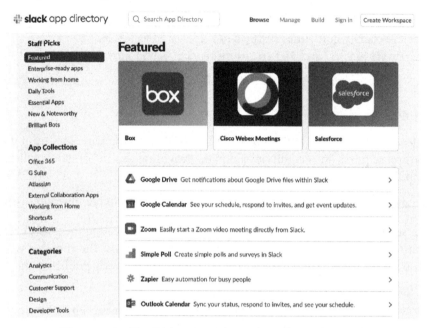

Figure 12.9 – The Slack App Directory through your browser

After you've completed all the preparation steps and checked everything off the checklist, it's time to officially submit your app for review. To do this, follow these steps:

1. Head to your app's settings dashboard.

2. Click to go to the **Submit to App Directory** page.

3. Complete the provided checklist we discussed in the prepping process and select the **Preview Submission** button.

4. Verify everything is correct on the **Review Your App Submission** modal, and then click the **Submit** button.

With these preceding steps completed, your app is officially undergoing the reviewing process! Once your app is reviewed, you'll receive an email from the App Directory team on the status of your application. If your app has been approved, you can then choose to publish to the App Directory by returning to the app's settings dashboard.

Once published, your app will be formally listed in the Slack App Directory. While this may seem like the end of the road for your efforts of creating and posting your app, it is far from it. Your app will belong not only to you and your team now but also to many others who will rely on its efforts on a day-to-day basis. It is your responsibility, as the creator, to keep your app functioning and up to date throughout its life on the directory.

Maintaining, updating, or discontinuing your published app

The many processes you go through to get your app published in the directory are to ensure that Slack is offering credible, reliable, high-quality material to its users. While your app being published is a great achievement, it is by no means the end of this process. Like any application, the way it's created for the present won't always be its most advanced version. Apps require updates to work out kinks and modernize with the times. Your app wasn't created on its own and it won't update on its own either.

In order to offer your app's users the highest quality experience throughout its lifetime on the App Directory, you as the creator are expected to maintain the app's quality, performance, maintenance, support, and security standards consistently. Let's take a look at some of the expectations required of you as an app creator, even after the app has been published.

Expectations for your published app

Your app is your baby and in order for your baby to evolve and thrive, you have to consistently take care of it over time as it grows. This includes caring for your app through maintenance, support, and the occasional upgrade when necessary. To have a successful app on the directory long after its original publication, always strive to meet the following expectations:

- **Your app's listing is kept up to date**: Any changes that occur to functionality, pricing, and visual appearance should be accurately reflected in your app's listing.

- **Your app's functionality and customer experience match or exceed the quality of experience at submission**: You must continually maintain your app's performance.

- **You provide timely support to customers**: If customers complain that they are not getting responses to their support requests/concerns, the App Directory team may reach out. If they don't receive a response from you, they could decide to de-list your app.

- **You regularly update your app to ensure that it makes use of the newest platform security features**: Slack is constantly adding new security features to their API. You can stay up to date on these changes by subscribing to Slack's changelog.

- **You keep your app contact details up to date and are responsive to messages from Slack**: Slack will occasionally contact you, the app creator, with questions about the app or to resolve any pending issues. It's important that your information is up to date so that you receive these notifications.

- **You must add a collaborator to your app**: Having only one person in charge of your app's configuration risks losing control if that person chooses to leave the workspace. To edit your creator list, head to your app's dashboard page and click to go to the **Collaborators** page.

- **You must resubmit your app for review when you make substantial changes or updates to the features, purpose, or functionality of your app**.

- **Your app is being actively used**: If your app is published, but not being actively used, the Slack App Directory team will reach out to see what your plans are. If you don't choose to update the app and no activity seems to occur, the team will de-list your app after further communication.

Use these guidelines as a consistent basis for improving your app's design, functionality, and outreach. The App Directory team is constantly looking for apps that are outperforming others to feature in the **Featured** category of the directory. If you can make it to **Featured**, you can make it anywhere.

To reach and sustain this level of excellence, you first need to learn how to actually update your app. Easier said than done; updating your app isn't really all that different than its original creation. Typically, updates are only for minor features that adjust the performance and design of the app from personal or peer feedback or simply just to keep up with the times. In the next section, we'll focus on the process of updating your app and resubmitting it for review prior to republication.

Updating your published app

Your app may have been perfect upon submission, but like anything, with time, what was once perfect becomes outdated. When it comes time to revamp your app and make settings changes, you can do so safely in the app's dashboard. Changes made in the dashboard won't affect your live app until you submit the app for re-review and the review is deemed successful. You can view the settings that apply to the published app under the **Published app setting** section of your dashboard.

Any changes in your app's functionality require that you resubmit your app for review and approval. As we learned in *Chapter 10*, *Building Your Own Bot*, before you officially undergo the submission process, once again, you should always test and develop your changes through a separate workspace, such as a designated channel or a sandbox. Testing your bot prevents any hiccups from making their way to the live version that Slack users other than you and your team are using in their own workspaces.

To resubmit your app for review, follow these steps:

1. Open your app's settings dashboard.

2. Select **Submit changes for review**.

3. Complete the submission checklist once again.

4. Add any information about the functionality changes under the **Help us review your app** section in the **Other notes** field.

5. Click the **Preview Submission** button.

6. Verify everything is correct on the **Review Your App Submission** modal and click **Submit**.

Similar to the original submission process, your app will again be manually reviewed by the App Directory team to make sure your app's improvements or new features are still up to par with Slack's API Terms of Service, Developer Policy, and Brand Guidelines.

If your updates still meet these standards, you'll again receive an email that you passed and you can go ahead and re-publish your app live. Your live app will immediately update from the original structure to the new and improved version. This cycle is endless as long as your app continues to keep its place on the directory.

Removing or discontinuing your app from the directory

Sometimes updating and maintaining an app becomes too much work. Or maybe what you built your app for originally is no longer useful or needed on a day-to-day basis within your workspace. No matter your reasoning, personal or professional, there comes a time when the best option may just be to remove or discontinue your app from the directory.

While it may be sad to see your creation taken away from its public life on Slack, it's better to remove your work before it becomes neglected or misused. You can remove your app from the directory by heading to the **Published App Settings** section of your app's settings dashboard and following the proper steps to dismiss your app from the directory's available app options.

If you're no longer actively maintaining or updating your app, you should ensure that it's adequately removed from the directory's options by either completely removing it before it reaches a point where it may be de-listed by Slack's team, reaching out to the App Directory team directly via email at `feedback@slack.com`, appropriately contacting your active customers, and deleting and revoking any tokens your app generated.

Summary

In this chapter, we learned about a new function of the Slack App Directory and how to use it to spread awareness and the use of your completed app. We prepped your app by going through the checklist and understanding what factors make an app suitable for public use across the platform. We submitted the app for approval and, once receiving the go-ahead, pushed it live by publishing it to the directory. We learned how to maintain our live app by keeping it constantly updated and if we reached a point where we could no longer take care of it, how to completely remove it from the app directory. We worked from the ground up, learning about and understanding the many features, tools, and skills of Slack, and now, you're on your own.

You've officially completed your journey through Slack. To summarize the entire book, you developed a basic understanding of Slack as a communication platform in *Chapter 1, Getting Started with Slack*, and the benefits of using Slack over email. You constructed a workspace of your very own in *Chapter 2, Setting Up Your Slack Workspace*, by inviting members of your team, creating different roles, and establishing different levels of access and permissions. You shopped for the best Slack plan for your organization in *Chapter 3, Slack Features, Tips, and Tricks*, and learned about the use of private versus public messages and channels as well as how to connect with your users directly through mentions and productivity tricks. You set up your team for success by customizing your workspace's design, channels, and privacy in *Chapter 4, Onboarding Your Slack Team*, in addition to creating a workspace language with text style and emojis. You incorporated outside members such as guests, clients, and partners into your established channels with interactive, inclusive sessions in *Chapter 5, Using Slack Externally with Live Chats, Guests, and Partners*.

That's when things got a little more advanced.

You discovered the bot in Slackbot in *Chapter 6, Your Workspace Slackbot*, and how the automated helper exists within your space to assist with basic bot functions. You brought some of your favorite tools that you know and love and some that are new to you into your workspace in *Chapter 7, Integrating Your Favorite Tools*, such as Google Drive, Donut, Giphy, and Zoom. You integrated Zapier into your workspace in *Chapter 8, Automate Your Workflow with Zapier*, to connect your existing, external work and important information to your communal communication space. You mastered some of the best tools Slack has to offer in *Chapter 9, Slack API, Webhooks, Block Kit, and Sandbox*, by taking the beginning steps in developing your own content through coded blocks and frameworks. You achieved the ultimate Slack test by learning how to create your own bot in *Chapter 10, Building Your Own Bot,* and learned when it's best to purchase an already-made app or hire someone to create one for you in *Chapter 11, Buying, Building, and Outsourcing Your Bot.*

This book has provided you with all the right tools to now create your own Slack experience. Everyone uses Slack for their own purpose. Whether your company is a new start-up or worthy of Enterprise Grid, there's a place in the Slack community for you and your team to thrive and grow. Take these tips and tricks to individualize your Slack workspace. Construct an efficient, productive, inclusive, creative, unique communication space. The boundaries are only limited by how far you're willing to push them.

Happy Slacking!

Packt.com

Subscribe to our online digital library for full access to over 7,000 books and videos, as well as industry leading tools to help you plan your personal development and advance your career. For more information, please visit our website.

Why subscribe?

- Spend less time learning and more time coding with practical eBooks and Videos from over 4,000 industry professionals

- Improve your learning with Skill Plans built especially for you

- Get a free eBook or video every month

- Fully searchable for easy access to vital information

- Copy and paste, print, and bookmark content

Did you know that Packt offers eBook versions of every book published, with PDF and ePub files available? You can upgrade to the eBook version at packt.com and as a print book customer, you are entitled to a discount on the eBook copy. Get in touch with us at customercare@packtpub.com for more details.

At www.packt.com, you can also read a collection of free technical articles, sign up for a range of free newsletters, and receive exclusive discounts and offers on Packt books and eBooks.

Other Books You May Enjoy

If you enjoyed this book, you may be interested in these other books by Packt:

Hands-On Microsoft Teams

Joao Ferreira

ISBN: 978-1-83921-398-4

- Create teams, channels, and tabs in Microsoft Teams
- Explore the Teams architecture and various Office 365 components included in Teams
- Perform scheduling, and managing meetings and live events in Teams
- Configure and manage apps in Teams
- Design automated scripts for managing a Teams environment using PowerShell
- Build your own Microsoft Teams app without writing code

Implementing Microsoft SharePoint 2019

Lewin Wanzer

ISBN: 978-1-78961-537-1

- Understand changes to the platform and how to migrate from other versions of SharePoint

- Explore infrastructure planning and governance relating to collaborative environments

- Install and configure network components, servers, and desktops

- Use SharePoint services and other Microsoft product servers and apps

- Monitor and troubleshoot SharePoint after it is implemented

- Discover the tools that can be used with SharePoint 2019 for BI and reporting

- Attack web and database servers to exfiltrate data

- Delve into social features and collaboration

- Maintain, monitor, and support the rollout of the platform in your enterprise

Packt is searching for authors like you

If you're interested in becoming an author for Packt, please visit `authors.packtpub.com` and apply today. We have worked with thousands of developers and tech professionals, just like you, to help them share their insight with the global tech community. You can make a general application, apply for a specific hot topic that we are recruiting an author for, or submit your own idea.

Leave a review - let other readers know what you think

Please share your thoughts on this book with others by leaving a review on the site that you bought it from. If you purchased the book from Amazon, please leave us an honest review on this book's Amazon page. This is vital so that other potential readers can see and use your unbiased opinion to make purchasing decisions, we can understand what our customers think about our products, and our authors can see your feedback on the title that they have worked with Packt to create. It will only take a few minutes of your time, but is valuable to other potential customers, our authors, and Packt. Thank you!

Index

Symbols

@ activity 60
@channel notification 58
@everyone alert 59
@here notification 59
@[name] notification 58

A

account maintenance 70
action 167
admin 44, 70
Amazon Lex 234, 235
Android Slack application 32, 33
App Collections 150
App Directory
  unsuitable apps 253, 254
application option
  Android downloads 35
  desktop downloads 34
  downloading 34
  iOS downloads 35
apps
  about 13, 27
  integrating, with Slack workspace 138
  usage tips 142, 143
  using, in Slack 140-142
apps, in workspace
  sorting, ways 137
app submission checklist 254-261
Ask me Anything session
  preparing 110
automatic speech recognition (ASR) 234

B

block elements
  about 192
  button 193, 194
  checkbox groups 194, 195
  date picker 195
  image 196
  time picker 197
Block Kit
  blocks, building 190-192
  using 189-224
blockquotes 55
blocks
  action block 198
  context block 198
  file block 198

Made in United States
North Haven, CT
16 February 2023

32647655R00167